D1564767

Prefaces to Canon Law Books in Latin Christianity

Prefaces to Canon Law Books in Latin Christianity

Selected Translations, 500–1245

Commentary and translations by
Robert Somerville
and Bruce C. Brasington

Yale University Press   New Haven and London

Set in Adobe Caslon type by Tseng Information Systems, Inc.
Printed in the United States of America.

Library of Congress Cataloging-in-Publication Data
Prefaces to Canon Law books in Latin Christianity : selected
translations, 500-1245 / commentary and translations by Robert
Somerville and Bruce C. Brasington.
p. cm.
Includes bibliographical references and index.
ISBN 0-300-07146-9 (cloth : alk. paper)
1. Canon law—History. 2. Law, Medieval. 3. Prefaces.
I. Somerville, Robert, 1940-   . II. Brasington, Bruce Clark, 1957-
LAW <CANON Pref 1998>
262.9—DC21   97-36931
CIP

A catalogue record for this book is
available from the British Library.

The paper in this book meets the guidelines
for permanence and durability of the Committee
on Production Guidelines for Book Longevity of
the Council on Library Resources.

10 9 8 7 6 5 4 3 2 1

CONTENTS

Preface   vii

1. INTRODUCTION   1

2. LATE ANTIQUITY AND THE EARLY MIDDLE AGES   19
Pope Siricius to Bishop Himerius of Tarragona   36
The Collections of Dionysius Exiguus   46
The Concord of Canons of Cresconius   50
The Chapters of Martin of Braga   53
The Spanish Collection   55
The Irish Collection of Canons   58

3. COMPILERS, REFORMERS, JURISPRUDENTS:
THE EARLY MIDDLE AGES   59
The Penitential of Halitgar of Cambrai   76
The False Capitularies of Benedict the Deacon   78
The Collection of "Isidore Mercator"   82
The Chapters of Bishop Isaac of Langres   91
The Two Books concerning Synodal Investigations and
Ecclesiastical Instructions of Abbot Regino of Prüm   92
The Collection Dedicated to Anselm   94
The Canons of Abbot Abbo of Fleury   97
The Decretum of Bishop Burchard of Worms   99

4. THE ERA OF REFORM: 1050–1140   105
The Breviary of Cardinal Atto of St. Mark's   118
The Book of Canons of Cardinal Deusdedit   122
The Polycarpus of Cardinal Gregory of S. Grisogono   129

The Tripartite Collection   131
The Prologue of Ivo of Chartres   132
The Collection in Ten Parts   158
The Second Collection of Châlons-sur-Marne   164
The Book On Mercy and Justice of Alger of Liège   165

5. GRATIAN AND THE DECRETISTS   170
The *Summa* of Paucapalea on Gratian's *Decretum*   180
The *Stroma* of Rolandus on Gratian's *Decretum*   185
The *Summa* of Rufinus on Gratian's *Decretum*   189
The *Summa* of Stephen of Tournai on Gratian's *Decretum*   194
The *Summa "Parisiensis"* on Gratian's *Decretum*   201
The *Summa "Antiquitate et tempore"* on Gratian's *Decretum*   202

6. PAPAL DECRETALS AND THEIR COLLECTORS:
1190–1245   213
The Breviary of *Extravagantia,* or the First Compilation,
by Bernard of Pavia   230
The *Summa decretalium* of Bernard of Pavia on the
First Compilation   231
The Collection of Decretals of Rainier of Pomposa   232
The Decretals of the Lord Pope Innocent, or the Third
Compilation, by Peter of Benevento   233
The Fifth Compilation, by Tancred   234
The Compilation of Decretals of the Lord Pope Gregory IX,
by Raymond of Peñafort, O.P.   235
Revision by Bartholomew of Brescia of the Ordinary Gloss
to Gratian's *Decretum* by Johannes Teutonicus   236

Select Bibliography   237
Index   239

PREFACE

The texts presented in this volume are for the most part translated in their entirety; in the few instances where this seemed impractical the gaps are clearly designated. Biblical passages were translated by the authors, and the format of texts into paragraphs is editorial, not always following the divisions of the Latin. In addition to the comments in the introductions to each chapter, some annotation is provided in notes to the translations, that is, identifying many of the citations and occasionally commenting on the Latin or on obscurities in the passage at hand. The intention, however, is to offer less rather than more in the way of substantive commentary. One goal of this work is to allow readers to confront a variety of introductions to canon law books on their own or in the classroom, and to form a judgment as to how this evidence can be understood.

All translations were newly done, and both editors had a hand in everything. B.C.B. had primary responsibility for chap. 2, nos. 5–6; chap. 3, nos. 1, 4–5, and 7; chap. 4, nos. 1, 4–5, and 7; and chap. 5, nos. 3 and 6; and R.S. for chap. 2, nos. 1–4; chap. 3, nos. 2–3 and 8; chap. 4, nos. 2–3; chap. 5, nos. 1 and 4–5; and the texts in chap. 6. Both worked on chap. 3, no. 6 and chap. 4, no. 6. The translations of chap. 4, no. 8 and chap. 5, no. 2 are based on drafts by Kären Sorensen, M.Phil., Department of Religion, Columbia University, who kindly allowed her work to be used. The introductions to chaps. 3, 4, and 5 were formulated by B.C.B., and those for chaps. 1, 2, and 6 by R.S.

The authors are grateful for the support and help they received in the course of preparing this book. Jaroslav Pelikan took an early interest in the project and brought it to the attention of Yale University Press, and the reception of the idea, and eventually the finished product, by the Press's anonymous reviewers and its editorial board made the book possible. Milton McC. Gatch, John Hine Mundy, and Michael Stoller read and greatly helped to clarify some of the chapter introductions. Kenneth Pennington generously made available for use in chap. 6 portions of his unpublished work on decretal collections, written for the *History of Medieval Canon Law*, and he also suggested including the preface to the decretal collection of Rainier of Pomposa. A number of colleagues and students helped to sharpen the translations, but thanks are due especially to Anders Winroth and, above all, to Carmela Franklin for her suggestions about how obdurate post-classical Latin constructions can be rendered as readable English. Kären Sorensen, who knows a great deal about medieval prefaces, read through many of the translations and made valuable suggestions. Professor David Weiss-Halivni kindly answered various questions about biblical and Talmudic law; Gregory Sherr's computer wizardry made disks written in one program in Canyon, Texas, legible in another in New York City; and Karen Green cheerfully put the resources of Columbia University's Electronic Text Service in Butler Library at the disposal of the authors on more than one occasion. Eliza Childs has been the copy editor every author dreams of encountering. Finally, R. S. is grateful to Professors Carl Gerold Fürst and Hartmut Zapp of the Kanonistisches Seminar and to Professor Hubert Mordek of the Historisches Seminar of the Albert-Ludwigs Universität, Freiburg im Br., for their cordial hospitality during summer 1995, when finishing touches were being applied to this book. None of the above, it should be added, bear any responsibility for the work, which rests solely with the authors.

I

Introduction

The Christian Church, in all the manifestations to which the name can apply, views itself as an institution suspended between heaven and earth, balancing eternal truths, on the one hand, with the realities of the human condition on the other. As with all institutions, however, the Church cannot live by transcendence alone. It requires norms according to which it is defined and constituted, and procedures by which it operates. That is to say, the Church requires laws. Although the tension between "law" and "gospel" has been part of Christianity from the apostolic age to the present day,[1] the Church repeatedly has devoted painstaking attention to formulating belief systems, setting in place ecclesiastical structures, and delineating boundaries of proper action. Saint Paul's admonitions to the Corinthians, the Pastoral Epistles, resolutions of councils, decretals of medieval popes, Martin Luther's critique of the Roman sacramental sys-

---

1. See, e.g., the discussion by Stephan Kuttner, "Reflections on Gospel and Law in the History of the Church," *Liber amicorum Monseigneur Onclin* (Biblioteca Ephemeridum theologicarum Lovaniensium 42; Gembloux, 1976), 199–209 (rpt. in Kuttner, *Studies in the History of Medieval Canon Law* [Variorum Collected Studies CS325; Aldershot, 1990]). Legal historians will be especially interested in the work of Rudolf Sohm, who saw a contradiction between "law" and "Church" and who devised an elaborate thesis to explain the progressive capture of Christianity by legalism: see Jean Gaudemet, *Eglise et cité: Histoire du droit canonique* (Paris, 1994), 35. For an introduction to Sohm in English, see Stanley Chodorow, *Christian Political Theory and Church Politics in the Mid-Twelfth Century: The Ecclesiology of Gratian's Decretum* (Publications of the Center for Medieval and Renaissance Studies, UCLA, 5; Berkeley, 1972), 7–16.

tem, the Barmen Declaration (1934), and modern papal encyclicals are a few examples in a vast tradition which has persistently been concerned with defining, organizing, and regulating.

The label often given to this body of norms, and even to the accompanying structures, is "canon law." Whatever its degree of sophistication and however much it treats ephemeral issues, that law never can be totally rational, for it belongs to an entity which professes to exist by divine plan and whose earthly forms aspire to mirror heavenly perfection. *Kanon* is a Greek word originally meaning a straight rod for measuring, hence it came to mean "rule." The term was appropriated to designate the list of writings which were regarded as "the measure" of the faith—that is, sacred scripture—but which also can specify any rule which applies to the Church. Canon law (etymologically perhaps a redundancy) is thus what defines the Church as an institution, governing its beliefs, ceremonies, organization, and its interactions with society at large. This, of course, is a general characterization. The details must be sought in particular branches of Christianity, for example, canon law of Latin Christianity before the sixteenth-century Reformation, Russian Orthodox canon law, Anglican canon law, Lutheran canon law, and so forth, and the diversity of both sources and content of religious law throughout Christian history is enormous and can surprise those encountering it for the first time. The demarcation, for example, between the study of law and theology which emerged in the schools of twelfth-century Europe would be anachronistic for earlier periods. Canon law can treat belief, ritual, and structure, but it can also deal with politics, the institutions and mores of society, the history of education, and even the survival of pagan practice.

This volume is not intended to be a general history of Western canon law, neither of canonical sources nor doctrines. It is unlikely to be a work where users can find answers to such questions as, "What was 'the law'?" or "How did canon law work?" It will, nonetheless, introduce the history of Church law in the Latin tradition through the mid-thirteenth century, but in a more modest and particular way. Many collections of ancient and medieval canon law began with introductions or prologues of various types, conveying information about the author, his purpose in writing or compiling the work, his sources, and the like. There is no substitute for reading a book in its entirety in the language in which it was composed, but it probably is fair to say that legal compilations generally are read in segmented fashion, according to need, and that this was the case even during the centuries of scholastic study of canon law. Then as now, prefaces could orient a user approaching what are formidable tomes. Yet despite this potential, such introductions have been largely excluded from sourcebooks in medieval and religious history, and there has never been an anthology of them in any language. This selection of translations aims to fill that lacuna, giving readers access to churchmen and canon lawyers who flourished between the sixth and the mid-thirteenth centuries, speaking (with the translators' help) in their own words about their works. But before moving to those texts, something more should briefly be said about the nature of Church law and its formative stages in antiquity.

The Sources. The "canons" of canon law are a miscellany of statements, derived from many different places, which are meant to be normative. It is important to distinguish between what are termed "material sources" (*fontes materiales*), on the one hand, and "formal sources" (*fontes formales*), on the other. Material sources are the "original sources," that is, the Biblical passages, papal decrees, conciliar canons, patristic writings, and so on which can be regarded as sources of law. Formal sources are the vehicles through which the law is transmitted, that is, the books and collections where someone can find it. A material and a formal source might be identical, if, for example, an official chancery register was used to supply a papal text, but canon law evolved in great part through the use of formal sources where this overlap did not occur. An eleventh-century author's or judge's material source might be a decree from the Council of Nicaea, but by the eleventh century the official acts of Nicaea were long lost (if they ever existed as such),[2] and the formal source whence the text was drawn would be one of the many collections of Church law which transmitted the ruling. Canonists generally used formal sources rather than returning to material sources, even when they were available and could have been used.

Material sources sometimes are called "constitutive," or even "legislative," sources,[3] and an attempt to catalogue their variety risks incompleteness. The use of biblical citations in the letter of Pope Siricius to Himerius of Tarragona (see chap. 2) illustrates that moral and ceremonial precepts from the Old Testament, and disciplinary and institutional excerpts from both the Gospels and the Epistles, were used from ancient times as legal points of reference. Pseudo-apostolic works also appear early on, treating discipline and ecclesiastical organization and purporting to represent a nonbiblical tradition extending back to Jesus and the apostles. Forged texts—"lying for the Lord," as it has been termed[4]—are a persistent fact in the history of

2. See Norman P. Tanner, S.J., *Decrees of the Ecumenical Councils* (London, 1990), 1:2. (The two volumes of this work are an English translation, together with the original on facing pages, of Giuseppe Alberigo et al., *Conciliorum oecumenicorum decreta*, 3d ed. [Bologna, 1972].)

3. See Reynolds, "Law, Canon," 395—an excellent article which has been utilized at many points throughout this introduction—and Van de Wiel, *History of Canon Law*, 20.

4. This compelling phrase was used in a personal letter written by the classical scholar Revilo Oliver. Forgery in canon law is a vast topic,

the Church. In the legal tradition they are represented perhaps most spectacularly and influentially by the ninth-century Pseudo-Isidorian corpus (see chap. 3), but forgery also encompassed less flagrant deception, such as changing attributions to texts and altering a few words in a canon to produce a more favorable reading. Theological writings also entered the reservoir of material sources for canon law as the Church moved through antiquity into the Middle Ages, as did liturgical and monastic regulations, hagiographical extracts, episcopal statutes, and even texts from secular law. Yet notwithstanding this richness, conciliar and papal texts were the most significant elements for the development of Western canon law.

Councils. The evolution of Christianity over the first three centuries produced an "orthodox consensus" among different groups about belief and practice.[5] The hallmarks of this consensus, "weapons" of orthodoxy against heresy as Henry Chadwick designates them,[6] were formulation of credal statements summarizing the tenets of the faith, gradual circumscribing of the New Testament canon of scripture, and a hierarchical organization in which bishops—the word derives from the Greek word *episkopos,* meaning "overseer"—emerged as the head of Christian communities. By the end of the second century the Church had bishops in its leading centers, and from then until

---

and a wealth of information about it can be found in *Fälschungen im Mittelalter II: Gefälschte Rechtstexte—Der bestrafte Fälscher* (Monumenta Germaniae Historica, Schriften 33.2; Hannover, 1988).

5. This term is used by Jaroslav Pelikan to refer to general agreement East and West in the late fifth and sixth centuries (notwithstanding "noteworthy" exceptions) about normative theology (*The Emergence of the Catholic Tradition, 100–600* [Christian Tradition 1; Chicago, 1971], 332ff.). The notion is borrowed here for an earlier period in Christian history.

6. Henry Chadwick, *The Early Church* (Pelican History of the Church 1; Baltimore, 1967), 42–44.

the sixteenth-century Reformation it was universally organized on an episcopal model.[7]

From very early times (cf. Acts 15), and clearly by the mid-second century in the face of the Montanist crisis in Asia Minor, bishops had convened to deliberate on questions of doctrine and discipline. These assemblies, which are called synods or councils (the terms can be used as equivalents), are characterized by the belief that they operated under the guidance of the Holy Spirit. Information about synods before the fourth century is scarce, but from the time of the Emperor Constantine onward, with the emergence of Christianity as a tolerated and then as the dominant religion in the Roman world, the Church flourished. Regional, provincial, and local synods throughout the Empire treated a multiplicity of questions, and many enactments from these assemblies survive (designated as "canons," but by a variety of other names, too, for example, "decrees," "statutes," and "constitutions"). In theology, discipline, and structure, these councils helped to define an evolving orthodoxy about the content of the faith and the operation of the institution, and synods at all levels of ecclesiastical organization continued to play a fundamental role in canon law throughout the Middle Ages.

The most famous council of antiquity and probably the most renowned in history is the great gathering of bishops convened at Nicaea in Bithynia in the year 325 by Constantine. The Council of Nicaea is the first of the so-called ecumenical councils. "Ecumenical" means "universal" or "worldwide," yet how this idea was applied to synods is a complex matter which has been fiercely debated.[8] Different branches of

7. The point holds, although some nuances are in order, e.g., the structure of early Irish Christianity.

8. For orientation on this questions in the medieval Church, see Robert

the Church apply different criteria and accord ecumenicity or a similarly exalted status to a different number of gatherings, although Nicaea, Constantinople I (381), Ephesus (431), and Chalcedon (451) often are viewed in a special light, and in many quarters these are recognized as the first four ecumenical councils. Each treated fundamental questions of Trinitarian theology; Nicaea, Constantinople, and Chalcedon promulgated disciplinary canons; and Pope Gregory the Great compared the councils to the four Gospels as building blocks of the faith. From early on, certainly by the mid-fifth century and long before Pope Gregory's day, the Roman Church saw papal approbation as the decisive factor in conciliar acceptance.[9] During the Middle Ages many assemblies in the West were termed "general" councils (sometimes even the adjective "universal" was used), and this institution was one of the significant legislative forces in medieval Christianity.[10]

Papal Acts. Bishops, in council and individually in their churches, were formulators and guardians of the faith, and

---

Somerville, "Papal Councils, 1049-1179," in *History of Canon Law,* ed. Wilfried Hartmann and Kenneth Pennington (Catholic University of America Press, forthcoming).

9. The most recent and best consideration of this development is by Hubert Mordek, "Der Römische Primat in den Kirchenrechtssamm-lungen des Westens vom IV. bis VIII. Jahrhundert," *Il primato del vescovo di Roma nel primo millennio* (Pontificio Comitato di scienze storiche, Atti e documenti 4; Vatican City, 1991), esp. 535ff.

10. Only after the Catholic Reformation did a series of nineteen synods, from Nicaea through the Council of Trent (1545-63), come to be accepted in the Roman Catholic Church as "the ecumenical councils." Vatican I (1869-70) and Vatican II (1962-65) subsequently became the twentieth and twenty-first entries, but this list has never been given official papal approbation. The decrees and acts of these gatherings are available in English translation in Tanner, *Decrees* (see n. 2, above).

legislators and interpreters of rules about structure and practice in the community.[11] The bishops of the Church at Rome were part of this collegiality, yet early in Christian history they were singled out in a special way. The story of the evolution of papal authority cannot be told here, but decisions from Roman bishops which had an impact beyond Rome are known even in the pre-Constantinian age. From the second half of the fourth century onward, papal letters survive which present responses to questions on ecclesiastical issues addressed to Rome from outlying churches. The antiquity of this practice is unclear, as is its relation to the analogous work of the Roman imperial chancery in issuing "rescripts," that is, written responses to questions, instructions to judges, and similar statements.[12] Papal rescripts come to be called "decretal letters," or simply "decretals," although these texts, as with conciliar canons, carry a variety of names in the sources. The verb "to decree," and the nouns "decree" and "decretal," all stem from the past participle (*decretum*) of the Latin verb *decernere*, which means "to decide, to judge, or to decree"; thus a decretal, in contrast to other types of papal correspondence, is an instrument which conveys a legal decision. From the mid-twelfth century, decretals play a predominant role in canon law, and exactly which papal letters should be classed as such, and their range of applicability, were

11. For the juridical role of bishops in the early Church see the essays by Guilio Vismara, "La giurisdizione civile dei vescovi nel mondo antico," and Wilfried Hartmann, "Der Bischof als Richter nach den Kirchenrechtlichen Quellen des 4. bis 7. Jahrhunderts," in *La giustizia nell'alto medioevo (secoli v–viii)* (Settimane di Studio del Centro italiano di studi sull'alto medioevo 42; Spoleto, 1995), 225-51 and 805-57.

12. Gaudemet, *Les Sources*, 59, writes that perhaps the imperial model inspired papal procedure but that similar needs could have generated comparable processes without direct borrowing. The development of legal principles in early papal decretals is treated by Landau, "Kanonisches Recht."

questions treated in detail by scholastic canonists. But such letters existed in the fourth century, and the principles which defined their special nature were even older.

Both by analogy to secular law and because of the preeminence of the Roman Church, the practice of turning to Rome for advice about issues which arose in local churches is not especially surprising. Discussing the sphere of application of early decretals, Jean Gaudemet has written that without forming a strict "code," these letters "constitute a guide for the daily activity" of the clergy to whom they are addressed.[13] Papal texts could be sent to more than one bishop, and even to all prelates in a region such as the bishops in Apulia and Calabria, and letters dispatched to one church might also circulate elsewhere. In the famous fourth-century decretal from Pope Siricius to Bishop Himerius of Tarragona (see chap. 2), the pope spoke of "general decrees sent to the provinces" by his predecessor Pope Liberius and also asked Himerius to disseminate the lengthy letter which he had now received.

Canon Law Collections. Pastor, politician, teacher, and judge, the bishop in the early Church stood at the crossroads of classical and Christian cultures. He needed to be literate and to know the Christian tradition in order to teach and defend it.[14] Canon law was an element in that tradition. As Pope Celestine I (422–32) wrote: "No priest may ignore the canons or do something that could obstruct the rules of the Fathers. What of worth will be preserved by us if the norm of established decretals be shattered at the whim of certain people?"[15] But whoever is to know

13. Gaudemet, *Les Sources,* 63–64.

14. JK 447: Pope Leo I (440–61) to the clergy and people of Constantinople.

15. JK 371, c. 1; Paul Kehr and Walther Holtzmann, *Italia pontificia,* 9 (Berlin, 1962), 272–73, no. 2 (Pope Celestine I to the bishops of Apulia and Calabria). See also Siricius to Himerius, sec. 20 (see chap. 2).

the law obviously needs access to it. In a remarkable statement, Pope Siricius told Bishop Himerius of Tarragona that Christian priests were expected to know both papal directives and the canonical tradition.[16] The general question of the education of the clergy in antiquity and the Middle Ages, and specifically the nature and extent of the training in law afforded them, are beyond the scope of this volume. Siricius's letter was transmitted in a number of widely diffused compilations, and the aforenoted stipulation from Celestine I was repeated by popes and synods across the centuries.[17] The Church's success in turning such counsels into practice, to whatever degree it happened, is due in no small part to the fact that the canons were collected into books whose number and circulation imply an abiding interest on the part of churchmen in having access to the law.

The diverse array of formal sources which made up Church law are not, of course, represented in all collections, and the source material included in canon law tends, not surprisingly, to become more variegated as the Church grows into a more complex institution. The earliest compilations were collections of pseudo-apostolic material composed chiefly in the East, and the small manual of ecclesiastical order and discipline known as the Teaching of the Twelve Apostles (or simply the *Didache*, i.e., "Teaching"), written at the turn of the second century, could be designated in a general way as the earliest canonical collection known.[18] Such works had limited influence in the West, with one noteworthy exception. In the sixth century Dionysius

16. See chap. 2, Siricius to Himerius, toward the end.

17. See Mordek, *Kirchenrecht*, 1, to whom these comments are indebted, for other examples and for bibliography on clerical education. See also the information in Brasington, "Prologues," where general bibliography on prologues and their function in the Latin tradition can be found.

18. E.g., Reynolds, "Law, Canon," 397, and Brundage, *Medieval Canon Law*, 5.

Exiguus translated from Greek into Latin fifty of the so-called Canons of the Apostles (see chap. 2). These short statements on ecclesiastical ritual and discipline stem from a pseudonymous work written in Syria at the end of the fourth century, the so-called Apostolic Constitutions, but through Dionysius's translation many of them flowed deeply into medieval Latin canon law.

It is plausible that Western representatives at the great fourth-century synods carried home texts of the decrees, and that Latin versions of these canons—together with local and regional rulings—circulated here and there in the West. By the early fifth century it is possible to identify such collections, although, as has been said, "the exact origin of each is sometimes unknown or is controverted."[19] At about the same time, texts issued by the bishops of Rome began to be collected as authorities, and then gathered together with synodal decrees. The instruments through which canon law would be available in the West were developing. The Church's law, as James Brundage writes, "had begun to emerge as not only an important element of Christian religious life, but also as an autonomous legal system complementary to the legal system of late Roman government."[20] In these early stages, however, it is difficult to see much that is systematic, at least consistently so, about the canon law, and it is very difficult to assemble details of the procedures by which law was formulated and used. Its preservation and diffusion in collections can be observed, yet the process unfolded without an overriding plan. Only in the eleventh and twelfth centuries did canon law begin to be rationalized and universalized in the name of the papacy; until the early thirteenth cen-

19. Reynolds, "Law, Canon," 398; for a summary of scholarly opinion on the development of early collections of both conciliar canons and decretals in the West, see Gaudemet, *Les Sources,* 73–91.
20. Brundage, *Medieval Canon Law,* 17.

tury all collections, however important and widespread, were private. Even when official papal collections emerged, neither the works themselves nor commentators on them claimed that papal law simply abrogated the traditions of the previous millennium, during which the law was, for the most part, a local phenomenon controlled by bishops.

Format. The organization of books of canon law and the accompanying nomenclature deserves some attention.[21] Some collections do not lend themselves to easy classification, and in others the principles of organization no longer can be retrieved. Two broad categories often are used to illustrate basic formats. The earliest compilations in the West are termed "chronological" or "historical" collections. Here the contents are arranged more or less in order of enactment, with texts copied in their entirety. The value of such a work rests on the comprehensive presentation of a certain set of information, such as the enactments of a series of councils or the full texts of a group of papal letters.

The difficulty in using a book of this type as a reference tool is obvious. Unless its contents are well known from memory, or unless a reader is prepared to read from beginning to end—say, from the first canon of the Council of Nicaea through the last canon of Chalcedon—something relevant can easily be missed. Thus from the fifth century onward systematic collections were made which grouped texts in thematic fashion, for example, by means of a series of titles. Canons would be distributed under those headings, and a reader could locate what suited his needs more expeditiously, and perhaps even compare different statements that appeared together under one title. But opportunities for comparison could mean trouble, leading to the discovery that two canons speak inconsistently on an issue, or that a ruling

21. See Reynolds, "Law, Canon," 396–97, and the general remarks by Gérard Fransen, *Les Collections canoniques* (Typologie des sources du Moyen Age occidental 10.A-III.1*; Turnhout, 1973), 13-14.

which a compiler deemed applicable under title "A" seemed to a reader appropriate only to the subject treated under title "B." The resolution of such problems is a fundamental characteristic of scholasticism in the High Middle Ages, but earlier writers were not unaware of these issues (see chap. 2, Canons of Cresconius and Irish Collection of Canons). It would be wrong, however, to see the appearance of thematic collections as an innovation which quickly superseded historical compilations, and as late as the middle of the ninth century a chronological schema was used for the Pseudo-Isidorian decretals. Significant production of new historical collections appears to dwindle soon thereafter, but interest in the great chronological works — books sometimes referred to simply as "the corpus of canons" (*corpus canonum*) — continued throughout the Middle Ages, as witnessed by the surviving manuscript copies of the Spanish Collection and Pseudo Isidore.

Authority. Decisions from a council were binding in the churches where the attending bishops presided, but when gathered in collections they gained wider circulation. In addition, conciliar canons might be ratified by emperors, thus becoming imperial law and acquiring the applicability granted to such texts.[22] By means of collections, papal decretals also reached an audience wider than the locality to which they were initially dispatched. Yet as far as is known, throughout the first millennium of Christianity no official papal compilations of Church law were made; only at the beginning of the thirteenth century, in the pontificate of Innocent III (1198–1216), does such a book appear. The authority of earlier collections depended essentially on the authority of the "legislators" of the canons assembled

22. Gaudemet, *Eglise et cité*, 119–20 (see n. 1, above); see also the editorial commentary to the proceedings of the first four ecumenical councils in Tanner, *Decrees* (see n. 2, above).

therein, that is, on the authority of the individual material sources which were amassed. The volumes where such rulings were gathered — as opposed to the great codes of civil law prepared for the Emperors Theodosius and Justinian — were private: they were not known to have been made or promulgated as an act of legislation; they were not declared to be binding by a pope, council, or other authority; and they were not authorized in any way. They had no force of law other than that of their separate elements. Dionysius Exiguus prepared his last translation of the Greek councils at the behest of Pope Hormisdas, to whom it was dedicated, but the work appears to have remained a private compilation; the individual texts were not injected with any special authority imparted by the collection. The same seems true of later collections assembled by cardinals of the Roman Church during the period of the eleventh-century papal reform (see chap. 4).

To modern eyes, works of canon law put together before the High Middle Ages, and especially those compiled before the eleventh century, can appear crude and unwieldy, even those of the so-called systematic variety. They are, in essence, accumulations of texts from which general legal principles can be extracted only with great difficulty, if at all, and where no effort has been made to resolve contradictions in the authorities gathered. Furthermore, until the mid-twelfth century and the development of a formal process of legal instruction in the schools, books of canons usually included no commentary, aside from isolated remarks which can be found here and there in manuscript copies. The transformation from this mass of variegated rules into a jurisprudential system composed mainly of papal laws claiming special authority is concomitant with the changes which took place in the papacy after the middle of the eleventh century. Exactly how the bishops of Rome before the time of Innocent III related to this evolution is, however, not clearly understood. What can be seen more readily is a clear relation between the development of jurisprudence and the study and teaching of law. Whatever its exact circumstances, Gratian's *Decretum* (see chap. 5) was assembled and succeeded in the world of nascent universities, becoming the foundation of a curriculum of systematic study of Church law which opened the door to the official compilations of papal decretals in the thirteenth century.

Introductions to Canon Law Books. Not all collections of canon law have introductions. Some simply began with the canons, providing no prefatory comment. Not even all of the most important compilations have prefaces. The influential *Collectio vetus Gallica* from sixth-century Lyon has none, nor does Gratian's *Decretum,* which was the most important compilation made before the thirteenth century.[23] But many such books do have prefaces or prologues, some bearing no title, some labeled *praefatio* or *prologus.* They can be cast in epistolary form, either in general without a named recipient or addressed to a specific person, perhaps the compiler's patron. A papal bull introduces the official collections of decretals in the thirteenth century, both authorizing them and revealing something of their genesis.

The prologue was not an uncommon feature of many types of medieval texts, with a function already well defined in ancient rhetorical theory: to introduce or explain the intent or content of the work to follow.[24] It was a self-conscious part of the book

23. This can appear strange given Gratian's pivotal importance, but it is not a simple issue. Perhaps Gratian viewed the first set of "distinctions" in his work—which sometimes is termed "The Treatise on Law"—as a kind of prologue to the rest of his book. Also, as Brasington points out, later writers composed prefaces for the book ("Prologues," 230). On the *Vetus Gallica* see the edition and analysis in Mordek, *Kirchenrecht.*

24. See Brasington, "Prologues," on which this section draws.

which it introduced and as such a valuable aid in discerning the individual behind the treatise or compilation (though an author always, to some extent, would express himself in rhetorical commonplaces). A prologue gave an author occasion to explain his purpose, his method of working, and anything else he cared to impart to readers. The content of many early medieval canonical collections overlaps in that they draw on a common dossier of sources, but the introductions are not simply pro forma and often yield insight about the particulars of a given work and its individual story. Some elements encountered in legal prefaces are, of course, venerable rhetorical devices found in prologues of all genres. Authors commonly show reverence for tradition and assure readers that they were not presuming to add anything of their own to it; yet variations of traditional themes can be found, as when the eighth-century compiler of the fascinating Irish Collection of Canons admitted that he was reconfiguring tradition and tried to explain something about why a new compilation was needed (chap. 2).

Nearly twenty years ago an eminent historian of canon law wrote: "Forewords to systematic and to historically arranged legal collections often give . . . information about the person of the author, and the real or imagined motives which led to composition of the work. . . . An investigation from the perspective of history of ideas of prefaces from Dionysius to Gratian—a work which remains to be done—would yield deeper insight into the ecclesiological assumptions of the ages being addressed, and show their attitude to the different sources of Church law."[25] This volume is not the scholarly study anticipated in that comment, but the editors share Hubert Mordek's assessment of the potential value of legal prologues as historical

25. Mordek, *Kirchenrecht,* 34, n. 96 (German text cited by Brasington, "Prologues," 229, n. 12).

sources. Behind the rhetorical flourishes inculcated into medieval authors by study of the *trivium,* prefaces can help to map out the contours and describe the evolution of collections of canon law from antiquity through the High Middle Ages. It is fortunate that so many of these introductions exist, for an editor can select the most revealing across a wide span of time—from the diversity of the early Middle Ages to canon law at the service of the popes and as a scholastic discipline in the thirteenth century.[26]

Some limitations to this project must be acknowledged. There are shortcomings to any translation, and it is important to bear in mind that many of the prologues translated here are not available in modern critical editions and had to be taken from early modern texts.[27] A decision was made not to incorporate manuscript research into this volume, nor to edit anew any of the sources used. It is worth repeating that this book is not, and should not be viewed as, a history of canon law or canonical doctrine. The editors are aware, furthermore, that at

26. It would be difficult to count the dozens of works from between the sixth and the twelfth centuries to which the label "canonical collection" applies. A rough idea can be gained from handbooks, such as Fournier-LeBras, *Histoire,* Stickler, *Historia,* Van de Wiel, *History,* and Van Hove, *Prolegomena,* although a more precise answer must also take account of modifications to compilations that produce what are essentially new collections. See Robert Somerville, "A Textual Link between Canterbury and Lucca in the Early Twelfth Century?" in *Cristianità ed Europa: Miscellanea di studi in onore di Luigi Prosdocimi,* ed. Cesare Alzati (Rome, 1994), 1:405–6.

27. See Charles Donahue, *Why the History of Canon Law Is Not Written* (London, 1986), 11–12, an essay which is stimulating reading for anyone interested in the history of canon law. It is not always possible to tell whether headings—e.g., *Praefatio*—found before prefaces in early modern editions are original parts of the text or editorial additions.

all points in the time period covered, but especially from the twelfth century onward, the range of material which can be classed under the heading "canon law" exceeds what can be neatly encompassed by the designation "canonical collection." Liturgical books come to mind for the early period, and in the High Middle Ages a wide range of forms emerged for legal discourse. Even in a larger book it would be difficult to encompass that diversity, and the decision to treat "collections"—expanding that term just enough to include early scholastic *summae*—is an editorial judgment about presenting a coherent selection of previously inaccessible material for a nonspecialized audience. A different and more comprehensive book would move beyond canon law and include for comparison prefaces from the great collections of Roman law and of scholastic theology. In the end, the authors make a plea analogous to that found in many of their prefaces: may readers find herein things that are useful and be indulgent about shortcomings, bearing in mind specifically the words of Bishop Martin of Braga, that "it is difficult for something to be translated sufficiently clearly from one language to another."

2

Late Antiquity and the
Early Middle Ages

This chapter presents introductions from seven canonical collections which can be dated between the year 500 and the early eighth century. The earliest are three dedicatory letters to compilations put together in Italy by the monk Dionysius Exiguus; the latest comes from the Irish Collection of Canons (*Collectio Canonum Hibernensis*). Dionysius was not the West's first compiler of Church law, but no previous collection exerted comparable influence, and no earlier prologues have been found which delineate the content, purpose, and structure of the accompanying work.[1]

What do these prefaces reveal? They describe the "stuff" of canon law, assess Latin translations of decrees promulgated originally in Greek, draw attention to certain problematic texts, relate the aims and organization of their collections, and even touch on the problem of discrepancies among canonical texts. No one introduction treats all of these points, and discussions

1. The fifth-century *Statuta ecclesiae antiqua* (C. Munier, ed., *Les Statuta ecclesiae antiqua* [Paris, 1960], 75ff., and Munier, *Concilia Galliae A. 314–A. 506* [Corpus Christianorum, Series Latina 148; Turnhout, 1963], 162ff.), composed in southern Gaul toward the end of the fifth century although transmitted as canons of the Fourth Council of Carthage, begin with a prologue which gives a discussion of the desirable qualities of a bishop, but no information about the genesis and intent of the compilation (see Klaus Zechiel-Eckes, *Die concordia canonum des Cresconius* [Freiburger Beiträge zur mittelalterlichen Geschichte 5; Frankfurt, 1992], 1:32, n. 10).

are not as detailed or as precise as a modern reader would hope, yet the prologues offer an informative entry to the early centuries of Latin Church law. The collections represented, for example, preserve many of the same canons, and certain themes appear more than once among the prefaces (e.g., concern about accurate translation of Greek texts, about the troublesome Canons of the Apostles [see chap. 1], and about how the law can be applied). Each prologue also depicts the attitudes of a regional church and illustrates the religious diversity of late antiquity and the early Middle Ages through the different emphases which emerge.

Although outside the category of prefaces per se, one of the earliest surviving papal decretal letters—the decretal sent in 385 by Pope Siricius (384–99) to Bishop Himerius of Tarragona, on the Mediterranean coast in northeastern Spain—is included in this section.[2] Despite the geographical distance between them, Himerius had posed a series of questions to Pope Damasus I (366–84), but the pope had not replied by the time of his death. That his successor did so, soon after election, indicates both Siricius's sense of continuity with his predecessor and the Roman Church's willingness to give advice. The pope's language is both stern and fraternal, offering an ecclesiology which accentuates papal dignity and authority and the obligation of others to recognize that status. Himerius's side of the correspondence has perished so his questions are known only from Siricius, but seemingly the church at Tarragona was struggling with heterodoxy, disciplinary problems, and a search for norms by which to operate (and it had to endure, it should be added, Siricius's

2. JK 255. The identity of the earliest surviving decretal has been debated; see Gaudemet, *Les Sources,* 61, and Landau, "Kanonisches Recht," 556, n. 7. On the origin of papal decretals and decretals as sources of law, see chap. 1.

disapproval of various local goings-on). Aside from vignettes of church life, noteworthy are: (1) Siricius's use of authorities, pre-eminently the Bible but also councils and enactments by Pope Liberius (352–66) for which general authority was claimed; and (2) the request for Himerius to circulate the letter to other regions. Whatever the church at Tarragona thought of Siricius's reprimands and counsel, the document is one of the earliest authentic papal letters subsumed into the canonical tradition; it was included in Dionysius, from whom it was taken by Cresconius and the Spanish Collection, and from the latter it came to Pseudo Isidore (see chap. 3). Through these channels the decretal was known in the High Middle Ages, and portions are found in Gratian's *Decretum* (see chap. 5).[3] Pope Siricius's letter is not a preface to a canonical collection nor a bull of promulgation, but is included as the earliest text translated, as a prelude to the development of law in the Latin Church.

To understand the early collections requires some knowledge of the Latin versions of conciliar canons, especially those from the Council of Nicaea. Sometime between the pontificates of Julius I (337–52) and Innocent I (401–17), but probably earlier rather than later, a Latin translation of the Greek text of the twenty canons of Nicaea became available in the Roman Church. To these Nicene decrees the canons of the Council of Sardica (343/344; modern Sofia) were appended without a

3. Despite such future prospects, it seems the letter was not included in the earliest collections of decretals, which were assembled in the fifth century before the pontificate of Leo the Great (440–461) and which appear to have gathered only fifth-century material: see Hubert Mordek, "Der Römische Primat in den Kirchenrechtssammlungen des Westens vom IV. bis VIII. Jahrhundert," *Il Primato del vescovo di Roma nel primo millennio* (Pontificio Comitato di scienze storiche, Atti e documenti 4; Vatican City, 1991), 545ff.

break.[4] This work is designated by modern scholars as the "Old Roman" version of Nicaea. The synod at Sardica, convened by the Emperors Constans and Constantius, was intended to be an assembly in the tradition of Nicaea, but it quickly split into Eastern and Western factions due to the theological and political tensions of the Arian Controversy. The Western bishops, under the presidency of Hosius of Córdoba, enacted a set of decrees which included establishing the bishop of Rome as a court of appeal in certain circumstances for accused bishops.

In the early fifth century an African priest named Apiarius in the diocese of Sicca Veneria, deposed by his bishop, appealed to Pope Zosimus (417–18) on the basis of what were said to be canons of Nicaea but in reality were from Sardica. The African church succeeded in obtaining a Greek text of the Nicene decrees, and a Latin translation was made of them plus those of other Eastern councils through Constantinople I (381), but whether in Rome or Africa has been debated.[5] Notwithstanding the possible existence of earlier local versions whose traces have vanished, the decrees of Eastern synods other than Nicaea can be documented in Latin here for the first time. They circulated thence in various combinations, eventually being used by the seventh-century Spanish Collection (this rendition thus is termed the "Spanish," or even the "Isidorian" version, given the possible connection of Isidore of Seville with the Spanish Collection). Before the end of the fifth century, however, another translation of the Eastern canons also was to be found

4. For what follows see Gaudemet, *Les Sources,* esp. 76–91; Mordek, "Römische Primat," 528ff.; and also his "Karthago oder Rom?" in *Studia in honorem em.mi Card. Alfons M. Stickler,* ed. R. J. Card. Castillo Lara (Studia et textus historiae iuris canonici 7; Rome, 1992), 359ff.

5. In "Carthago oder Rom?" Mordek opts for an African origin for the collection, which was revised in Rome to accentuate the role of papal authority in approving conciliar decrees.

in the Roman Church. This work is called the *Prisca* (i.e., "old," or "former"; sometimes also dubbed the "Italian version"). The label *Prisca* was bestowed by the early modern scholar Christophe Justel (+1649), following a reference in the prologue to his translation of the Greek councils by Dionysius Exiguus about the "confusion of the 'old translation'" (see below). The *Prisca* differs from the Spanish version in certain ways, such as adding the canons of the Council of Chalcedon (451) and retaining the decrees of Sardica joined to those of Nicaea.

This very brief summary of much that is complex and still debated by specialists leads directly to Dionysius Exiguus. Dionysius was a native of Scythia (present-day Romania) who came to Rome at the end of the fifth century.[6] He probably arrived in the reign of Pope Anastasius I (496–98), since he wrote at one point that he never saw Anastasius's predecessor Pope Gelasius I (492–96). The self-applied sobriquet *exiguus* ("small, insignificant") no doubt was engendered by monastic humility. Little is certain about the course of Dionysius's life. The time in which he was active at Rome was a period of turmoil, marked by the Acacian Schism between Rome and Constantinople and a local schism between Pope Symmachus (498–514) and his rival, the antipope Lawrence (+507/8). Nothing of Dionysius's involvement in these affairs is known, but Cassiodorus extols his excellent reputation and range of contacts, and it seems unlikely that he was sympathetic to those deemed schismatics. The aim of Dionysius in his scholarly work has been seen

6. For Dionysius, see Gaudemet, *Les Sources*, esp. 134–37, and Hubert Mordek, "Dionysius Exiguus," *Lexikon des Mittelalters* (1986), 3:1088–92. For a useful general survey of collections of canon law before the mid-twelfth century, see Jörg Müller, "Forschungsstand und aktuelle Aufgabenplanung in der vorgratianischen Kanonistik," *Österreichisches Archiv für Kirchenrecht* 43 (1994): 225–40.

as a desire to unite the Greek and Latin ecclesiastical traditions through reliable and clearly presented translations, thus promoting understanding and reinforcing the sense of Christian unity between East and West.[7] Fluent in both tongues and possessed of literary skill, he translated many important Greek works into Latin. He is also famous for revising the Church calendar and establishing a new method for calculating Easter. The date of his death is unknown but can be placed between the years 526 and 556.

Dionysius's legal work is often seen as a by-product of what is called the "Gelasian Renaissance," after Pope Gelasius I. How much, in fact, this pontiff's leadership was responsible for fostering research in canon law and inspiring new collections is debated, although his brief reign generated important papal texts which were significant elements in the medieval canonical and political tradition.[8] Whatever role Gelasius had in his work, the accomplishments of Dionysius rank him as one of the most significant figures in the history of canon law. He also is one of the few canonists before the High Middle Ages who both reveals himself by name as the author of his work and about whom something — however little it might be — is known (cf. below for Cresconius). The term "Dionysian Collection" (*Collectio Dionysiana*) is employed today in various ways, but especially to refer to a composite work made up of two separate chronological collections, one devoted to synodal decrees and the other to papal decretals. These works with their revisions and amplifications were one of the prime channels by which texts of early

7. See Mordek, "Dionysius," 1089, which draws on the work of H. Wurm.

8. Especially well known is his letter to the Emperor Anastasius (JK 632), delineating the separate responsibilities of clerical and secular powers, which has given rise to the term "Gelasian dualism"; for a partial translation see Tierney, *Crisis,* 13–14.

Church law came to later centuries. They can be considered under three headings.

1. A book of conciliar canons was assembled by Dionysius shortly after his arrival in Rome. It survives in two recensions. The second was dedicated to Bishop Stephen of Salona (on the coast of Dalmatia, present-day Solin), lauded as Dionysius's true inspiration in assembling the work, although "our dearest brother Lawrence"—whoever he was—seemingly "offended . . . by the confusion" of the *Prisca* translation had urged Dionysius to undertake the project. It is unknown what problems Lawrence had with the *Prisca*. Perhaps he was put off by mistranslations or upset by the unbroken sequence therein of the Nicene and Sardican canons, or by the fact that the *Prisca* ascribed canon 28 of the Council of Chalcedon—which accentuated the prestige of the church of Constantinople, which Pope Leo I (440–461) had refused to accept and which Dionysius would exclude—to Constantinople I (381). Other than Nicaea, in his preface Dionysius did not name the Eastern councils that issued the 165 canons which he translated and numbered. These post-Nicene synods are: Ancyra (314), Neo-Caesarea in Cappadocia (between 314 and 319), Gangra (343), Antioch (330 or 341), Laodicea (between 343 and 380), and Constantinople I. His scruples about authenticity and accuracy are revealed by Dionysius's caution to Stephen about the so-called Canons of the Apostles[9] and his care, lest he be suspected of promoting

9. It seems unlikely that the so-called Decree of Gelasius (*Decretum Gelasianum,* falsely attributed to Pope Gelasius I), listing which books should and should not be received in the Church, could have influenced Dionysius on this matter; the section of the decree which rejects the Canons of the Apostles seems to have been composed early in the sixth century in southern Gaul. See *Clavis patrum Latinorum,* 3d ed. (Turnhout, 1995), no. 1676, and Hubert Mordek, "Decretum Gelasianum," *Lexikon des Mittelalters* (1986), 3:624–25. See also n. 23, below.

deception, to give the Sardican canons and the canons from African councils separate from the others. Also noteworthy — and of value to users of this chronologically arranged book—is the index of title headings at the beginning of the work.

2. Another recension of the councils was commissioned by Pope Hormisdas (514–23), but a letter of dedication to the pope is all that survives from this interesting enterprise. Hormisdas had requested a bilingual text: Greek, with a word-for-word Latin translation. At the beginning of his preface Dionysius perhaps hinted that he found the need for a new rendering into Latin strange because he had already translated the Eastern decrees. He continued, however, and provided a context for Hormisdas's request when he noted that the Canons of the Apostles, the Council of Sardica, and the African canons were now excluded because the pope wished to know which texts were received in common by East and West.

3. Some scholars have contended that Dionysius had access to the papal archives. Whether or not that is so, he compiled a relatively small collection (on what principles remains unknown) of decretals from Popes Siricius, Innocent I, Zosimus, Boniface, Celestine I, Leo I, Gelasius I, and Anastasius II. That work is generally dated toward the end of the reign of Pope Symmachus and was dedicated to Julian, priest of the title church of S. Anastasia in Rome. Only the first part of the dedicatory epistle is given below (the remainder is a lengthy panegyric of Julian, of rhetorical interest but adding little if anything about the work). This collection of papal texts was not the first such compilation, but it is distinctive by its focus on legal content. Dionysius strove for clarity in highlighting this feature by not hesitating, as he wrote to Julian, to divide the decretals according to the "precepts" (*praecepta*) found in each. He composed titles for these subsections, and as with the conciliar collection,

since he knew that Julian approved, he placed an index of these rubrics at the beginning of the book.

Although his talent was highly valued in the Roman Church —witness the commission from Hormisdas—and there is evidence that his collections were used there as early as the reign of Pope John II in 534, Dionysius's books never were thought of as official codifications. Because compilers before him had also gathered conciliar and papal texts, he is not, furthermore, differentiated from others of his age in terms of the specific materials with which he worked. The distinction of Dionysius lies in his accuracy of translation, the quality of language used, and his organization of a substantial corpus of canons, which enabled readers to locate, with a degree of ease, what they wanted within a chronological schema. With his solicitude for accuracy, for authenticity, and for presenting a body of canons in a clear fashion, Dionysius set a new standard in assembling Church law, and the success of his works is understandable. With the exception of Martin of Braga's work, all the collections represented in this chapter appear indebted to his books.

In contrast to Dionysius, Cresconius is only a name attached to a collection.[10] The time and place of composition of the Concord of Canons (*Concordia canonum*) has been debated, with Italy or Africa and the sixth or the seventh centuries proposed. The work's modern editor, Klaus Zechiel-Eckes, argues for an Italian provenance and a date in the second half of the sixth

10. Zechiel-Eckes, *Concordia* (see n. 1, above), in his first volume, gives a full treatment of the collection, its sources, and the historical issue surrounding composition, whence these comments derive. In general, for the later section of this chapter much of value is found in Roger E. Reynolds, "The Organisation, Law and Liturgy of the Western Church, 700–900," in *The New Cambridge Medieval History II, c.700–c.900*, ed. Rosamond McKitterick (Cambridge, 1991), 587–621.

century, in large part because of Cresconius's heavy use of Dionysius. At one point in his preface Cresconius even refers to himself as *exiguus* among the servants of Christ.[11] The *Concordia* was undertaken at the request of a Bishop Liberinus, likewise unknown, and has been called "extraordinary for its time,"[12] given the manner in which a large array of texts are distributed systematically under numbered titles. These headings are listed in numerical order in a table of contents, with references to the canons found under each one. This systematic arrangement shows what a "concord" of canons meant to Cresconius. The preface is also extraordinary for its rich detail about the work it introduces.

Cresconius was confident about his book's pedagogical utility. He also believed that knowledge of the canons would help a judge decide whether to render a sentence "according to severity or leniency," although he did not elucidate principles for reaching that decision and his advice to rely on proven authorities remains vague. Throughout his preface Cresconius reacts to the Breviary of Canons (*Breviatio canonum*) compiled on episcopal order by Deacon Ferrandus of the church in Carthage around the years 546–547, soon after the Vandal invasion of North Africa.[13] Ferrandus referred to but did not quote decrees of Eastern and African councils in this handbook of 232 brief statements which summarized many canonical issues. Cresconius's skepticism about the utility of the Breviary is to the point:

11. Zechiel-Eckes, *Concordia*, 1:83, indicates, however, that this designation occurs in both Dionysius and in the work of Fulgentius (see n. 13, below).

12. Reynolds, "Law, Canon," 400.

13. For Ferrandus, see Reynolds, "Law, Canon"; Gaudemet, *Les Sources*, 137–38. Zechiel-Eckes, *Concordia*, 1:116, gives a wider span for dating Ferrandus's work, i.e., certainly after 523, perhaps at the beginning of the 530s, but before the end of the sixth century.

it might be helpful to someone already versed in the canons—who knew where to find them and how to read them—but frustrating to a novice.

The *Concordia* was well received in early medieval Europe, and churchmen no doubt found its systematic presentations of canonical tradition very useful. An expanded version was produced between 680 and 689 in northern Italy, probably as an orthodox initiative during final stages of the long-standing dispute over the "Three Chapters."[14] Cresconius's work also was known in the Carolingian Church and even beyond. It was cited in the preface to the *Collectio Anselmo Dedicata* (see chap. 3), where Cresconius is termed an "imitator" of Ferrandus, and as late as the twelfth century the *Summa "Antiquitate et tempore"* on Gratian gives two references to texts found "in Cresconius"[15] (see chap. 5).

Roughly contemporary with Cresconius, a small canon law collection was assembled in the northwestern corner of the

14. The "Three Chapters," the term used for three condemnations by the Emperor Justinian I in 543–44, and again at the Council of Constantinople in 553, in hopes of placating the Monophysites by a burst of anti-Nestorian zeal, were condemnations of: (1) the person and works of Theodore of Mopsuestia; (2) the writings of Theodoret of Cyrrhus against Cyril of Alexandria; (3) the letter of Ibas of Edessa to Bishop Mari of Hardascir in Persia.

15. Zechiel-Eckes, *Concordia*, 1:245–47 (and 246, n. 141, for the reference to Cresconius as an *imitator* of Ferrandus) and 292–93; see also Stephan Kuttner and Eleanor Rathbone, "Anglo-Norman Canonists of the Twelfth Century," *Traditio* 7 (1949–51): 300–301 (rpt. in Stephan Kuttner, *Gratian and the Schools of Law, 1140–1234* [Variorum Reprints CS185; London, 1983]). See also Peter Landau, "Vorgratianische Kanonessammlungen bei den Dekretisten und in frühen Dekretalensammlungen," in *Proceedings of the Sixth International Congress of Medieval Canon Law*, ed. Stanley Chodorow (Monumenta iuris canonici, Subsidia 9; Vatican City, 1992), 112–13, and the appendix, "Cresconius und die Summe 'Antiquitate et tempore.'"

Iberian peninsula by a bishop who also was troubled by inadequacies in earlier canonical works. Martin of Braga, like Dionysius, was both a monk and a native of an eastern region—Pannonia (modern Hungary).[16] He probably arrived in Galicia around the middle of the sixth century and was soon active in the conversion of King Chararich of the Sueves from Arian to orthodox Christianity. First abbot and then bishop at the monastery he established at Dumio near Braga, Martin was made archbishop of Braga between the first and the second synods in that city (561 and 572). He died there in 580. His canonical work is known as the Chapters (*Capitula*), which is equivalent to "stipulations" or "canons." The dedicatory letter addressed to Archbishop Nitigisius of Lugo and his province indicates that the work was assembled after 569, that is, after the separation of the ecclesiastical provinces of Lugo and Braga. Perhaps its composition was connected in some way with the Second Council of Braga, where both Martin and Nitigisius were participants, and to whose acts it is appended in manuscripts of the Spanish Collection.[17]

The dedicatory letter serves as a prologue for the collection and is explicit about its purpose. Translation, the author confessed, is a difficult task, and the available versions of the Greek

16. For Martin's life see Claude W. Barlow, *Martini episcopi Bracarensis opera omnia* (Papers and Monographs of the American Academy in Rome 12; New Haven, 1950), 2–8; and more recently, Jean Gaudemet, "'Traduttore, traditore'—Les Capitula Martini," *Fälschungen im Mittelalter, 2: Gefälschte Rechtstexte, Der bestrafte Fälscher* (Monumenta Germaniae Historica, Schriften 33.2; Stuttgart, 1988), 51–5; and J. M. Alonso-Núñez, "Martin von Braga," *Lexikon des Mittelalters* (1993), 6:343–44.

17. Gaudemet, "'Traduttore,'" 52, writes that the work was composed shortly after 572.

canons are faulty. Martin, whose education obviously included Greek, would try to do better. He assembled a small book of eight-four chapters divided into two parts—one dealing with clergy and the other with laity—in the hope that users could readily find what they wanted. Martin gave no attributions for his texts, nor are they chronologically ordered, although each chapter is introduced by a short title about its content. In a compilation of this size a separate index would have been almost redundant. The preface implies that only Eastern councils were taken into account, and although they predominate, Martin employed Western material too, for example, from the First Council of Toledo (397–400) and from the first at Braga. A few of his excerpts remain to be identified, perhaps because, as opposed to the care which Dionysius exhibited toward his texts, Martin took liberties with his, presenting items "more according to sense than to the letter."[18] The preface provides no insight as to whether his formal source contained excerpts or whether Martin adapted the canons for his own purposes.[19]

The *Capitula* of Martin are not known to survive on their own,[20] but they were deemed important enough to be incorporated into other works from the Iberian peninsula, especially the seventh-century Spanish Collection (*Collectio His-*

18. Stickler, *Historia*, 38.

19. Given the literal style of Martin's other translations, Barlow found it hard to accept that he had altered ecclesiastical law and wrote: "it must be conjectured that he had a different Greek original" (*Opera*, 84–85). It is unclear how tenable a view this is, and others see Martin as adapting the canons to his pastoral needs. See, e.g., García y García, *Historia*, 179, and Gaudemet, " 'Traduttore,' " 55ff. (see n. 16, above), and also *Les Sources*, 153.

20. For traces of the *Capitula* in others collections, see García y García, *Historia*, 179–80.

pana), which like the collections of Dionysius had a profound impact on later canon law.[21] Unlike the books treated so far in this chapter, the *Hispana* does not carry the name of an author. Yet on the basis of the great similarities between its preface and book VI, chapter 16 of Isidore of Seville's *Etymologies,* Bishop Isidore (+636) has been proposed for this role, although the matter is unresolved. The Spanish Collection is a vast historical compilation, beginning with councils—Eastern, through canon 27 of Chalcedon (and including Sardica distinct from Nicaea), African, Gallican, and Spanish. In its earliest form the Spanish series probably extended through Toledo IV (633). The work thus would date between 633 and the convocation of Toledo V in 636, but the list of synodal rulings was expanded in later recensions to include gatherings held through the seventh century. The conciliar section is followed by a sequence of papal texts in chronological order, from Damasus I through Gregory I (590–604), with Dionysius an important source (a dependence also clear in the work's preface).

The goal of the collection—in some ways similar to that of Dionysius—was to provide a large magazine of texts, especially from councils. The decrees are clearly identified, with titles summarizing their content preceding them throughout. The introduction does not ignore the work's organization, but this certainly was not its focus: aside from a comment about numbering the canons, no details are given either about how the work would facilitate learning or about finding and applying the law, although in a few lines borrowed from Dionysius a regimen

21. The *Hispana* is the object of a great scholarly project, still underway, to produce a critical edition: Gonzalo Martínez Díez, S.J., et al., *La Colección canónica Hispana* (Monumenta Hispaniae Sacra, Serie Canónica, 5 vols. to date; Madrid, 1966–).

of ecclesiastical discipline under the canons is lauded.[22] The prologue of the Spanish Collection is most concerned with assembling an ecclesiology which appears to mirror the Visigothic church after the conversion of King Recared from Arianism in 587. A period of close cooperation between Church and state then ensued, and beginning with the Third Council of Toledo in 589 a series of synods offered regular forums where bishops and secular leaders cooperated in regulating many facets of society.

In this environment the Spanish Collection was born, and the short conciliar history which opens the preface outlines the triumph of orthodoxy achieved in the Roman Empire through the cooperation of emperors and bishops in the four great ecumenical councils (see chap. 1). A rationale then is offered for subsequent synods, and the etymology which concludes the prologue reiterates, in a way which today can appear strange, the lasting importance of councils. Papal authority is not ignored; yet its acknowledgment, after the catena of synodal grandeur which dominates the first part of the text, could—but probably should not—be read as a backhanded concession. Unlike Dionysius, the Spanish compiler set aside the Canons of the Apostles. Their utility is conceded, but due to heretical stigma, and because they are said not to have received the approbation of tradition, either papal or conciliar, they are not authoritative.[23]

The last preface in this chapter belongs to an Irish collection. Celtic Christianity developed its own distinctive traditions because Ireland was never subject to direct Roman influ-

22. For a discussion of the preface and its sources, see Martínez Díez, *Colección*, 1:271–77.
23. Perhaps the so-called Decree of Gelasius influenced the compiler's attitude toward the Canons of the Apostles (see above, n. 9).

ence. Around the year 700 or a bit later a systematic collection was assembled there, the Irish Collection of Canons (*Collectio canonum Hibernensis*), which blended papal and conciliar texts of the sort available in the great Continental source books with a variety of other material. Some of these new sources were Irish, including penitential and synodal texts, and others derived from the Bible and patristic writings. Attributions can be tricky: a group of Insular sayings go under the name "Proverbs of the Greeks."[24] The use of theological and Biblical excerpts as "canons" is not totally new, but the extent of their use in the *Collectio canonum Hibernensis* is, and thus the work stands as a point of departure for a major expansion of the "collected" canonical tradition.[25]

The work is arranged by titles, and the canons which appear under them have often been edited significantly to suit the author's purpose. Maurice Sheehy has warned modern readers about glib evaluations of the collection: "How . . . external sources were used is something that requires the greatest caution. Unless the primary aim of the compilers is constantly kept in mind, the use, or apparent misuse, of these sources can be misunderstood. For a correct interpretation of this collection as thorough a knowledge as possible of native secular law and custom, and the conditions which prevailed when the earliest Irish law tracts were put to paper, is of paramount importance."[26]

24. Maurice P. Sheehy, "The Collectio Canonum Hibernensis—a Celtic Phenomenon," in *Die Iren und Europa im früheren Mittelalter,* ed. Heinz Löwe (Stuttgart, 1982), 1:528. The Latin is *proverbia Graecorum.*

25. See, e.g., Roger E. Reynolds, "Unity and Diversity in Carolingian Canon Law Collections: The Case of the *Collectio Hibernensis* and Its Derivatives," in *Carolingian Essays,* ed. Uta-Renate Blumenthal (Washington, D.C., 1983), 101 (rpt. in Reynolds, *Law and Liturgy in the Latin Church, 5th–12th Centuries* [Variorum Collected Studies Series CS457; Aldershot, 1994]).

26. Sheehy, "Collectio," 529.

Earlier Sheehy has denoted the aim of the compilers as "an attempt to draw-up a blueprint for all aspects of Christian living in an alien civilisation" where the influence of Continental Church law was not taken for granted.[27] The Irish Collection of Canons was, therefore, a work which harmonized Irish and non-Irish traditions, and Sheehy does not shy away from calling it "the most ambitious endeavor to codify Christian life of all the medieval canonical compilations."[28]

How much of this blueprint is visible in the preface? The answer would depend to an extent on a deeper familiarity with the collection proper than these comments can provide, but just as the Irish Collection of Canons differs significantly from the other collections that have been treated, so does its introduction. A short prelude to the actual preface, which occurs in at least one manuscript of those used for Wasserschleben's edition, admitted that the author expanded the range of the canons to encompass biblical and theologicial writings and forewarned readers to follow the greater authority if an inconsistency was spotted among rulings in the book. As with Cresconius's advice to base judgments on texts of confirmed authority, this counsel is not as lucid as a modern reader might like, yet no further help is provided and no hierarchy of authorities is given. The preface goes on to lament, with considerable bluntness, the difficulties in using the received synodal texts, which are likened to an enormous forest—an image that will reappear in the twelfth century in reference to papal decretals. An editor was needed to prune this jungle, and the author freely noted his intention to do so, by cutting, adding, and even recasting the texts. Nothing in this process was to be ascribed to personal whim, no doubt meaning that editorial work was undertaken to clarify what the

27. Ibid., 527.
28. Ibid.

tradition meant to say, although on what principle this was discovered is unstated. A concluding set of remarks alerts users to the compilation's organization into titles, with a numbered index of these headings found at the beginning of the book.

Martin of Braga seems to have exercised editorial license similar to that found in the Irish Collection of Canons, but he did not make a point of confessing it, whereas Cresconius by and large handled his texts faithfully.[29] The *Hibernensis* awaits a modern critical edition, so the details of its editorial procedures remain to be elucidated. As with Cresconius's *Concordia,* the work circulated on the Continent during the Carolingian period and exerted influence into the twelfth century, especially in central and southern Italy.[30]

TRANSLATIONS

1. Letter of Pope Siricius to Bishop Himerius of Tarragona, 385. Ed. Pierre Coustant, *Epistolae Romanorum pontificum* (Paris, 1721; rpt. Farnborough, 1967), 623–38.

Siricius to Himerius, bishop of Tarragona.

1. The account which you, brother, directed to our predecessor of holy memory Damasus, found me now installed in his see because the Lord thus ordained. When we read that [account] more carefully in an assembly of brethren, we found to the degree we had hoped to recognize things which ought to be praised much which was worthy of reprimand and correction. And since it is necessary for us to succeed to the labors and responsibilities of him whom, through the grace of God, we succeeded in honor, having first given notice, as was necessary, of my promotion, we do not refuse, as the Lord deigns to

29. Zechiel-Eckes, *Concordia,* 55 (see n. 1, above).
30. See Reynolds, "Unity" (see 135–35 for his conclusions).

inspire, a proper response to your inquiry in every point. For in view of our office there is no freedom for us, on whom a zeal for the Christian religion is incumbent greater than on all others, to dissimulate or to be silent. We bear the burdens of all who are oppressed, or rather the blessed apostle Peter, who in all things protects and preserves us, the heirs, as we trust, of his administration, bears them in us.

2. On the first page of your letter, therefore, you indicated that multitudes who were baptized by the impious Arians were hastening to the catholic faith, and that certain of our brothers wished to baptize these same people again. This is not allowed, since both the Apostle forbids[31] and the canons oppose doing it;[32] and after the Council of Rimini[33] was annulled, the general decrees sent to the provinces by my predecessor of venerable memory Liberius prohibit it. We unite these people, and the Novatianists and other heretics, to the assembly of catholics, just as it was constituted in the synod,[34] solely through invocation of the sevenfold Spirit by imposition of the bishop's hand. Indeed all the East and the West preserves this practice, and it is also inappropriate henceforth for you to deviate from that path, if you do not wish to be separated from our company by synodal sentence.

3. Then follows objectionable confusion, in need of correction, about those who are about to be baptized just as it pleases each and every one of them. Our fellow priests—we speak in indignation—not by reason of any authority but by temerity alone presume this, so that throngs of people, as you report, at-

31. Cf. Ephesians 4:5.

32. Van Hove, *Prolegomena*, 138, n. 1, refers this canonical prohibition to canon 8 of the Council of Arles, 314.

33. Summoned by the Emperor Constantius in the year 359.

34. See Coustant, *Epistolae*, 625, n. a, for the Council of Nicaea, canon 8, but Siricius says more than is found there.

tain the mystery of baptism randomly and freely at Christmas, or Epiphany, and also on the feasts of the apostles or martyrs, although both with us and in all churches the Lord's Resurrection and Pentecost claim this privilege specially for themselves. On these days alone through the year is it proper for the complete rites of baptism to be bestowed on those coming to the faith, but only on those select people who applied forty or more days earlier, and were cleansed by exorcisms, daily prayers, and fasts, so that the precept of the Apostle is fulfilled that with old leaven having been driven out, new dough comes into being.[35] But just as we say that sacred Paschal reverence in no way ought to be diminished, so we wish for the waters of sacred baptism to be of assistance with all speed to infants, who because of age are not yet able to speak, and to those for whom in any emergency it is needed, lest the destruction of our souls be at stake if, the salutary font being denied to those seeking it, someone departing from the world loses both the kingdom and life. Whoever, indeed, suffers the peril of shipwreck, the assault of an enemy, the uncertainty of a siege, or the despair of any bodily illness and demands to be supported by the singular help of belief, at the very same moment when they demand, the advantages of the sought for regeneration should follow. Enough error on this matter! All priests who do not wish to be torn from the solidity of the apostolic rock, upon which Christ built the universal Church, should now hold the aforementioned rule.

4. It was also added that certain Christians, crossing over into apostasy—which is abominable to be uttered—have been profaned by the worship of idols and the pollution of sacrifices. We order that they be cut off from the body and blood of Christ, by which formerly they were redeemed in new birth. And if coming to their senses at some point perhaps they turn

35. Cf. 1 Corinthians 5:7.

to grieving, they should do penance as long as they live, and in their final moments the grace of reconciliation ought to be given, because, as the Lord teaches, we do not wish the death of a sinner, only that he be converted and live.[36]

5. You also asked about marriage, whether someone can marry a girl who was betrothed to another. We forbid by all means that this be done because that blessing which a priest imposes to a girl who is to be married is, if it is violated by any transgression, a kind of sacrilege among the faithful.

6. Not improperly, beloved, you believed that the apostolic see should be consulted about those who, having performed penance, again hungered, just as dogs and swine returning to old vomit and wallowing ponds,[37] for the military belt, pleasures of the theater, new marriages, and forbidden liaisons whose manifest incontinence was shown by children born after absolution. Concerning them, because now they do not have the option of doing penance, we decided that this ought to be decreed. Inside church they can be united with the faithful only in prayer; they can be present for the sacred celebration of the mysteries, although they are unworthy, but should be excluded from the banquet of the Lord's table, so that reproached at least by this stricture they can castigate their faults within themselves and give an example to others that they may be drawn back from obscene desires. But since they fell by weakness of the flesh, we wish them to be supported by the gift of a viaticum through the grace of communion when they are about to depart to the Lord. We are of the opinion that this procedure should be observed also for women who, after penance, devoted themselves to such pollutions.

7. You indicate, furthermore, that certain monks and nuns,

36. Cf. Ezekiel 18:23.
37. Cf. 2 Peter 2:22.

having thrown off the life of sanctity, plunged into so much wantonness that they tangled themselves up in illicit and sacrilegious intercourse, first in secret, as it were under cover of the monasteries, but afterward, led on precipitously by abandonment of conscience they freely produced children with illicit partners, which both civil laws and ecclesiastical regulations condemn.[38] We command, therefore, that these shameless and detestable persons should be banished from the community of monasteries and the congregations of churches, so that having been thrust away in personal imprisonment, bewailing with constant lamentation so great an outrage, they can roast in the purifying fire of repentance so that at least at death, out of consideration of mercy alone, forgiveness through the grace of communion can assist even them.[39]

8. Let us come now to the most sacred orders of clerics, which we learn from your report, beloved, are thus so scorned and disordered throughout your provinces, to the injury of religion which should be venerated, that we should be speaking with the voice of Jeremiah, "Who will give water to my head, or a fountain of tears to my eyes? And I shall weep for this people day and night."[40] If, therefore, the blessed prophet says that tears are insufficient for him in lamenting the sins of the people, by how much grief can we be smitten when compelled to deplore the iniquities of those who are in our body, [we] to

38. In terms of Church law, see, e.g., canon 19 of the Council of Ancyra, 314.

39. For this passage see Edward M. Peters, "Prison before the Prison: The Ancient and Medieval Worlds," in *The Oxford History of the Prison: The Practice of Punishment in Western Society,* ed. Norval Morris and David J. Rothman (New York, 1995), 28. For the reenactment of this section of Siricius's letter at the Council of Tribur in 895, see J. D. Mansi, *Sacrorum conciliorum nova et amplissima collectio,* 18 (Venice, 1773), 145.

40. Jeremiah 9:1.

whom especially, according to blessed Paul, ceaselessly falls the daily concern and solicitude of all churches? "For who is weak and I am not weak? Who is offended and I do not burn?"[41] For we learned that many priests and deacons of Christ, long after their ordination, have produced offspring both from their own wives and even through filthy liaisons, and defend their sin with this excuse, that it is read in the Old Testament that the opportunity to procreate was given to priests and ministers.

9. Let him speak to me now, whoever is an addict of obscenities and a teacher of vices. If he thinks that here and there in the law of Moses the restraints of indulgence are relaxed by the Lord for sacred orders, why does He admonish those to whom the Holy of Holies was committed saying: "Be holy, because I, the Lord your God, am holy"?[42] Why indeed were priests ordered to live in the temple, far from their homes, in the year of their service? Just for this reason: so that they could not engage in physical contact even with wives, and that shining in integrity of conscience they might offer acceptable service to God. The period of service having been completed, use of wives was permitted to them for reason of succession alone, because no one from a tribe other than of Levi was directed to be admitted to the ministry of God.

10. Whence the Lord Jesus, when he enlightened us by his advent, testified in the Gospel that he had come to fulfill the law not to destroy it.[43] And he wished thus that the figure of the Church, whose bridegroom he is, radiate with the splendor of chastity, so that on the day of judgment when he comes again he can find her without stain and blemish, just as he taught through his Apostle.[44] All we priests and deacons are bound by

41. 2 Corinthians 11:29.
42. Leviticus 20:7.
43. Matthew 5:17.
44. Cf. Ephesians 5:27.

the unbreakable law of those sanctions, so that from the day of our ordination we subject our hearts and bodies to moderation and modesty in order that in every respect we might please our God in these sacrifices which daily we offer. "They who are in the flesh," says the chosen vessel,[45] "are unable to please God. But you are not now in the flesh but in the Spirit, if indeed the Spirit of God dwells in you."[46] And where can the Spirit of God dwell except, as we read, in holy bodies?

11. And because a considerable number of those of whom we speak, as your holiness reported, lament that they lapsed in ignorance, we declare that mercy should not be denied to them, with this condition: if henceforth they strive to conduct themselves continently, they should continue as long as they live in that office which they held when they were caught, without any advancement in rank. But those who lean on the excuse of an illicit privilege by asserting that this was conceded to them in the old law, let them know that they have been expelled by the authority of the apostolic see from every ecclesiastical office, which they used unworthily, nor can they ever touch the mysteries which ought to be venerated, of which they deprived themselves when they were obsessed with obscene desires. And because present examples forewarn us to be vigilant in the future, any bishop, priest, and deacon henceforth found in this situation—which we hope will not happen—should understand right now that every avenue of forgiveness from us for himself is blocked, because it is necessary that wounds which do not respond to the medication of a soothing compress should be excised with a knife.

12. We learned, furthermore, that men of unexamined life, who even had many wives, boldly and freely aspire just as they

45. Acts 9:15.
46. Romans 8:8–9.

please to the aforementioned ranks. We place blame for this not so much on those who reach for these things with immoderate ambition as on the metropolitan bishops specifically, who, when they close their eyes to forbidden strivings, disdain as far as is possible the precepts of our God. Let us be silent about what we suspect more deeply; but what of that which our God constituted in the law given through Moses, saying, "Let my priests marry once," and in another place, "Let a priest take a virgin as a wife, not a widow, not a divorced woman, not a prostitute"?[47] Guided by this the Apostle, a persecutor turned preacher, commanded that both a priest and a deacon should be made "the husband of one wife."[48] All of these things are thus despised by the bishops of your regions, as if they were decreed more in the opposite sense. And because we should not ignore presumptions of this sort, lest the just voice of an indignant Lord reproach us when he says, "You saw a thief and you ran with him, and you cast your lot with adulterers,"[49] what henceforth should be followed by all churches, what should be avoided, we decree by general pronouncement.

13. Whoever, therefore, vows himself to the services of the Church from his infancy ought to be baptized before the years of puberty and attached to the ministry of readers. From the beginning of adolescence up to thirty years of age he ought to be an acolyte and subdeacon, if he lives properly, content with only one wife whom he received as a virgin with a public benediction by a priest. Subsequently he should advance to the grade of deacon, if first, with continence leading the way, he proves himself worthy. If he performs this ministry laudably for more than five years he should attain the priesthood. From there,

47. Cf. Leviticus 21:13-14; Ezekiel 44:22.
48. 1 Timothy 3:2.
49. Psalm 49 (50):18.

after a decade, he is able to reach the episcopal office, provided that during these times the integrity of his life and faith was demonstrated.

14. But he who, having been called to the conversion of a better way of life already advanced in years, is in a hurry to move from the laity to the sacred militia, will not otherwise obtain the fruit of his desire unless when baptized he is attached at once to the rank of readers or exorcists, if, that is, it is clear that he had or has one wife and that he received her as a virgin. Two years after his initiation having elapsed, he can be made an acolyte and subdeacon for five more, and thus can be advanced to the diaconate, if during these times he was judged worthy. Then subsequently, with the passage of time, if election of the clergy and people designates him, he justly can obtain the priesthood and the episcopate.

15. Any cleric indeed who marries a widow or a second wife should thereupon be stripped of all privilege of ecclesiastical rank, with communion as only a layman conceded to him, which he can then have provided that he does nothing henceforth for which he should lose it.

16. We certainly do not allow women in the houses of clerics, other than those alone whom the synod of Nicaea, for reasons only of necessities, permitted to live with them.[50]

17. We also desire and wish that monks who are commended by depth of character and a holy pattern of life and faith be added to the ranks of clerics in this way. Those under thirty years of age should be promoted in minor orders over time through the individual ranks and thus reach the honors of the diaconate and the priesthood with the dedication of maturity. They should not ascend in a jump to the height of the epis-

50. Council of Nicaea, 325, canon 3.

copate, but only after having served the same periods of time which we established above for the individual ranks.

18. It is proper also for us to ensure that just as it is not conceded to any member of the clergy to do penance, thus after repentance and reconciliation it is not permitted to any layman to attain the honor of clerical office. For although they have been cleansed of the contamination of all sins, nevertheless those who formerly were vessels of iniquities ought not to take up any of the instruments of the sacraments.

19. And because for all these things which come under censure the singular excuse of ignorance is pleaded, for the moment, out of consideration of piety alone, it is necessary that we indulgently make allowances for it. Any penitent, any twice married man, any husband of a widow who improperly and unsuitably slipped into the sacred militia should understand that pardon has been bestowed on them by us with this condition, that it should be counted as a great benefit if, having removed from himself all hope of promotion, he remains with perpetual steadfastness in that order where he is. Hereafter the bishops[51] of all provinces will know that if they believe that anyone of this sort should in the future be taken into sacred orders, an appropriate judgment is to be given by the apostolic see concerning both their own status and that of those whom they promoted contrary to the canons and to our prohibitions.

20. We explicated, I believe, dearest brother, all the things which were set forth as being at issue, and we provided adequate replies, in my opinion, to the individual cases which you referred to the Roman Church, just as to the head of your body, through our son the priest Bassianus. Now, brother, we incite your spirit more and more for observing the canons and adher-

51. The text reads *summi antistites.*

ing to the constituted decretals, so that you make known to all our fellow bishops, and not only those situated in your region, what we wrote back in response to your questions. But these things which were set forth by us in salubrious fashion should even be sent by escort of your letter to all the Carthaginians, Baeticians,[52] Lusitanians,[53] and Gallicians,[54] and those who border you in neighboring provinces on either side. And although there is freedom for no priest of the Lord to be ignorant of the statutes of the apostolic see and the venerable decrees of the canons, it can, nevertheless, be helpful, and because of the antiquity of your see, beloved, exceedingly glorious for you, if those things of a general sort which were written to you by name are brought to the attention of all our brothers through your cooperative solicitude, so that the things which were salubriously established by us, not haphazardly, but prudently, with very great care and deliberation, might remain inviolate, and that in the future access to all excuses should be blocked, which according to us cannot be available now to anyone. Issued on February 11, in the consulship of Arcadius and Bauto.

2. Prefaces to the Collections of Dionysius Exiguus. Ed. Fr. Glorie, *Scriptores "Illyrici" Minores* (Corpus Christianorum, Series Latina 85; Turnhout, 1972), 29–51.

Preface to the first Collection of Councils (second redaction), c. 500: dedicatory letter to Bishop Stephen of Salona. Ed. Glorie, *Scriptores,* 39–42 ("recensio B").

52. The province of *Baetica* was in southern Spain, comprising Andulusia and part of Granada.
53. *Lusitania* was the western part of the Iberian peninsula, comprising most of Portugal and parts of the western Spain.
54. *Gallaecia* was that portion of the Iberian peninsula comprising Galicia and the northwestern part of Portugal.

Dionysius "exiguus" to the lord Bishop Stephen, a father who ought to be venerated by me, greetings in the Lord.

Although our dearest brother Lawrence, offended, I believe, by the confusion of the old translation,[55] urged us, insignificant as we are, with incessant and friendly exhortation to translate the ecclesiastical rules from Greek, I, nonetheless, undertook the imposed labor in consideration of your blessedness, to whom Christ, God omnipotent, providing for the people with accustomed compassion, conferred the dignity of the episcopate. Among the very many ornaments of virtue by which, with holiness of morals, you decorate the Church of the Lord, you also govern the clergy and people with a perfect regimen, preserving inviolate the most sacred laws set forth by bishops convened through the grace of God. Not at all content with the custom of our age by which we desire more readily to know what is right than to do it, but helped by divine assistance, by carrying out beforehand the things which you command to be done you thus benefit the faithful by a most efficacious example. Great indeed is the authority of a commander who first performs the very things which have been commanded, so that the discipline of ecclesiastical order, remaining invulnerable, might offer to all Christians a gateway for gaining the eternal prize, by means of which both the holy bishops can be fortified with paternal rules, and the obedient people can be imbued with spiritual examples.

In the beginning, therefore, we translated from Greek the canons which are called "of the apostles." We did not want your holiness to be ignorant of the fact that many have not given ready assent to them, although subsequently certain enactments of bishops seem to have been taken from those very canons.

55. For comments on *confusione priscae translationis,* see the introduction to this chapter.

Next we presented in numerical order, that is from the first canon up to the one hundred and sixty-fifth, just as it is in the Greek authority, the rules of the synod of Nicaea and successively of all councils, whether held before or after that one, up to the synod of 150 bishops which convened at Constantinople. Then adding on the decrees of the Council of Chalcedon, with these we brought to an end the Greek canons. Furthermore, so that we are not believed to want to suppress something from your attention, the statutes of the Council of Sardica and of Africa, which were promulgated in Latin, are considered by us to be separate with their own numbers.

Arranging concisely after this preface the titles of all the decisions, we put those things which were promulgated dispersedly in individual councils in one list so that we have provided a kind of compendium for searching out each subject.[56]

Preface to the Collection of Papal Letters, c. 514: dedicatory letter to the priest Julian. Ed. Glorie, *Scriptores*, 45.

Dionysius "exiguus," to the lord priest Julian, venerable to me.

Excited by your holiness's assiduous attention to duties, in which you neglect to investigate absolutely nothing of those things which pertain to ecclesiastical discipline, I collected with what care and diligence I could the enactments of the former bishops of the apostolic see, and arranging them in order I divided them up by means of suitable titles. In this way I could encompass within one numerical sequence however many precepts I found of individual pontiffs and could append to the end of this preface all of the titles. Translating the canons of the Fathers from Greek a little while ago I ordered things in this way, which I recognized to have pleased you greatly. . . .

56. The translation follows the text in the first column of "recension B" at this point.

Preface to a second Collection of Councils, 514–23: dedicatory letter to Pope Hormisdas. Ed. Glorie, *Scriptores*, 51.

Dionysius "exiguus" to the lord pope most blessed Hormisdas.

I acknowledge that, insignificant as I am, some time ago with a certain amount of zeal on my part the rules of the holy bishops, which your blessedness now compels me to present word for word from the Greek, had been translated. Not putting up with the arrogance of certain people who fancy themselves most expert on the Greek canons but who, questioned about any ecclesiastical enactment, seem to respond from within themselves, just as from a hidden oracle, your veneration deigned, by the power with which you are eminent above other bishops, to command that I should strive with what diligence I am able not to deviate in Latin from the Greek, and on every page, divided into equal columns, should give both directly opposite each other. This especially [is to be done] on account of those who believe with a certain temerity that they can violate the canons of Nicaea, and substitute for them certain other enactments.

Complying, therefore, with the orders of your apostolic office, I displayed the full truth of the Greek canons, just as I faithfully translated [them], beginning with the definitions of Nicaea and ending with those of Chalcedon. But the canons which are called "of the apostles," and those of the council of Sardica and of the African province, which everyone has not accepted, I too omitted in this work, because (as I mentioned above), I included them in that first translation, and because you, father, sought to know the authorities[57] by which the Eastern churches are bound.

57. The text at this point gives an ablative singular, *auctoritate*, which the editor makes accusative, *auctoritate<m>*, and here is translated in the plural.

3. Introductory Notice and Preface (dedicatory letter to Bishop Liberinus) to the Concord of Canons of Cresconius, second half of the sixth century. Ed. Klaus Zechiel-Eckes, *Die concordia canonum des Cresconius,* 2 (Freiburger Beiträge zur mittelalterlichen Geschichte 5; Frankfurt, 1992), 419–22.

Presented here is a concord of canons of the councils and Roman bishops listed below, that is, the Canons of the Apostles, Nicaea, Ancyra, Neo-Caesarea, Gangra, Antioch, Laodicea, Chalcedon, Sardica, Carthage, and also of the bishops Siricius, Innocent, Zosimus, Celestine, Leo, and Gelasius.

Here ends the introductory notice about the canons of the holy Fathers.

[There follows, which will not be translated, the preamble in elegiac distich to the version of the Council of Nicaea found in Dionysius.]

Here begins the preface.

Cresconius, of the servants of Christ "exiguus," to the lord pontiff Liberinus, truly holy and always blessed.

The incomparable splendor of your episcopate, in which you shine exceedingly with purity of faith and probity of life, does not cease to admonish you to struggle solicitously after and to provide most carefully for the things which are useful to the Lord's flock, whose government you undertook. In fulfilling this, your office, you expect no less diligence from your subjects, and accordingly, it is necessary that you nourish them generously, as the Lord's very own flock, with the sustenance of spiritual bread. Whence, considering that the regimen of human life rests on earthly and divine laws, and that the precepts of worldly law constrain the steps of the wayward with rather strict reins but that ecclesiastical sanctions have fixed for pious and faithful souls the framework of living correctly, putting aside those secular things,[58] you command that we collect for you into one [work] all the canonical enactments which both the holy apostles and apostolic men promulgated from the very beginning of the Christian struggle through the course of time, and arranging a concord of them and inserting title headings, make them available more clearly.

You undoubtedly see that due to the magnitude of such a thing this work exceeds our powers. When very often I wished to excuse myself from it, with paternal authority you insisted, promising most faithfully that divine assistance would help us. Such an escape being blocked to me, I similarly proposed that this handbook of canons already had been prepared by a most reverent man, Ferrandus, deacon of the church of Carthage, and that it ought to suffice for our instruction, lest in seeking another we be found to detract in some way from his wisdom. For totally undermining this excuse of ours you likewise countered that you were not inclined to request this to find fault with that most wise man, but instead, desiring assiduously to increase our smattering of knowledge.

These things having taken place, guarding now against pleading any excuse at all to Christ speaking in you, fortified

58. Cresconius's text reads *illis floralibus subrelictis.* Zechiel-Eckes, *Concordia,* 1:39, n. 20 (see n. 1, above), points out that the *Floralia* (the rites celebrated annually in honor of the Roman goddess Flora) symbolized in Christian polemic the height of indecency, and thus Cresconius was setting up an opposition between lawless pagan times and the Christian way of life governed by the canons. Anders Winroth has proposed that the somewhat enigmatic *floralibus* be emended to *foralibus,* i.e., "public matters" (strictly, "matters of the forum"). This inventive reading would clarify the opposition between the two laws which Cresconius noted as governing human affairs. The word *foralibus* does not occur as a variant reading in this passage, but curiously, in three manuscripts *floralibus* is followed by *iudiciis* (see the edition in Zechiel-Eckes, *Concordia,* 2:420).

with heavenly assistance I chose to obey your commands and, with God's favor, to comply with your wishes most willingly. I had become challenged especially by the fact that the afore-mentioned venerable man is known to have made this hand-book to refresh the memory of those who learned these things and already were well acquainted with them, so that through it they can remember what they want, whenever they want. But it is clear, as I would say, that study in the same work by the unlearned, of whom there is a very great number, is excluded, since he sent them to hunt for those things which neither are found by all, nor having been found are read through without trouble on their part.[59] For indeed no one doubts that it is most annoying for a reader, when he avidly hopes for knowledge of some matter, to be referred to a book which either he has not read or whose whereabouts he does not know. Thus, with praise of the aforementioned man having been offered, in accordance with your command I considered it necessary, serving the de-velopment of the young, to present in this volume complete ecclesiastical "enactments," as they are called, which came to our attention, with attributions, under a sequence of titles, and to remove the uncertainty of doubt for those able and willing to learn them thoroughly, so that their full understanding depends not on trouble with the compiler, but now on the tenacity of the reader.[60]

From such a work, furthermore, with God's help, this bene-fit results: when an exceedingly fair judge personally ascertains

59. That is, because Ferrandus only summarized canons, his work was difficult for beginners. Those who wanted full texts had to find them elsewhere, and then try to understand them.

60. That is, not on Ferrandus and his lack of complete texts, but on the work a reader is willing to devote to comprehend full texts. The word Cresconius emphasizes, translated as "enactments," is *constituta*.

that every canonical decree by which a proceeding at a given moment is conducted is applicable in various ways, he can learn by careful examination whether he ought to form his opinion according to severity or leniency. That scrutiny will especially convey such instruction to the one who would make a decision if he is guided by the rulings of many [texts], and particularly those of confirmed authority. Whence I pray that with this redoing of the canonical handbook, just as that distinguished doctor of ours declared, "The learned can be indulgent lest the unlearned be injured; for it is preferable to give to one who has than to bewilder one who does not have."[61] But indeed I implore your sanctity that if perchance you see here that your wish has not been fulfilled, may you pardon genuine ignorance and commend rather devotion. Pray for me and remember me always, worthy pontiff in God's sight.

Here ends the preface.

4. Preface to the Chapters of Martin of Braga, late sixth century (after 569): dedicatory letter to Bishop Nitigisius of Lugo. Ed. Claude W. Barlow, *Martini episcopi Bracarensis opera omnia* (Papers and Monographs of the American Academy in Rome 12; New Haven, 1950), 123–24.[62]

Chapters from the Synods of the Eastern Fathers Collected and Arranged by Bishop Martin.
Bishop Martin to the most blessed lord Bishop Nitigisius, brother in Christ, who ought to be received with the honor

61. Augustine, *De baptismo,* 2.1.1 (Corpus scriptorum ecclesiaticorum Latinorum 51, ed. M. Petschenig [Vienna, 1908], 174, lines 18–20).
62. García y García comments on the deficiency of Barlow's edition in not including Spanish manuscripts (*Historia,* 179, n. 54). See also Gaudemet, "'Traduttore,'" 54 (see n. 16, above).

due an apostolic see, and to the entire province of the church of Lugo.[63]

The holy canons which were constituted in parts of the East by the ancient Fathers were first written in Greek, afterward, however, with the passage of time, they were translated into Latin. But since it is difficult for something to be translated sufficiently clearly from one language to another, plus the fact that in such circumstances scribes, either not understanding, or sleeping on the job, overlook much, certain things in those canons thus appear obscure to the unlearned. It seemed, therefore, that with all diligence I should reformulate more clearly and accurately both the things which were stated obscurely through the translators, and the things which were changed through the scribes, at the same time taking care that those matters which pertain to bishops and to all clergy are copied in one section, and that those which pertain to laity are immediately added, so that anyone can locate more quickly whatever chapter he wishes to know about.

63. The text reads *Domno beatissimo atque apostolicae sedis honore suscipiendo in Christo fratri Nitigisio episcopo vel universo concilio Lucensis ecclesiae Martinus episcopus.* There are two problems. (1) Bishop Nitigisius is given the honor of an apostolic see. Possibly this simply means that he should be honored as bishop, particularly the metropolitan bishop of the newly formed church province of Lugo. See *Mittellateinisches Wörterbuch,* 1 (1967), 764, for the adjective *apostolicus -a -um* in the early Middle Ages to refer to bishops. More likely, however, Martin was advocating apostolic foundation of Lugo, and that other churches such as Braga itself in ancient Galicia also might be apostolic: see A. García Conde, "Lugo," *Diccionario de historia eclesiastica de España,* 2 (1972), 1355. (2) The words *universo concilio Lucensis ecclesiae* pose a second problem. As Barlow, *Opera,* 86, indicated, this might mean a synod to be convened at Lugo, or, more probably, it is a reference to the province (cf. subscriptions to the Second Council of Braga [*Opera,* 123], where participants from the province of Lugo are identified *ex sinodo Lucensi*).

5. Preface to the Spanish Collection, c. 633. Ed. Gonzalo Martínez Díez, S.J., and Félix Rodríguez, S.J., *La Colección canónica Hispana III: Concilios Griegos y Africanos* (Monumenta Hispaniae Sacra, Serie Canónica 3; Madrid, 1982), 43–6.

The canons of the general councils began from the time of Constantine. For in preceding years, with persecution raging, there had been little opportunity to teach the people. Christianity then was torn into various heresies, since there was no freedom for the bishops to gather together until the time of the aforementioned emperor. He gave Christians the opportunity to meet freely. Under him, the holy Fathers gathered together from the whole world in the Council of Nicaea, and delivered the second confession, after the apostles, following the evangelical and apostolic faith.

These are the four principal councils from which the Church holds the fullest teaching of the faith, concerning both the divinity of the Father, Son, and Holy Spirit, and the incarnation of the aforementioned Son, our Savior. The first of these is the synod at Nicaea of 318 bishops, held when the august Constantine was reigning. Condemned therein was the blasphemy of Arian treachery, which the same Arius asserted about the inequality of the Holy Trinity, and the same holy synod defined through a confession that God the Son is consubstantial with God the Father. The second synod, of 150 fathers, gathered at Constantinople under Theodosius senior. Condemning Macedonius, who denied that the Holy Spirit was God, it demonstrated that the same Paraclete is consubstantial with the Father and the Son, and gave a more extensive form of the confession which the entire Greek and Latin worlds preach in the churches. The third synod, of 200 bishops, the first at Ephesus, was held under the younger august Theodosius.[64] It condemned with a just anathema Nestorius, who asserted that there are two persons in Christ and showed that the one person of the Lord Jesus Christ remains in two natures. The fourth synod, of 630 bishops, was held at Chalcedon under Emperor Marcian. Therein one voice of the Fathers vehemently damned Eutyches, abbot at Constantinople, who claimed that the Word of God and the flesh were one nature, his defender Dioscorus, former bishop of Alexandria, and, again, Nestorius, with the rest of the heretics. The same synod proclaimed that Christ is God, thus born of a virgin so that we may confess in him the substance of divine and human nature. These are, as we said above, the four principal and venerable synods embracing the entire catholic faith. But if there are any [other] councils which holy Fathers, filled with the spirit of God, sanctioned, after the authority of these four they should remain fixed with all firmness, and their acts are preserved in this work.

At the beginning of this volume we put the synod of Nicaea, because of the authority of that same great council. Then we placed in the course of this volume [the acts] of various Greek and Latin councils, whether they were held before or after [Nicaea], arranged in chronological order with their canons separately numbered, also appending decrees of the Roman bishops, in which, because of the eminence of the apostolic see, an authority exists not unequal to the councils. Thus by the discipline of ecclesiastical order gathered and arranged by us into one, both the holy bishops may be instructed with paternal rules, and the obedient ministers and people of the Church may be imbued with spiritual examples.[65] But the canons which are called "of the apostles," because neither the apostolic see

64. Emperor Theodosius II was the grandson of the Emperor Theodosius I.

65. Cf. the preface to Dionysius Exiguus's first collection of councils.

receives them nor the holy Fathers offered approval to them, since they are known to have been written by heretics under the name of the apostles, although certain useful things are found in them, nevertheless, their acts clearly are lacking in canonical and apostolic authority and are to be relegated among the apocrypha.

"Canon" in Greek is called "rule" in Latin. It is called rule because it directs rightly, nor does it ever lead in a different direction. Others have said that it is called rule since it rules, or because it shows a norm of living rightly, or because it corrects what is distorted and evil. "Synod" is translated from Greek as "company" or "assembly." The term "council" is derived from "common intent," since all direct the gaze of the mind onto one thing. *Cilia*, in fact, belong to the eyes,[66] whence those who disagree among themselves do not make a council, since they do not agree. A "meeting"[67] is a "convention"[68] or a "congregation,"[69] [derived] from "meeting together,"[70] that is, from "convening"[71] as one. Whence the name "convention," because men agree together there,[72] just as "convention," "meeting" and "council" [derive] from the union of many as one.

Here ends the preface.

66. The etymologies which follow may seem odd to a modern reader, and whatever care is taken to retain the sense of the original, it is impossible to replace the crispness of the Latin. This particular derivation depends on the word *concilia* = "councils," made up of the prefix *con-*, from the preposition *cum* = "with" and *cilia* = "eyelids." Thus a "council" is composed of those who direct "the gaze of the mind" in common.

67. *coetus*
68. *conventus*
69. *congregatio*
70. *coeundo*
71. *conveniendo*
72. The text reads *unde et conuentum est nuncupatum quod ibi homines conueniant.* The meaning hinges on the fact that *convenire* means both "to convene" and "to agree."

6. Preface to the Irish Collection of Canons, early eighth century. Ed. Hermann Wasserschleben. *Die irische Kanonensammlung*, 2d ed. (Leipzig, 1885), 1.[73]

Here begins the most pleasing collection of canons, which, fortified with the testimonies of Scripture and the sayings of the saints, edifies readers. If something therein seems discordant, the text that is judged to be of greater authority should be chosen.[74]

Considering the immense number of synodal texts, and seeing almost useless obscurity in most of those clumsy products and a discordant diversity more destructive than constructive in the rest, I assembled into one volume from an enormous forest of writings a brief, full, and harmonious exposition. I added many things, abbreviated many things, preserved many things just as they were, liberated many things, disregarding the sequence of words, from one sense to another, and strove in all for this alone, that what appeared as recommended in these texts should not be ascribed to my judgment. I have placed the name of each author in front of each testimony, lest it be unclear and uncertain who said what. But the reader should not neglect, when having recourse to the general titles which, out of necessity, we placed at the beginning, to pay careful attention to the numbers, and those having been observed, he will find without any delay the subject which he wishes.[75]

Here ends the prologue.

73. For the deficiencies of this edition, see Paul Fournier, "De l'influence de la collection irlandaise sur la formation des collections canoniques," *Novelle revue historique de droit français et étranger* 23 (1899):28ff. (rpt. in Fournier, *Mélanges de droit canonique*, ed. Kölzer, 2:94ff.)

74. This introduction occurs in one of the three manuscripts in which Wasserschleben found the preface and is included here for its comment on discordance.

75. After the preface the edition gives a list of sixty-seven titles, which will not be translated here.

3

Compilers, Reformers, Jurisprudents: The Early Middle Ages

Texts in this chapter dating from the ninth to the early eleventh centuries reflect the efforts of canonists to preserve canonical tradition and—in a new impulse awakened during the reign of Charlemagne (771-814)—to employ it to reform Church and society.[1] Reform was central to Charlemagne's conception of his role as a Christian king. His advisers, men like Alcuin of York and Paul the Deacon, believed that the Church had experienced a decline that could be remedied only by a cultural and spiritual renewal led by the king. Since many aspects of the faith were bound up in learning, if scholars reformed and purified texts—from law to liturgy to theology—God's Church might be well administered, proper worship offered to him, and his word effectively studied.[2]

1. See Gerhart B. Ladner, *The Idea of Reform: Its Impact on Christian Thought and Action in the Age of the Fathers* (Cambridge, Mass., 1959). On the Carolingian period specifically, see Rosamond McKitterick, *The Frankish Church and the Carolingian Reforms, 789-895* (London, 1977); J. M. Wallace-Hadrill, *The Frankish Church* (Oxford, 1983); and Roger E. Reynolds, "The Organisation, Law and Liturgy of the Western Church, 700-900," in *The New Cambridge Medieval History II, c.700-c.900,* ed. Rosamond McKitterick (Cambridge, 1991), 587-621.

2. For bibliography on Carolingian education, see John J. Contreni, "Inharmonious Harmony: Education in the Carolingian World," *Annals of Scholarship: Metastudies of the Humanities and Social Sciences* 1 (1980): 81-96. Much of the literature is not in English. See Josef Fleckenstein, *Die Bildungsreform Karls des Grossen als Verwirklichung der Norma Rectitudinis* (Bigge-Ruhr, 1953). For a general survey of education in the period, see

For canon law, this reform moved on both a royal and local level.[3] From the court at Aachen came commands for greater ecclesiastical discipline and fidelity to the canons. At the heart of this program was a desire to normalize the sources of law along ancient models. Purity lay in the texts—conciliar canons, judgments of theologians, papal decretals, and so on—authored in the holy past, before the pre-Carolingian decline and uncertainty. The standards of antiquity, when Constantine miraculously converted and the great ecumenical synods convened, were to be restored and observed.

Toward this end, Charlemagne asked Pope Hadrian I in 774 for a book of canon law. He received an enlarged version of Dionysius Exiguus's collections of decretals and councils, which scholars now call the *Collectio Dionysio-Hadriana*. What Charlemagne gained was, in retrospect, neither a complete nor satisfactory book of canon law, but it was ancient and came

---

Pierre Riché, *Les Ecoles et l'enseignement dans l'Occident chrétien de la fin du Ve siècle au milieu du XIe siècle* (Paris, 1979); for the difficult question of how canon and Roman laws were taught, see Harald Zimmermann, "Römische und kanonistische Rechtskenntnis und Rechtsschulung im frühen Mittelalter," in *La scuola nell'occidente latino nell'alto medioevo* (Settimane di studio del Centro italiano di studi sull'alto medioevo 19; Spoleto, 1972), 767–94, and Pierre Riché, *Enseignement du droit en Gaule du VIe au XIe siècles* (Ius romanum medii aevi 1.5.b.bb; Milan, 1965).

3. See Rosamond McKitterick, "Knowledge of Canon Law in the Frankish Kingdoms before 789: The Manuscript Evidence," *Journal of Ecclesiastical History* 36 (1985): 97–117, and Roger E. Reynolds, "Unity and Diversity in Carolingian Canon Law Collections: The Case of the *Collectio Hibernensis* and Its Derivatives," in *Carolingian Essays*, ed. Uta-Renate Blumenthal (Washington, D.C., 1983; rpt.in Reynolds, *Law and Liturgy in the Latin Church, 5th–12th Centuries* [Variorum Collected Studies Series CS457; Aldershot, 1994]). Fundamental is Mordek, *Kirchenrecht*, and see also his "Kirchenrechtliche Autoritäten im Frühmittelalter," in *Recht und Schrift im Mittelalter*, ed. Peter Classen (Vorträge und Forschungen 23; Sigmaringen, 1977), 237–55.

from Rome, and that was what mattered. Copies were made and distributed to churches and monasteries throughout the realm, while the original was kept at Aachen.[4]

In the provinces, the call to reform prompted not only the reception and study of new collections like the *Dionysio-Hadriana* but also renewed copying and reworking of such older compilations as the Spanish Collection, the *Concordia* of Cresconius, the Irish Collection of Canons, and others.[5] Reform and renewal in canon law did not automatically mean that older collections were discarded, or that the *Dionysio-Hadriana*, equipped, as it were, with Charlemagne's seal of approval, forced out older compilations. This expanded version of the work of Dionysius Exiguus never became a code of law for the

4. For the *Dionysio-Hadriana*, see Reynolds, "Law, Canon," 403–4. On Charlemagne's similar concern for authenticity and conformity in his secular legislation, the capitularies, see McKitterick, *Frankish Church*, esp. 1–79 (see n. 1, above), and, more recently, her *The Carolingians and the Written Word* (Cambridge, 1989). Many manuscripts of the *Dionysio-Hadriana* carry a metrical dedication from Pope Hadrian to Charlemagne: see the edition by Friedrich Maassen, *Geschichte der Quellen und der Literatur des canonischen Rechts im Abendlande. Die Rechtssammlungen bis zur Mitte des 9. Jahrhunderts* (Graz, 1870; rpt. Graz, 1956), 965–67. See also Mordek, *Kirchenrecht*, 157ff., and in general for the *Dionysio-Hadriana*, 151–52.

5. See Reynolds, "Law, Canon," 403, and, e.g., for canonical activity at Salzburg, Reynolds, "Canon Law Collections in Early Ninth-Century Salzburg," in *Proceedings of the Fifth International Congress of Medieval Canon Law*, ed. Stephan Kuttner and Kenneth Pennington (Monumenta iuris canonici, Subsidia 6; Vatican City, 1980), 15–34 (rpt. in Reynolds, *Law and Liturgy in the Latin Church, 5th–12th Centuries* [Variorum Collected Studies Series CS457; Aldershot, 1994]). See also Rosamond McKitterick, "Some Carolingian Lawbooks and Their Function," in *Authority and Power: Studies on Medieval Law and Government Presented to Walter Ullmann on His Seventieth Birthday*, ed. Peter Linehan and Brian Tierney (Cambridge, 1980), 13–27, who considers the knowledge of Roman law at various sites throughout the empire.

Church in the Carolingian realm or elsewhere. That achievement lay in the future with the Decretals of Pope Gregory IX. In short, the texts of Carolingian canon law were spread throughout a variety of collections, for what the court at Aachen wanted was not always available or even appropriate in other places. Church law continued to be, to use the image noted earlier from the prologue to the Irish Collection of Canons, a dense and tangled forest. Although Charlemagne and his advisers were concerned with increasing conformity of usages in the Frankish kingdom, this ideal simply could not be achieved with any consistency. Literate culture remained isolated and dispersed. Until the ecclesiastical reform movement of the eleventh century, local or regional orientation continued to predominate in canon law, a sign of the bishops' control of the canons and the weakness of any centralized authority.

Emperor Louis the Pious (+840) continued his father Charlemagne's religious and cultural reform. At his side were like-minded men who did their best to realize this dream of an earthly empire reflecting, however faintly, the perfect harmony and order of heaven. As Bishop Agobard of Lyons put it, clothing Saint Paul in Frankish dress: "There is now neither Gentile nor Jew, Scythian nor Aquitanian, nor Lombard, nor Burgundian, nor Alaman, nor bond nor free. All are one in Christ."[6] This unity could not, of course, be realized amid the brutal realities of civil war and invasion that soon descended upon Louis and his successors, but it does suggest the goals that motivated the reformers gathered around the emperor. These are some of the hopes and expectations underlying the prefaces selected for this chapter.

The Penitential (*Penitentiale*) compiled by Bishop Halitgar

6. R. H. C. Davis, trans, *A History of Medieval Europe from Constantine to Saint Louis,* 2d. ed. (London, 1992), 147.

of Cambrai, at the request of Archbishop Ebbo of Reims, illustrates the interests of a bishop committed to reform. Halitgar governed his church from 817 to 831, turbulent years that witnessed the eruption of civil war between Louis and his sons. His Penitential comprises five books but is, in fact, best understood as a modified collection of penitential regulations.[7] Although most characteristic of the Celtic and, later, Anglo-Saxon churches, these handbooks of penitential practice which regulated virtually every aspect of life, from sexual behavior to proper worship, also could be found throughout the Frankish world, especially in regions visited by insular missionaries.[8] Many manuscripts of Halitgar include a sixth book as an appendix containing excerpts from another work, the so-called Roman Penitential.[9] In addition to these sources from the penitential tradition, Halitgar also drew texts from works like the *Dionysio-Hadriana,* from an earlier Carolingian compilation known as the *Collectio Dacheriana,* and from such authors as Pope Gregory the Great.

7. Raymund Kottje, *Die Bussbücher Halitgars von Cambrai und des Hrabanus Maurus: Ihre Überlieferung und ihre Quellen* (Beiträge zur Geschichte und Quellenkunde des Mittelalters 8; Berlin, 1980). See also, in general, Cyrille Vogel, *Les "Libri paenitentiales"* (Typologie des sources du Moyen Age occidental 27; Turnhout, 1978), where, on p. 81, he notes that Ebbo's request probably came in the year 829.

8. The penitentials are an important episode in early medieval religious history, the literature is vast, and a number of these texts have been made available in English translation. For an older introduction and a wide selection of translations, see John T. McNeill and Helena M. Gamer, *Medieval Handbooks of Penance* (Columbia Records of Civilization 29; New York, 1938; rpt. 1990); for selections from Halitgar, see 295ff. For further translations, see the editions with accompanying English in Ludwig Bieler, *The Irish Penitentials* (Scriptores Latini Hiberniae 5; Dublin, 1963).

9. See the notes to the preface to Cardinal Atto's collection in chap. 4 and cf. McNeill and Gamer, *Medieval Handbooks* 295.

Halitgar's collection is prefaced by both Archbishop Ebbo's request and his reply. The latter is a typical dedicatory letter, filled with protestations of incompetence and unworthiness and offering a justification of the new work. The success of Halitgar in striking an appealing tone is demonstrated by Burchard of Worms's use of the letter to Ebbo almost two centuries later as a source for the introduction to his own collection.

The four compilations collectively called "Pseudo-Isidore" form one of the most well-known and, indeed, infamous episodes in medieval canon law, and one of the most intriguing.[10] These collections, which include a Gallican version of the Spanish Collection named after a manuscript from Autun (*Hispana Gallica Augustodunensis*); the *Capitula*, or Chapters, of Angilramnus; the Capitularies of Benedict the Deacon (or the Levite—*Benedictus Levita*); and the False Decretals, have together been labeled "Pseudo-Isidorian" since the late nineteenth century, although the anonymous compiler of the forged papal decretals was the only author whom medieval audiences identified as "Isidore." Some manuscripts refer to the compiler of the Decretals as "Isidore the Merchant," a confusion possibly arising from the fifth-century African friend of Saint Augustine, Marius Mercator, who translated and replied to the writings of the heretic Nestorius. Others assume that the compiler was the seventh-century Visigothic Bishop Isidore of Seville,

10. See Horst Fuhrmann, "False Decretals (Pseudo-Isidorian Forgeries)," *New Catholic Encyclopedia* (New York, 1967), 5:820–24. Fuhrmann's monumental three-volume study is the standard scholarly work on these forgeries: *Einfluss und Verbreitung der pseudoisidorischen Fälschungen von ihrem Auftauchen bis in die neuere Zeit* (Monumenta Germaniae Historica, Schriften 24.1–3; Stuttgart, 1972–74). See also Reynolds, "Law, Canon," 405–6. All the collections discussed in this chapter and the next are discussed in Fournier and LeBras, *Histoire,* 1:121ff., and in vol. 2, although in some cases the views expressed there are obsolete, e.g., that Le Mans was the home of the Pseudo-Isidore.

perhaps because of the connection of Isidore to the Spanish Collection and the importance of a version of that work for Pseudo Isidore (see chap. 2). Included among the texts translated in this chapter are the introductions to Benedict the Deacon and to the Decretals.

Forged papal letters and conciliar canons were nothing new in the ninth century.[11] But the magnitude, variety, and interdependence of the forged materials in these four collections was extraordinary and probably indicate an enterprise undertaken in the province of Reims during the late 840s. Civil war had ended whatever concord existed among bishops and secular rulers earlier in the century, and various reform councils—for example, at Paris in 829—had failed to restore harmony. A few bishops had even been deposed for political reasons. The division of the empire of Charlemagne and Louis into three kingdoms by the Treaty of Verdun in 843 did not so much signal peace as certify the fragmentation of the Carolingian world. In this precarious society bishops could be vulnerable. Trapped between rapacious counts, on the one hand, and ambitious and powerful archbishops (metropolitans), on the other, episcopal partisans decided, so it seems, to defend their rights, as they saw them, through the creation of a body of law demonstrating the way things ought to be. The result was the Pseudo-Isidorian collections.

Within this myriad of authentic and forged materials, there are common themes, above all the consistent defense of suffragan bishops' rights against *chorepiscopi* (rural bishops),[12] metro-

11. A comprehensive survey down to Gratian's *Decretum* is provided by Peter Landau, "Gefälschtes Recht in den Rechtssammlungen bis Gratian," *Fälschungen im Mittelalter, 2: Gefälschte Rechtstexte. Der bestrafte Fälscher* (Monumenta Germaniae Historica, Schriften 33.2; Hannover, 1988), 11–49.

12. On the chorepiscopi, see Fuhrmann, *Einfluss*, 1:179.

politans, and secular lords. The *chorepiscopi* are judged to be no better than simple priests; the metropolitans not only cannot act without the consent of their diocesean bishops, but also must now submit to a higher ecclesiastical office, the primate or patriarch, a dignity essentially invented by the forgers to transcend any authority found in one ecclesiastical province. Any process against a bishops became automatically a case reserved to Rome. The definition and delineation of these rights and procedures were based on supposedly authentic witnesses from the past. The recourse to past models which was found within earlier Carolingian canon law now operated in an extreme way, as the forgers created the "old law" they needed for their particular purposes.

The collection attributed to an unknown deacon named Benedict is considerable, containing over 1,300 forged capitularies. The work purports to be a continuation and supplement to the ninth-century compilation of capitularies by Abbot Ansegisus of Fontanelle. Benedict begins with a genuine letter of Saint Boniface, the revered missionary and reformer of the previous century, but what follows is a mix of authentic and spurious texts, all purporting to transmit the judgments of Frankish rulers. They were supposedly discovered in the archive of Mainz cathedral, at a conveniently discrete distance from Reims. The compiler claimed that he was following the orders of Archbishop Otgar of Mainz (826–47), which suggests a date in the late 840s. Benedict offers his metropolitan and secular opponents the model of Church-state cooperation that the bishops had hoped to achieve at their reform councils, and that they believed Charlemagne actually had achieved.

The False Decretals—which, in fact, comprise both decretals and conciliar texts—were an even more ambitious, and ultimately more successful, creation. Their popularity is demonstrated by the nearly one hundred complete medieval manuscripts that survive. A variety of sources were pieced together like a mosaic by the author(s), preeminent among them the *Hispana Gallica Augustodunensis*, but also the *Collectio Dionysio-Hadriana* and even the Irish Collection of Canons. The defense of episcopal rights in these decretals and synodal rulings, presented basically in two groups in chronological order, some authentic, some forged, and some mixed, represented the highest earthly authority. The confected decretals were ascribed to the saintly popes of the age of persecution. Text after text is presented, asserting the papacy's authority to supervise the law and the organization of the Church, to defend the bishops against ecclesiastical or secular lords who might disturb them, and, in general, to support the diocesan bishops in a variety of ways. The influence of this work, and of other Pseudo-Isidorian products, too, extended far beyond the immediate context of its composition. In the turmoil of eleventh- and twelfth-century ecclesiastical reform, the papacy would find in these apparently ancient texts proof and guarantees of its unique juridical power over not only the hierarchy of the Church, but also secular rulers. What began as a weapon in the hands of beleaguered Carolingian churchmen became a cornerstone of papal ecclesiology.

In sum, the prefaces to Halitgar, the Pseudo-Isidorian Decretals, and Benedict the Deacon introduce compilations influenced in one way or another by the Carolingian ecclesiastical reform movement. All demonstrate a conviction that the Church must be restored to the standards of purity and discipline established by the Fathers. Halitgar desired correct penitential practice. Benedict confronted declining ecclesiastical and secular authority with ideal laws that would restore harmony and peace. In the Decretals, precedents not uncovered in earlier collections were forged against archbishops and others who, in the opinion of the compilers, had more power than tradition warranted.

Taken together, these collections—and especially the products of the Pseudo-Isidorian workshop—demonstrate the force of sacred precedent at work in early medieval canon law, a vision of a golden age whose norms could be recovered and applied to reform the present.

The introduction to the Chapters (*Capitula*) compiled by Isaac, bishop of Langres (859–880), reveals a bishop's efforts on the diocesan level to reform his church.[13] Despite the invasion and strife marking the end of Charles the Bald's reign as West Frankish king and emperor (840–877), Isaac participated in councils at Troyes, Soissons, and elsewhere. Derived from the earlier work of Benedict the Deacon, Isaac's work is further evidence of a commitment to ecclesiastical discipline even under the most trying circumstances. His collection is, furthermore, thematically arranged. Thus as opposed, for example, to the bulky Pseudo-Isidorian Decretals in chronological sequence, the Chapters provide a more readily usable volume for locating a desired text.[14]

13. See the introduction to the new ed. by Rudolf Pokorny, in Rudolf Pokorny and Martina Stratmann (unter Mitwirkung von Wolf-Dieter Runge), *Capitula episcoporum* (Monumenta Germaniae Historica, Capitula episcoporum 2; Hannover, 1995), 180ff., and also P. Schreiner, "Isaak von Langres," *Lexikon des Mittelalters,* (1991), 667; Hubert Mordek, "Isaak der Gute in Freiburg i. Br. Ein neuer Textfund und die Capitula des Bischofs von Langres überhaupt," *Freiburger Diözesan-Archiv* 100 (1980): 203–10; and M. Csáky, "St. Isaac the Good of Langres," *New Catholic Encyclopedia* (New York, 1967), 7:662. In general on episcopal *capitula*, see Peter Brommer, *"Capitula episcoporum": Die bischöflichen Kapitularien des 9. und 10. Jahrhunderts* (Typologie des sources du Moyen Age occidental 43; Turnhout, 1985), 52, for discussion of Isaac. For the meaning of the title *Capitula*, see the comments in chap. 2, above on Martin of Braga's collection, and for medieval use of the title *Canones Isaac,* see Mordek, "Isaak," 204, n. 7.

14. See the remarks on format in chap. 1.

The preface to Regino of Prüm's Two Books concerning Synodal Investigations and Ecclesiastical Instructions (*Libri duo de synodalibus causis et disciplinis ecclesiasticis*) reflects this same turbulent era and emphatically reiterates the conviction that the canons were not only to be preserved, but also used to discipline and reform the Church.[15] Regino was born near Speyer in 840 and died at Trier in 915. He became abbot of Prüm in 892, and in 899 Archbishop Rathbod of Trier named him abbot of the monastery of St. Martin's, where he remained until his death. In addition to his canonical collection, Regino's literary fame rests on work in musical theory and on a world chronicle.

The Two Books date from 906 or a bit later and were undertaken at Archbishop Rathbod's request. Regino took his texts from a variety of collections, including the Spanish Collection and the false Decretals of Pseudo-Isidore. Like Isaac's Chapters, the work is topically arranged. The first book treats diocesan administration and canonical procedure; the second concerns the laity. Regino can be said to continue, at least in spirit, the Carolingian reform, for the beginning of the first book treats the guidelines to be followed by a bishop conducting a visitation of his diocese, thus showing that a century after the time of Charlemagne the ideal of a well-ordered Church had not been forgotten. The collection's preface brims with deferential rhetoric praising the virtues of Archbishop Hatto of Mainz (+913), to whom the Two Books were dedicated. The introduction also makes clear that belief in the rule of law in Church

15. On Regino's work, see Gerhard Schmitz, "Ansegis und Regino: Die Rezeption der Kapitularien in den Libri duo de synodalibus causis," *Zeitschrift der Savigny-Stiftung für Rechtsgeschichte*, Kanonistische Abteilung 74 (1988): 94–132, esp. p. 96 for discussion of the preface. See also Reynolds, "Law, Canon," 406–7.

and society had not wavered to the point of total disregard, despite what are termed "unheard of" evils of Regino's world.

The Collection Dedicated to Anselm (*Collectio Anselmo dedicata*) was compiled by an unknown Italian cleric sometime in the late ninth century and dedicated to Archbishop Anselm of Milan (882–896).[16] It is divided into twelve parts, with subjects ranging from ecclesiology—beginning with texts concerning the primacy of the Roman see (anticipating the direction of canon law in the second half of the eleventh century)—to the treatment of heretics and schismatics. The delineation of content for each section, with which the preface closes, offers, in fact, a table of contents which influenced Burchard of Worms's presentation of content in the preface to his *Decretum*.[17] The *Anselmo Dedicata* drew texts from a variety of sources, among them Pseudo-Isidore, the letters of Gregory the Great, and scattered texts from classical Roman law. The dedicatory letter even alludes to Cresconius. In the century after its compilation the collection was used both in Italy and north of the Alps and was influential in the work of Bishop Burchard of Worms.

In the course of the tenth century, distressed by lax standards in monasteries and abuses in the Church such as simony, centers of reform began to sprout in such cloisters as Gorze in Lotharingia and Cluny in Burgundy. They recalled the emphasis which Carolingian reformers like Benedict of Aniane (+821) had placed on the purification of the monastic life through a

16. For an edition of the first book, with commentary, see "Collectio Anselmo Dedicata liber primus," ed. Jean-Claude Besse, *Revue du droit canonique* 9 (1959): 207–96. On the intricate history of modern scholarship concerning the collection, see Fuhrmann, *Einfluss*, 2:425, n. 7 (see n. 10, above); see also Reynolds, "Law, Canon," 406; and, most recently, Horst Fuhrmann, "Fragmente des Collectio Anselmo dedicata," *Deutsches Archiv* 44 (1988): 539–43.

17. Gérard Fransen, "Les Sources de la Préface du Décret de Burchard de Worms," *Bulletin of Medieval Canon Law* 3 (1973): 1.

closer observance of the Benedictine Rule.[18] The final pair of texts presented in this chapter, from Abbot Abbo of Fleury and Bishop Burchard of Worms, reflect this renewed impulse for reform, not only in the cloister but in the secular Church as well.

Abbo was born near Orléans around the year 940 and was given as a child to the monastery of St.-Benoît-sur-Loire at Fleury, renowned as the house which enshrined the bones of the founder of the Benedictine order.[19] There Abbo received his basic education in the trivium—grammar, rhetoric, and dialectic—and subsequently continued his studies in the cathedral schools of Paris and Reims, and also for a time at Ramsey Abbey in England, where he would have encountered the monastic reform movement initiated by Archbishop Dunstan of Canterbury. Given the widely dispersed schools of the day, Abbo thus had a remarkably extensive education. Eventually he returned to Fleury and became involved in the turmoil that brought the Capetian dynasty to power. At first, Abbo chose wisely in supporting Hugh Capet in his rise to the throne, but subsequently fell from favor with Hugh's son Robert. He met a martyr's fate in 1004 when, during an inspection of the priory of La Réole in Gascony, he was beaten to death by the irate monks who resented his attempts to reform their house.

18. Among the many studies on Cluny and the Cluniac reform, see two works by Barbara Rosenwein, *To Be a Neighbor of Saint Peter: The Social Meaning of Cluny's Property, 909–1049* (Ithaca, 1989), and *Rhinoceros Bound: Cluny in the Tenth Century* (Philadelphia, 1982). Benedict of Aniane's influence is discussed by Wallace-Hadrill, *Frankish Church,* 229ff. (see n. 1, above).

19. See Reynolds, "Law, Canon," 407; T. Kölzer, "Mönchtum und Kirchenrecht," *Zeitschrift der Savigny-Stiftung für Rechtsgeschichte,* Kanonistische Abteilung 69 (1983) 125, 135ff.; and in general, M. Mostert, *The Political Theory of Abbo of Fleury: A Study of the Ideas about Society and Law of the Tenth-Century Monastic Reform Movement* (Middeleeuwse Studies en Bronne 2; Hilversum, 1987).

Abbo championed the reform of Benedictine monasticism. He passionately defended monastic rights and properties against encroachments by secular lords, but especially by bishops. As he notes in the preface to his Canons (*Canones*), compiled around the year 1000, he has searched canonical tradition and secular laws to find texts that justify and guard monastic customs against all adversaries. The collection is made up of fifty-two chapters, under which are arranged both canons and some of Abbo's own thoughts. It would be a mistake to exaggerate the systematic nature of the endeavor, but as Fournier indicated, in this combination Abbo's work was ahead of its time, anticipating the great changes in Church law which occur in the late eleventh century.[20] The preface introduces a reformer working through the sources of law, confident that they support his call for monastic *libertas,* that is, the freedom from interference and oppression by ecclesiastical or secular lords. Abbo's carefully worded appeals for support from the crown demonstrate, however, the harsh political realities of his world. Without powerful protection, an abbot was vulnerable. Abbo's preface proclaims his commitment to reform; his fate shows that this could come at a terrible price.

The *Decretum*[21] compiled by Burchard, bishop of Worms from 1000 to 1025, was one of the most successful canonical collections—not only of the eleventh century, but of the Church's first millennium—and remained influential beyond the eleventh century (see chap. 5 for use of Burchard by the Decretists in the late twelfth century).[22] Like Halitgar of Cam-

20. Fournier and LeBras, *Histoire,* 1:324–25, 329–30. See also Reynolds, "Law, Canon," 407, and Gaudemet, *Les Sources* (Paris, 1993), 38–39.

21. No one English word can properly render the Latin *Decretum* when used as a title of a collection. "Decree" is inadequate.

22. For Burchard, see Reynolds, "Law, Canon," 407–8 (with bibliography), and Brundage, *Medieval Canon Law,* 32–34. See also the

brai, whose preface influenced his introduction,[23] Burchard was a canonist with extensive experience in ecclesiastical politics and pastoral life. Named bishop by Otto III, he earned a reputation as an outstanding pastor and vigorous defender of his see. He was an active participant in regional ecclesiastical reform and attended various provincial councils that passed decrees attempting to enforce tighter discipline. The *Decretum* reflects this commitment.

Burchard compiled his collection during the middle years of his episcopacy, with the book taking final form by 1015. It is a far more extensive and comprehensive work than the other compilations whose prefaces are presented in this chapter, excepting the Pseudo-Isidorian Decretals. Containing more than 1,700 canons arranged in twenty books, its size and comprehensive treatment of tradition are reminiscent of such great early medieval compendia as the Spanish Collection, although the *Decretum*'s systematic format would make it more readily usable. The variety of formal sources used in the compilation demonstrates Burchard's considerable knowledge of canon law, for he drew on an array of collections, among them Regino's Two Books, the

fundamental work on the manuscripts of Burchard by Hartmut Hoffmann and Rudolf Pokorny, *Das Dekret des Bischofs Burchard von Worms: Textstufen, Frühe Verbreitung, Vorlagen* (Monumenta Germaniae Historica, Hilfsmittel 12; Munich, 1991).

23. On Burchard's preface in general, see Kalb, *Studien*, 23–24, with a survey of previous literature. On the preface and its manuscript tradition, see Fransen, "Préface," 1–9 (see n. 17, above), at p. 3 for Halitgar's influence, and at p. 1, for the influence of the preface of the *Anselmo Dedicata*. See also Horst Fuhrmann, "Zum Vorwort des Dekrets Bischof Burchards von Worms," *Società, istituzioni, spiritualità: Studi in onore di Cinzio Violante* (Centro italiano di studi sull'alto medioevo, Collectanea 1; Spoleto, 1994), 1:383–93, and Robert Somerville and Anders Winroth, "'Collecting Tidbits': Aulus Persius Flaccus and Bishop Burchard of Worms," *Studia Gratiana* 27 (1996): 507–16.

Collection Dedicated to Anselm, and Pseudo-Isidore, as well as venerable authors like Pope Gregory the Great. The nineteenth and twentieth books, devoted to penance and to theological issues respectively, were especially popular and sometimes can be found copied apart from the rest of the collection.

Burchard's prologue reveals his motivations and goals in considerable detail. While often employing the elaborate rhetoric of justification characteristic of these introductions, such as defending his right to collect and arrange sources, he also explicitly claims an educational purpose for his work. Earlier compilers had made ignorance of the canons part of their reason for compiling, though their rhetoric often gives the impression of affectation. For Burchard, the pedagogic intent of his compilation transcends rhetorical flourish for a practical concern. He emphasizes that the book was specifically created for his clergy; it need not leave his diocese to be successful in Burchard's view, although its many extant manuscripts demonstrate widespread diffusion. Furthermore, it can be noted that Burchard's protestations about adding nothing to the canons which he collected is a matter of protesting too much, for he was a consistent tamperer with his texts and their inscriptions, even forging what he needed when it could not be located in his sources.[24]

The compilation of the Pseudo-Isidorian Decretals was the last great collection arranged in a chronological order. With the collections of the early tenth century, the vastly more ac-

---

24. Fournier and LeBras, *Historie*, 1:378–81, and see Hoffmann-Pokorny, *Dekret*, 158–59. Taking liberties with texts would, of course, be characteristic of most authors in this period (see, e.g., Fournier and LeBras, *Histoire*, 1:256–59, for Regino). As Hoffmann-Pokorny point out, the twelfth-century methods of textual reconciliation are not yet available, so "retouching" canons is one way that a churchman like Burchard could try to reconcile laws from across centuries of the Christian tradition.

cessible and more sophisticated thematic format came to dominate, and such subsequent writers as Burchard built on this approach by fashioning more elaborate systematic structures for their compilations. Yet while the format of the collections was changing in this period, the compiler's prologue continued to provide a forum for jurisprudence. As in earlier prefaces, for example, to the Spanish Collection and to Cresconius's *Concordia,* authors continued to deal with the authenticity of their sources and debts to predecessors. In particular, compilers repeatedly took pains to acknowledge dependence on tradition in order to defend themselves against possible critics. Echoes and allusions to some of these earlier prefaces can be found in the texts presented in this chapter, but there is also innovation in jurisprudence, as demonstrated in the historical and contextual sensitivity of Regino of Prüm or in the musings about proper canonical procedure by the unknown author of the remarkable prologue to the Pseudo-Isidorian Decretals.

With Burchard's compilation, a kind of watershed had been reached in early medieval canon law. His *Decretum* was the most widely received and subsequently used of a series of collections assembled from the tradition to meet local needs. His preface captured themes at work in each of the texts presented in this chapter: to collect the canons, to arrange them in a convenient format for the reader, and to present them for the discipline and reform of Church and world. During the next century the demands of ecclesiastical reform would lead to a revolution in that process—a revolution perhaps hinted at in the Canons of Abbot Abbo of Fleury—thus enabling the scholastic jurisprudence of the High Middle Ages to emerge.

1. Letter of Archbishop Ebbo of Reims to Bishop Halitgar of Cambrai requesting a penitential book, and Preface (dedicatory letter to Ebbo) to the Penitential, c. 829. Ed. E. Dümmler, Monumenta Germaniae Historica, *Epistolae,* 5 (*Epistolae Karolini aevi,* 3) (Berlin, 1898–99), 617.[25]

In the name of the Lord, Ebbo, unworthy bishop, to the most reverent brother in Christ and son, Bishop Halitgar, greetings.

I do not doubt that your charity knows the extent to which concern for ecclesiastical discipline occupies us, and with how many needs of our subjects and, moreover, with what burdens of worldly things we are daily afflicted. Therefore, as I told you, I was unable to gather together from the sayings of the Fathers and also the decrees of the canons a penitential book for the benefit of our fellow priests because the mind, while it is divided among many things, is made weaker for each one. And this is what greatly concerns me in this matter: in the handbooks of our priests the judgments for those doing penance are so confused, and so varied and in disagreement among themselves, and supported by the authority of no one, that because of the discord they scarcely can be disentangled. Whence it happens that for those fleeing to the remedy of penance, because both of the confusion of the books and lack of skill [of the priests] help in no way is at hand for them.

You, therefore, dearest brother, who in most perfect serenity have always flourished in divine studies with an ardent spirit and with special care for contemplation of scripture, do not deny yourself to us. Take, I beseech you, without a word of ex-

---

25. Another edition of these letters is found in Hermann Joseph Schmitz, *Die Bußbücher und das kanonische Bußverfahren* (Düsseldorf, 1898), 2:265.

cuse, the weight of this load, indeed, imposed by me on you, but which should be eased by the Lord whose burden is light.[26] And do not fear nor be in awe of the magnitude of this work, but confidently undertake it, since he will be with you who said, "Open your mouth and I shall fill it."[27] You know well that little things are sufficient for children, and that the crowd of the poor is unable to approach the table of the great.[28] Do not withdraw the knowledge of your piety from us. Do not place the light burning in you under a bushel, but place it on a high candelabra, so that it may shine on all your brothers who are in the house,[29] and as a learned scribe show to us what you have received from the Lord.[30] Along the path of this labor you will be accompanied by the grace of him who joined himself on the road as a third companion to two disciples traveling, and opened their mind so that they might understand the holy scriptures.[31] Dearest brother, may the Holy Spirit illumine your heart with every teaching of truth, and with perfect knowledge of charity. Farewell.

Halitgar, the least servant of Christ, to the lord and venerable father in Christ, Archbishop Ebbo, greetings.

Venerable father, when I received the letter from your blessedness, in which you deigned to urge me that I should not allow my mind to be inert and sluggish, but should commit myself vigilantly to daily consideration of and meditation on sacred scripture, and, moreover, should collect in one volume a peni-

26. Cf. Matthew 11:30.
27. Psalm 80 (81):11(10).
28. A source of these images, whose aptness here is obscure, has escaped detection.
29. Cf. Matthew 5:15.
30. Cf. Matthew 13:52.
31. Luke 24:13ff.

tential from the ruling of the holy Fathers and the canons, the command that I should undertake this burden, which I knew had been relinquished by more prudent men, was severe, very difficult, and terrifying to me. Not from obstinacy, but mindful rather of my own lowliness, I strongly resisted your wish, and, indeed, troubled by this concern I judged it necessary that I should hold off for a little while from the risk of writing. But just because I weighed the difficulty of the work enjoined, I did not on that account wish, nor should I, to resist altogether the authority of the one enjoining it, certain that your grandeur of commanding will help my weakness much more than the difficulty of my ignorance will impede it. Farewell.

2. Preface to the False Capitularies of Benedict the Deacon, post 847. Ed. G. H. Pertz, Monumenta Germaniae Historica, *Leges*, 2.2 (Hannover, 1837), 39–40.

Here begins the preface of the following capitularies.

The preceding four books contain a good number of capitularies of the most glorious emperors Charles and Louis, which in their time were collected and brought together in the aforesaid books by Abbot Ansegisus, just as is said in the preface to the same books. But because, as we estimate, perhaps less than half were discovered and collected by him, in order for them to be available to those in authority[32] everywhere it was necessary

---

32. Benedict used the word *fideles* on several occasions, e.g., twice in this sentence. The obvious translation, "the faithful," in the sense of the body of believers, is not what was intended, for the text appears to designate leaders, both ecclesiastic and lay. See Jürgen Hannig, *Consensus fidelium* (Monographien zur Geschichte des Mittelalters 27; Stuttgart, 1982), 195–99, for *fideles* in mid-ninth century Frankland referring to the great men of the realm (a reference kindly provided by Hubert Mordek). Translating the word readily into English is problematic, and inadequate as it is, "those in authority" has been chosen.

that [these] be sought out, and, because of the memory of such great princes and the utility of their capitularies, be assembled, put into manuscripts, and kept in mind by those in authority.[33] Wherefore, for the love of omnipotent God, and for the utility of the holy Church of God, its servants, and the entire people, we took pains carefully to investigate and in three subsequent books separately to assemble, with their own title headings, those which either he was unable to find, or perhaps was unwilling to present, and those of Pepin, Charles, and Louis which we discovered were not inserted later by those in authority in the holy Church of God into [his] aforementioned books. They should be retained and handed on to those who are in authority over all Christians,[34] [and] we did not hesitated to write [this] to the most noble kings Louis, Lothar, and Charles, the sons, that is, of the most pious emperor Louis, so that they would know how they are expected, with the Lord's help, to rule the clergy and people committed to themselves according to the standard of [their] grandfather, great-grandfather, and father, following the will of the Lord just as those men did.

These capitularies which we zealously assembled in the following three books we found here and there in diverse places and diverse copies,[35] just as they were promulgated in diverse synods and judicial assemblies. And of greatest importance were those which we discovered had been preserved in the archive of the holy metropolitan church of Mainz by Riculf, metropolitan of the same holy see, and then had been found by Autgar, his kinsman and second successor, which, in line with what has

33. *a fidelibus memoriae conmendarentur.* Benedict could hardly be suggesting that his extensive collection be committed to memory.

34. *omnium christianorum fidelibus.*

35. See Fournier and LeBras, *Histoire,* 1:157ff., drawing on the fundamental research on Benedict by Emil Seckel, for discussion of the *scedulae* ("copies"), indicated.

been stated above, we chose to insert in this work. We warn the readers, however, that if they come across the same capitularies two or three times they should not attribute this to our ignorance, because, as we said, we found them in diverse copies and for that reason were unable to edit them very quickly, but left these things needing correction to all those readers brimming with knowledge. We saw, furthermore, that some of them have the same beginnings and a different ending, some have the same endings but not the same beginnings; in some there was more, in some less, and for that reason we left those just as we found them. We also implore everyone that if, henceforth, they come across more of these which the aforesaid Ansegisus did not include, and which up to now we were unable to locate, they should not hesitate to insert them, distinct from the others, in a fourth and a fifth book. By so doing they would have God's grace, and the clergy and the people would not lack the benefits of these capitularies, since they are very useful and will be especially helpful for those wanting to know which things ought to be held with the strongest authority as law, both ecclesiastical and secular.

In the first place, therefore, we provided some short verses of poetry composed in praise of the aforenoted princes. Title headings for the first book then follow, with their own numbers added, so that the ruling which is sought can be found more easily. These things thus taken care of, at the beginning of the first book is placed the letter of Pope Zachary directed to all bishops, to the remaining grades of the ecclesiastical order, to all dukes and counts, and to all those fearing God throughout Gaul and the provinces of the Franks, just as it says therein. So that everyone knows that these capitularies of the aforementioned princes are confirmed especially by apostolic authority, this is followed by two synods, which the legate of the holy Roman and apostolic Church Boniface, archbishop of the said church of Mainz, representing the previously noted Pope Zachary, held canonically together with Carloman, prince of the Franks. The things which follow these [councils] also are fortified, on the one hand, by the same maximum authority which we described, and, on the other hand, by the assent of all the leaders of the Franks, of each order.

At the beginning of the second book, after enumeration of the title headings, some selections[36] excerpted from divine law are included, just as we found them in different places mixed in with the capitularies of those [princes]. Thus no one can be ignorant of the fact that these capitularies harmonize with divine laws and canonical rules. In the third book, after enumeration of the title headings of the same book, some selections are inserted from the canons here and there collected by Bishop Paulinus,[37] Master Alcuin, and the rest of the masters, by order of the most invincible prince Charles. With some things in between, others congruent to the monastic rule follow.[38] Finally, those capitularies which come next are transcribed just as they are found in the same book, for the utility of the holy Church of God, its servants, and the entire Christian people.

We also implore all readers, judges, and wise men that they deign not at any time to explicate these things with a "left-handed" interpretation,[39] or to judge anyone unjustly, or to find fault because some of them are not composed according to the rules of grammar. But they should be zealous to pray for these princes, for those in authority faithful to them and to the holy

36. The word used here is *capitula*, the same term translated as "capitularies" and "title headings."

37. Paulinus of Aquileia (+802): see Fournier and LeBras, *Histoire,* 1:148, for this passage.

38. See ibid., 1:168, for this passage.

39. The term is *sinistra interpretatione;* see also the preface to the collection of Isaac of Langres (see below).

Church of God who, together with them, transacted these same [capitularies], and for us, who struggled to collect and transcribe them. And let them, the Lord assisting, strive equally with us and with them [i.e., the princes and their collaborators] to venerate, to love, and to hold the aforesaid capitularies as laws, so that all on this account would deserve an equal reward. Amen.

3. Preface to the Collection of "Isidore Mercator," c. 850: dedicatory letter to the reader. Ed. Paul Hinschius, *Decretales Pseudo-Isidorianae et Capitula Angilramni* (Leipzig, 1863; rpt. Aalen, 1963), 17–20.

Here begins the preface of Saint Isidore for this book.[40] Isidore Mercator, servant of Christ, obedient in the Lord to the faith, to the reader, his fellow servant, greetings.[41]

I am compelled by many, both bishops and the rest of the servants of God, to collect the sentences of the canons and to assemble them in one volume, and to make one out of many. Yet

40. Hinschius's edition has certain problems at the beginning of the preface, which cannot be taken up here. See Emil Seckel, *Die erste Zeile Pseudoisidors, die Hadriana-Rezension In nomine domini incipit praefatio libri huius und die Geschichte der Invokationen in den Rechtsquellen* (Aus dem Nachlass mit Ergänzungen von Horst Fuhrmann), *Sitzungsberichte Berlin*, Klasse für Philosophie, Geschichte, Staats-, Rechts- und Wirtschaftswissenschaften, 1959, no. 4 (Berlin, 1959), esp. 15–24. For the combination of "St. Isidore" and "Isidore Mercator" at the beginning of the preface see ibid., 39–40. A study of the sources of this preface—Horst Fuhrmann, "Pseudoisidor und die Bibel"—will appear in the *Proceedings of the Tenth International Congress of Medieval Canon Law* (Syracuse, N.Y., August 1996).

41. *Isidorus Mercator servus Christi lectori conservo suo et parens in domino fidaei salutem.* This greeting contains a number of ambiguities, only one of which will be noted. Perhaps *parens* should be translated as "parent," for *parenti* occurs as a variant, i.e., "parent to the reader, his fellow servant."

this especially disturbs me: different translations create varying sentences, and although there might be one sense, nevertheless there are different sentences, some longer, some shorter. Indeed we find those councils which were published in Greek translated and copied more than three or four times. But if truth ought to be sought from much diversity, we should follow the mode of expression of the Greeks and should copy their usages and models. If not, let those who have as many models as they have manuscripts speak and expostulate. It seems to us, however, that since [the texts] disagree in our language, unity and truth should be sought from those in whose tongue they are known to have been published. And we did this, and just as we learned from true masters of these things we took pains to incorporate into the volume to which this little preface is attached.

"Canon" in Greek is called "rule" in Latin.[42] It is called rule because it directs rightly, nor does it ever lead in a different direction.[43] Others have said that it is called rule since it rules, or because it shows a norm of living rightly, or because it corrects what is distorted and evil. "Synod" is translated from Greek as "company" or "assembly." The term "council" is derived from "common intent," since all direct the gaze of the mind onto one thing. *Cilia*, in fact, belong to the eyes, whence those who disagree among themselves do not make a council, since they do not agree. A "meeting" is an "convention" or a "congregation," [derived] from "meeting together," that is, from "convening" as one. Whence the name "convention," because all agree together there, just as "convention," "meeting" and "council" [derive] from the union of many as one.

42. Cf. the preface to the Spanish Collection (chap. 2).
43. The text reads *ne quando aliorsum trahit*, with the expected *aliquando*, as found in the preface to the Spanish Collection, as a variant reading for *quando*.

At the beginning of this volume we have set out how a council is celebrated among us, so that those who wish to follow our order know how to do it. But whoever would elect to do this better should do what they decide by just, canonical, and most wise counsel. Then, on account of their authority—although by certain people they are called apocryphal—we placed before the rest of the councils the canons which are called "of the apostles," since many receive them, and the holy Fathers corroborated their statements with synodal authority and set them among the canonical constitutions.[44] Next we inserted the decrees from certain letters of the popes, that is of Clement, Anacletus, Evaristus, and the rest of the pontiffs up to Pope Silvester whose letters thus far we have been able to find. Thereafter we put the synod of Nicaea because of the authority of this same great council. Then we placed in the course of this volume [the acts] of various Greek and Latin councils, whether they were held before or after [Nicaea], arranged in chronological order with their canons separately numbered, also appending the remaining decrees of the Roman bishops up to Saint Gregory and certain letters of his, in which, because of the eminence of the apostolic see, an authority exists not unequal to the councils. Thus by the discipline of ecclesiastical order gathered and arranged by us into one, both the holy bishops may be instructed with paternal rules, and the obedient ministers and people of the Church may be imbued with spiritual examples[45] and not deceived by the depravities of wicked men.

Many, sunk in depravity and greed, have oppressed priests with accusations. The holy Fathers on that account composed

44. Note the reversal in attitude here toward the Canons of the Apostles from what occurs in the preface to the Spanish Collection.
45. Cf. the preface to Dionysius Exiguus's first collection of councils (chap. 2) and the preface to the Spanish Collection (chap. 2), although the final clause of this paragraph is not found in either.

laws which they named holy canons. Many, therefore, by this means, accuse others, so that either through them they take pressure off themselves, or they become enriched by their goods. But very many good Christians are silent and endure the sins which they know of others, because they often are lacking in documents with which they could prove to ecclesiastical judges the things which they know, since although certain things might be true, yet unless they are demonstrated with sure evidence, proven in an open investigation, and made public in a judicial proceeding, they ought not to be believed by judges.

No one who is despoiled of his own goods, or expelled from his own see by force or terror, can, according to canonical teaching, be accused, summoned, judged, and condemned before everything stolen from him is legally restored to him, and he has use of his possessions peacefully, for a long period, and having been restored to his own see in proper fashion, freely holds his office over a span of time. Whence the ecclesiastical history composed by Eusebius, bishop of Caesarea, says of a certain woman who was accused by her husband regarding chastity: "It was commanded and imposed by the emperor in a published law that first she should be permitted freely to manage the household for a long period, and then finally should respond to the charges."[46] All laws, both ecclesiastical as well as secular and public, command this. If all of their converging statements were set forth, the day would run out before these examples, and an excessively prolix letter would be produced. From many, nevertheless, we decided to insert here some of them for the consideration of others. For Saint Leo, bishop of the Roman Church, in a letter sent to the Council of Chal-

---

46. Eusebius of Caesarea, *Historia ecclesiastica*, bk. 4.17, trans. Arthur Cushman McGiffert, *Select Library of Nicene and Post-Nicene Fathers*, 2d ser., 1 (New York, 1904; rpt. Grand Rapids, 1961), 195.

cedon which begins in this way, "Leo, bishop, to the synod of Chalcedon. I had wished, indeed, most beloved, etc.,"[47] among other things asserts the following, saying: "We are not unaware that the status of many churches was troubled through perverse rivalries, and that very many brothers were unjustly expelled from their sees and banished, and that in place of those still alive others were substituted. First of all, the medicine of justice should be applied to these wounds: let no one, therefore, lack his own possessions, lest one uses what belongs to another. Let all thus forsake that error, so that no one's office ought to perish, but for the former bishops their own rights, with every privilege, should be reestablished." And the ancient popes who were earlier than the synod of Nicaea decreed the same things. The synod which was held in Lampsacus under Valentinian says the same things.[48] Very many Roman synods testify to the same things. Pope Symmachus[49] and the rest of the holy Fathers decreed the same things. Avoiding the prolixity of these statutes, we have deferred inserting them here. If, however, anyone wishes to know and to read about this more fully, he can locate and read [them] thoroughly for himself in his own texts.

But let these things suffice for us in this little preface. And just as for a foot soldier, from among many weapons those which he can bear conveniently on his person suffice, thus for us: from many statements one or two or as much as is necessary at the time suffices, since just as with a spear or two we vanquish an enemy, so we overcome an adversary with one or two statements full of authority. For if these things were established for women and secular men, by how much more were

47. JK 473.

48. Synod of Lapsacus (364) held by Emperor Valentinan I.

49. See in Jaffé and Wattenbach, *Regesta,* the false acts of the synod listed under the year 503.

they conceded to ecclesiastical men and priests. Ecclesiastical laws order and secular laws command these same things. Similarly, the accusers and accusations which secular laws prohibit canonical authority utterly rejects. The authority of congregating synods was committed by special right to the apostolic see, nor do we read that any synod is valid which was not congregated or supported by its authority.[50] Canonical authority bears witness to these things; ecclesiastical history corroborates these things; the holy Fathers confirm these things.

It is necessary, however, that you, the eighty bishops who compelled me to undertake and to carry out this work, and all the rest of the priests of the Lord, know that we found from the synod of Nicaea more than those twenty canons which are held among us, and in the decrees of Pope Julius we read that there ought to be seventy canons of the same synod.[51] We placed that letter, which should be examined by those investigating these things and by all wishing to know them, in its proper order among the rest of the decrees of the popes. In many places it is found that there are more than twenty canons of the Council of Nicaea. For it thus is read in the Council of Constantinople: "It is clear that a synod of the province itself should regulate those matters which belong to each individual province, just as it is known to have been decreed in the Council of Nicaea."[52] And in the letter of Pope Innocent directed to Bishop Vitricius of Rouen it is read thus: "If there are cases

50. This statement, of great importance for the development of conciliar theory, might seem oddly placed here. Perhaps the idea, based on the secular-ecclesiastical comparisons given, is that although the emperors of antiquity convened councils (see the list, taken from the Spanish Collection, at the end of the preface), the authority of popes to do so was preeminent.

51. JK +195.

52. Council of Constantinople (381), canon 2.

or disputes which have arisen among the clerics and laity, or among clerics of a major order, or even a lower one, according to the synod of Nicaea it was resolved that when all the bishops of the same province have been congregated, a judgment should be determined, etc."[53] Even Bishop Theophilus of Alexandria of holy memory[54] remembered in his letters that it was decreed in the Council of Nicaea that whenever the new moon is born in the interval from eight days before the Ides of March until the Nones of April, that is for twenty-eight days, this serves to mark the beginning of the first month. He wrote that the fourteenth day is carefully to be searched out, from twelve days before the Kalends of April until fourteen days before the Kalends of May, even if it falls on Saturday, and to celebrate

53. JK 286.

54. Theophilus was patriarch of Alexandria, 385–412. The complexities of the discussion which follows about the date of Easter cannot be taken up here: see the detailed treatment by Henri Leclercq, *Dictionnaire d'archéologie chrétienne et de liturgie*, 13.2 (Paris, 1938), 1521ff., and the shorter articles by J. Ford, *New Catholic Encyclopedia* (New York, 1967), 5:8–9, and in the *Oxford Dictionary of the Christian Church*, 2d ed., ed. F. L. Cross and E. A. Livingstone (Oxford, 1974), 1037–38. The details are incidental to the forger's purpose, which is to emphasize that the well-known twenty canons do not comprise the totality of the proceedings from the Council of Nicaea. The first calculations given are problematic. Eight days before the Ides of March is March 8, and the Nones of April is April 5. Employing the Roman practice of inclusive reckoning, i.e., counting both the beginning and end days, it is twenty-nine, not twenty-eight, days, a difficulty probably caused by the fact that a lunar month is not exactly twenty-eight days long: see Leclercq, 1556. To find the possibilities for the fourteenth day of the first month (i.e., the day on which the Jewish Passover begins), counting fourteen days from March 8 and from April 5 gives March 21 and April 18, i.e., twelve days before the Kalends of April, and fourteen days before the Kalends of May, counting inclusively in both cases.

Easter on the following Lord's day, that is [even] on the fifteenth day of the lunar month.[55] And if the fourteenth day of the same lunar month, that is of the first month, falls on the Lord's day, he wrote to celebrate Easter without doubt when this week has moved along to another Lord's day.

From these and very many other examples it is clear that there are more than twenty canons of the Council of Nicaea, and that the letter of the aforementioned Pope Julius is true. Moreover certain Easterners from the fellowship of our brethren bore witness to us that they had seen [a text of] the Council of Nicaea having the size of the four Gospels, containing sessions of the bishops, presentations and judgments of quarrels, definitions and constitutions, and also subscriptions to these. They confirmed that [the acts of] the great Council of Chalcedon were recorded in imitation of this, and afterward [those of] others assembled at Constantinople, namely one under Emperor Justinian[56] against the assaulters of God—Origen, Didymus, and Evagrius—and another in the time of Pope Agatho and Emperor Constantine[57] against Bishop Macharius, his disciple Stephen, and the rest of the bishops who sowed in the churches tares for grain, mixed wine with water, gave unbridled destruction as a drink to their neighbor, as wolves mendaciously pretended to be lambs, and truth was repressed as a lie.

It is also necessary to know that although others are not invalidated, there are four principal councils from which the churches hold the fullest teaching of the faith, concerning both the divinity of the Father, Son, and Holy Spirit, and the in-

55. Leclercq, *Dictionnaire,* 1528, for the Roman practice of not celebrating Easter before the sixteenth day of the lunar month.

56. The Second Council of Constantinople, 553.

57. The Third Council of Constantinople, 680–81.

carnation of the aforementioned Son, our Savior.[58] The first
of these is the synod at Nicaea of 318 bishops, held under the
august Constantine. Condemned therein was the blasphemy
of Arian treachery, by which the same Arius asserted the inequality of the Holy Trinity, and the same holy synod defined
through a confession that the Son of God is consubstantial with
God the Father. The second synod, of 150 fathers, gathered at
Constantinople under Theodosius senior. Condemning Macedonius, who denied that the Holy Spirit was God, it demonstrated that the same Paraclete is consubstantial with the Father
and the Son, and gave a more extensive form of the confession which the entire Greek and Latin worlds preach in the
churches. The third synod, of 200 bishops, the first of Ephesus,
was held under the younger august Theodosius. It condemned
with a just anathema Nestorius, who asserted that there are two
persons in Christ, and showed that the one person of our Lord
Jesus Christ remains in two natures. The fourth, of 630 bishops, was held at Chalcedon under Emperor Marcian. Therein
one voice of the Fathers vehemently damned Eutyches, abbot
at Constantinople, who claimed that the Word of God and the
flesh were one nature, his defender, Dioscorus, former bishop
of Alexandria, and, again, Nestorius, with the rest of the heretics. The same synod proclaimed that Christ is God, born thus
of the Virgin so that in one substance both divine and human
natures may be confessed. These are, as we said above, the four
principal and venerable synods embracing the catholic faith.
But if there are any [other] councils which holy Fathers, filled
with the Spirit of God, sanctioned, after the authority of these
four they should remain fixed with all firmness.

At the beginning, as was said above, an order for celebrat-

58. For what follows, see the preface to the Spanish Collection (chap.
2) and the notes given at that point.

ing a council is inserted, and afterward in their place follow the canons "of the apostles," the decrees of the first popes, that is, from Saint Clement up to Saint Sylvester, and the various councils.

4. Preface to the Chapters of Bishop Isaac of Langres, 859–880. Ed. Rudolf Pokorny and Martina Stratmann (unter Mitwirkung von Wolf-Dieter Runge), *Capitula episcoporum* (Monumenta Germaniae Historica, Capitula episcoporum 2; Hannover, 1995), 180.

Here begins the preface of the following work.

When ecclesiastical need demands that a pastoral judgment be brought forth against the delinquent and erring, it often happens that remedies which are prepared with the height of charity and the ardor of piety by concerned fathers are rejected by sons languishing toward their ruin. And since they pay heed neither to the compassion of physicians nor, as they should, to their own danger of damnation, they scorn what was offered them and despise the remedies, because they are familiar, as ineffective.

Therefore, due to the tenacity of certain agitators and their complaint against pastoral solicitude, and also due to the insolence of the impudent, who prattle that all things spoken for their correction and caution have been made up, contrived, or invented by us, I, Isaac, unworthy bishop of Langres, judged[59] it useful to repeat some chapters of the most healthful sanctions which the legate of the holy Roman and apostolic Church, the venerable Boniface, Archbishop of Mainz, vicar of Pope Zachary, together with the orthodox Carloman, prince of the Franks, formulated to the honor and benefit of the Church at two councils of bishops—texts which the same Pope Zachary

59. The verb is in the plural, *duximus.*

also confirmed with apostolic authority in the year of the Lord's incarnation 742, and decreed to be held inviolably by all the faithful of the Church of God. I considered it useful for me and for my people to collect and gather into one small work some of these things on subjects most often in dispute, so that if they[60] should misrepresent our work, or try by "lefthanded" interpretation[61] to destroy it, curbed equally by apostolic and royal authority, let them henceforth be silent and, even unwillingly, acquiesce in healthful cures when the occasion demands.

5. Preface to the Two Books concerning Synodal Investigations and Ecclesiastical Instructions of Abbot Regino of Prüm, 906: dedicatory letter to Archbishop Hatto of Mainz. Ed. F. G. A. Wasserschleben, *Libri duo de synodalibus causis et disciplinis ecclesiasticis* (Leipzig, 1840; rpt. Graz, 1964), 1–2.[62]

Here begins the preface of the following work.[63]
To Hatto, archbishop of the holy see of Mainz and primate of all Germany, Regino, the least but most devoted dependent of your sublimity, prays for your prosperity in this life and the glory of future blessedness.

Knowing that your great prudence not only takes care of the whole province according to the sanctions of the holy canons, but also labors with watchful care for the advantage of the

60. Presumably this refers to the "agitators" and "the impudent" of the first line, but are they among Isaac's "people," i.e., his parishioners, just noted?

61. *sinistra interpretatione labefactare temptaverint.* See the preface to the False Capitularies of Benedict the Deacon, above.

62. Another edition of this preface is found in F. Kurze, *Regionis abbatis Prumensis Chronicon cum continuatione Trevernensi* (Hannover, 1896), xix–xx.

63. Wasserschleben indicated that this introductory line occurred in only one of the manuscripts he used (Wasserschleben, ed., *Libri*).

whole kingdom, I sent your exaltedness a little book concerning synodical cases and ecclesiastical discipline, which, by the order and encouragement of the most reverend Lord Archbishop Rathbod, I collected and brought together with great zeal from diverse councils and decrees of the holy Fathers. I did not rashly decide either that a supply of all kinds of books was lacking on your shelves, or that something was unknown to the wisdom of your excellent intellect—you, who by the dignity of nobility adorns with renowned praise the place committed from on high to your magnificence, who are so great in every type of philosophy that you alone display to us in this worn-out age the skills of the philosophers about which learned Roman antiquity boasted. But since your great wisdom is constantly engaged in taking care of public matters, it seems perhaps burdensome that many volumes of councils always should be carried along with you far and wide. Therefore I sent this handbook to your lordship so that you might have it as a guide when the abundance of your books is not at hand.

However, if someone is disturbed about why I have used a greater number of texts from our own councils—namely of Gaul and Germany—let him receive a reply, and know that I took great care to insert those texts which I considered more necessary to these perilous times of ours, and which have appeared to pertain to the business at hand. It must also be added that many kinds of disgraceful things were perpetrated, and are being perpetrated, in the Church at this most evil time, things unheard of in early times because they were not done and were thus not written down or condemned by fixed decrees. These have been condemned, and are being condemned daily, by the recent rules of the Fathers. And it should be known that just as various people differ amongst themselves in type, customs, language, and laws, thus the holy universal Church spread through the whole world, though joined in unity of faith, differs from one place to another in ecclesiastical customs. Indeed, some customs in ecclesiastical operations are found in the kingdoms of Gaul and Germany, others are found in the eastern kingdoms in regions across the seas. Moreover, scripture warns that the boundaries, that is, the laws and decrees which our Fathers established, must be observed in all ways, never transgressed by any rash presumption.[64] Wherefore, following the footsteps of our predecessors, I arranged in order[65] a variety of statutes from various Fathers, leaving to the judgment of the reader what he prefers to select and approve as most important. Let your worthiness thus receive this little work with that kindness with which, in devotion, it was sent by my unworthiness. May the glory of your blessedness prevail here and in the future. Amen.

Here ends the preface of the following work.

6. Preface to the Collection Dedicated to Anselm, 882–96: dedicatory letter to Archbishop Anselm II of Milan. Ed. Jean-Claude Besse, "Collectionis 'Anselmo Dedicata' Liber Primus," *Revue du droit canonique* 9 (1959): 212–13, and idem, *Histoire des textes du droit de l'Eglise au Moyen-Age de Denys à Gratien: Collectio Anselmo Dedicata, Etude et Texte (Extraits)* (Paris, 1960), 3–4.

To the most magnificent lord, most vigilant pastor, and most eminent archbishop, Anselm, I, the least little lamb of his flock, and in a certain way his own small servant, invoke his pontifical grace and unspeakable merit with diligent petitions.

O famous pastor, the acumen of your praiseworthy wisdom, worthy of imitation, provides for the good of the Church pru-

64. Cf. Proverbs 22:28, and JK +86 of Pseudo Calixtus I, c. 12. This represents a well-known maxim in early medieval canon law.

65. *in ordine digessi.* The arrangement of the two books of his collections (see the discussion above) shows what Regino meant by this general phrase.

dently and expertly, always contending both inwardly and out-wardly for the communal growth of the flock entrusted to you. You did not refuse frequently to admonish me, though least among the rest of your servants, and to spur me to higher studies, in every way directing and enjoining that, according to the measure of my slight talent, I should diligently gather and arrange together in one work the teachings of the sacred canons, which from the earliest days of the Christian faith the masters of the holy, catholic Church, namely, the apostles and the popes, have set down in their writings for the instruction of posterity. Fully conscious of my lack of skill, my unimportance, and my weakness, I would not have presumed to undertake such a difficult work from any temerity or audacity—especially since it is certain that abler and more discerning men, Greeks as well as Latins, have labored at this very thing—but only because the censure of your judgment compelled [me]. For in one place Fer-randus, deacon of the church of Carthage, and in another a cer-tain Cresconius, an imitator of that work, appear to have made a kind of harmony of ecclesiastical sanctions. And I should be especially cautious, lest perchance by patching together the very same, the infamy of being either a "compiler" or a detractor be laid against me.[66] But so that I can at least partly satisfy your command, which compels me beyond measure, and your most ardent love, I pray that above all, after divine assistance, the ap-proval of your paternal blessing be with me, so that among the other sons under your rule I shall not appear utterly devoid of

66. In classical Latin *compilator* was not a neutral term. Its basic meaning could best be translated by "plagiarist." Only gradually did the modern senses of "compiler" and "compiling" emerge from the origi-nal negative meaning, which is preserved here. See Neil Hathaway, "Compilator: From Plagiarism to Compiling," *Viator* 20 (1989): 19–44, and with concentration on the term in canonistic prologues, Brasington, "Prologues," 226–42.

your most sagacious estimation, even if not for my own labor at least for what belongs to another.[67]

Therefore, to carry out this little work of mine to which I am inadequate, as the Lord, the maker of all good things deigned to grant increase, I decided to divide all the pages of the canons, councils, and decretals of the Fathers into twelve parts, following the model of apostolic pedigree,[68] and in each section appropriate headings are placed in front of [the canons]. These prefaced statements, just as specific and most truthful witnesses, offer clear testimony and point to an open entrance for the eager reader to find what he seeks. I ask him not to be annoyed if I do not improvidently add what individual teachers believe about each issue, since a position supported by the authority of many judges seems more certain and unshaken.

The first part of this work which, with God's assistance, I am undertaking, deals with the primacy and dignity of the Roman see and of other primates, patriarchs, archbishops, and metropolitans.

The second part deals with the appropriate honor and different occupation of bishops and chorbishops.

The third part deals with celebrating a synod and convocation to a synod, with accusers and accusations, with witnesses and testimonies, with those unjustly despoiled, and with ecclesiastical and secular judges and judgments.

The fourth part deals with the proper dignity and the different occupation of priests, deacons, and the remaining ecclesiastical orders.

67. The idea seems to be that however carefully done (see n. 66 on the fear of being a "compiler"), the collection still must be derivative from the work of others.

68. An arrangement according to a number with such special significance is not unique. The eleventh-century Collection in Twelve Parts likewise followed the "apostolic number."

The fifth part deals with the formation, support, and quality of life of clerics.

The sixth part deals with the vocation of monks and the profession of nuns and widows.

The seventh part deals with laity, namely, emperors, princes, and the remaining ranks "in the world."[69]

The eighth part deals with the standard of the Christian faith, the grace of Christ, and fulfilling diving commands.

The ninth part deals with the sacrament of baptism, those about to be baptized, and those having been baptized.

The tenth part deals with the disposition of "temples" of worship,[70] both cult and estates, and with offerings, oblations, and tithes.

The eleventh part deals with the solemnity of Easter and the remaining festivals and holidays.

The twelfth part deals with heretics, schismatics, Jews, and pagans.

7. Preface to the Canons of Abbot Abbo of Fleury, c. 1000: dedicatory letter to King Hugh Capet and his son Robert.
Ed. Jean Mabillon, *Vetera analecta* (Paris, 1723), 133–34
(rpt. in J.-P. Migne, *Patrologia Latina*, 139
[Paris, 1853], 473–474).

Here begin the canons of the lord abbot Abbo, and of both King Hugh and his son Robert, kings of the Franks, excerpted from other canons.

To my most glorious lords, kings of the Franks, Hugh and his son Robert, a worthy example of governing power, the humble Abbo, rector of Fleury, [wishes] the gift of eternal salvation in Christ.

69. *reliquis seculi ordinibus.*
70. *templorum divinorum.*

After you assumed the leadership of the kingdom, by virtue of divine clemency, by the hidden but not unjust judgment of God you endured, for the purpose of testing, many calamities. Nor was this [done] by foreign peoples, but by the leading men of the kingdom, so that the beginning of your reign was agitated. But because the omnipotent Lord has delivered you from all these things, remember the goodness and piety of God, remember the good kings, your predecessors, remember just judgments and always be inclined to spare the lowly and subdue the proud.

Certainly, most serene lords, since I have learned that you are benevolent toward our [monastic] order, I placed in one sequence title headings, copied below,[71] from books of canons and secular laws, together with opinions, partly my own, partly from others. And dedicating it to your name, after making use of [my] *Apologeticus* against adversaries,[72] I laid out concisely in one volume the things collected. In these I described the height of your office, and have not kept silent as to how the leading men of the kingdom ought to keep faith with you. I have compiled many things for the defense of the monastic order, I who desire and have desired that the "senate" of the monks,[73] whose most pious defenders and advocates you indeed are, always be secure. Have mercy, therefore, on the monks and at the same time on your Abbo, so that God enables you to find his mercy, both here and in eternity with his holy kings. Farewell.

71. In the edition the preface is followed by a list of fifty-two titles, which will not be translated.

72. Abbo had written his *Apologeticus* as a defense against critics and rivals seeking to turn the French king and his son against him, and to urge the elimination of such abuses as simony. The ideas which Abbo delineates here are not especially easy to follow. The *Apologeticus* must have been a source for "opinions" which he inserted into the collection.

73. *monachorum senatum.*

8. Preface to the *Decretum* of Bishop Burchard of Worms,
early eleventh century: dedicatory letter to Provost
Brunicho of Worms. Ed. Gérard Fransen, *Burchard von
Worms, Decretorum libri XX* (ergänzter Neudruck der Editio
princeps Köln 1548, herausgegeben von Gérard Fransen und
Theo Kölzer) (Aalen, 1992), 45–49.

In the name of Christ, here begins the little preface of this
little book.[74]

Burchard, in name alone bishop of Worms, to Brunicho his
vassal, namely the provost of the same see, greetings in Christ
the Lord.

For a long time now, intimate and most dear brother, in person you frequently urged that with a careful mind I should compile into one corpus from various useful things—from the statements of the holy Fathers, from the canons, and from diverse
penitentials—a little book for the work of our fellow priests.
And for this reason especially:[75] because in our diocese the laws
of the canons and the judgments for those doing penance are
confused, varied, and disordered, just as if they were completely
neglected, and are both greatly in disagreement among themselves and supported by the authority of almost no one, so that
because of the discord they scarcely can be disentangled by experts. Whence it frequently happens that for those fleeing to
the remedy of penance, both on account of the confusion of the
books and also the ignorance of the priests, help in no way is
at hand.

74. Burchard used the word *libellus* both here and in the preface itself
to designate his collection. The word is not unusual and can mean a
variety of things, including simply "book." But the topos of humility
probably was at work, and the choice was made to use the literal meaning,
"little book."

75. For some of what follows, see the letter from Ebbo of Reims to
Halitgar of Cambrai which prefaces Halitgar's Penitential (above).

Why is this? I believe that it happens especially because the canons do not prescribe for each and every offense the gravity of the sin and the amount of time for doing penance carefully, clearly, and fully enough in order to tell for individual cases how each sin should be corrected, but, rather, they state that it ought to be left to the judgment of an understanding priest. Wherefore, because this cannot be done except by the wise and those learned in divine law, you, beloved, requested that I deliver this little book, now at last concisely assembled, to young boys for study, so that what our coworkers, today in their maturity, had neglected due to the ineptitude of our predecessors, is handed over to those now of tender age and to others willing to learn. Indeed let them first be made apt students, and afterward both teachers and leaders of the people, and let them learn in schools what some day they ought to say to those committed to themselves. Your desire and petition, brother, seemed just to me, and I give thanks for such a wish. I also offer many thanks to him who provided one such as you for me, because I have recognized that you have exerted yourself assiduously on behalf of the state of our church.

But that I put off for such a long time your exhortation, often pressed upon me, I do not wish you to attribute to my laziness and lack of enthusiasm. I was unable to proceed for two reasons: because of various and inevitable ecclesiastical obligations, which emerge daily just as waves of the sea, and, moreover, because of responsibility for secular affairs relating to imperial commands. These greatly blunt the mind of one zealous and striving toward higher things, because the mind of anyone, while it is divided among very many things, will be weaker for each one. Obedient, nonetheless, to your holy requests, I collected, God granting, synodal precepts and holy statutes both from the rulings of the holy Fathers and from the canons, and, just as I was able, linked them together in one corpus and divided the same corpus into twenty books. And if any diligent reader carefully examines them, he will find therein many useful things for our ministry.

The first book deals with the power and primacy of the apostolic see, with the patriarchs, and with the rest of the metropolitan primates, with celebrating a synod and convocation to a synod, with those accused, and both accusers and witnesses, with those unjustly despoiled, with judges, and with every proper honor, dignity, and with the diverse labor and ministry[76] of bishops.

The second book deals with the proper dignity, and with the diverse formation, support, quality of life, and the different labor and ministry of priests, deacons, and the rest of the ecclesiastical orders.

The third book deals with the disposition of houses of worship, both cult and status, with tithes, oblations, and the rights of individuals, and which books should be accepted in the sacred catalogue and when they ought to be used, but which are apocryphal.

The fourth book deals with the sacrament of baptism, and with ministry both to those about to be baptized and to those having been baptized, and to those about to be confirmed and to those having been confirmed.

The fifth book deals with the sacrament of the body and blood of the Lord, and with both their reception and regulation.

The sixth book deals with murders committed voluntarily

76. Burchard uses the word *ministerium* at several points in describing the contents of the *Decretum*'s books. It consistently will be translated as "ministry," although at times "duty" or "responsibility" perhaps renders more clearly in modern English what is intended.

and involuntarily, with patricide, fratricide, those who kill their legitimate wives and their elders, with the murder of ecclesiastics, and with both the regulation and penance for each.

The seventh book deals with the incestuous union of consanguinity, and within which degree of kinship the faithful ought to be married and separated, and with both the correction and penance for each.

The eighth book deals with men and women dedicated to God, with those contravening the sacred way of life, and with both their correction and penance.

The ninth book deals with virgins and widows not veiled, with their abductors and separation from them, with the union of legitimate marriages, with concubines, and with both the sin and penance for each.

The tenth book deals with magicians, soothsayers, prophets, fortune-tellers, various illusions of the devil, curses, the contentious, conspirators, and with the penance for each.

The eleventh book deals with those who ought to be excommunicated, with those excommunicated, with thieves and plunderers, and with their disobedience, contempt, disrespect, reconciliation, and penance.

The twelfth book deals with perjury and its penance.

The thirteenth book deals with the veneration and observance of the holy fast.

The fourteenth book deals with gluttony, drunkenness, and their penance.

The fifteenth book deals with emperors, princes, the remaining laity, and with their ministry.

The sixteenth book deals with accusers, judges, defenders, false witnesses, and with the penance of each.[77]

The seventeenth book deals with fornication and incest of

77. Compare the contents of book 1, dealing with bishops.

different sorts, and with the penance for both genders and different ages.[78]

The eighteenth book deals with the visitation, penance, and reconciliation of the sick.

The nineteenth book, which is called the Corrector [and the Physician],[79] deals with the corrections of bodies and the medicines of souls, and teaches each and every priest, even the simple, how and in what measure he is able to help each and every one: ordained or without order, poor, rich, young boy, youth, aged, decrepit, healthy, ill, at every age, of both genders.[80]

The twentieth is called a book of Explorations, for it probes into divine providence and predestination, the advent of Antichrist, his works, the resurrection, day of judgment, damnation, and the felicity of eternal life.

Whence, brother, if one from all of these is lacking for those guiding their people, how are they able to train and to teach them? And even the title "priest" will hardly remain with them, because the evangelical warnings are exceedingly foreboding, in which it is said, "If the blind leads the blind, both fall into a ditch."[81] But what if there is some jealous little person who, after he has seen this, envies me, saying that I collect tidbits from the ears of others,[82] and make for myself an empty name from the work of others? Let it be so! I admit that I have col-

78. *utriusque sexus et diuerse etatis.* The text in the singular is translated in the plural.

79. This second title does not occur in all manuscripts collated by Fransen for his edition.

80. As in n. 78, here the singular *in utroque sexu* is translated in the plural.

81. Matthew 15:14.

82. This enigmatic passage is actually a quotation from Persius's *Satires:* see Fuhrmann, "Vorwort," and Somerville and Winroth, " 'Collecting Tidbits' " (as in n. 23, above).

lected these things from the work of others, since it is not permitted for me alone to make canons. It is permitted to collect them, which I did, God knows, not on account of some arrogance but for the need of our church.

So that the murmur of a detractor might be silenced, let the book,[83] of whatever sort it might be, be ours. I do not ask that it pass beyond the boundary of our bishopric, but let it remain to be studied by our own. But how and whence I assembled it I want you to hear, and I leave it to be determined by your judgment if any sin is involved. I added nothing of myself except labor, but I collected with great toil from inspired witnesses those things which you find herein. And I strove with greatest zeal so that those which I had brought together would be authoritative. For I selected some things necessary for our time from that core of canons which by some is called the "Corpus of Canons," some from the canon[s] "of the apostles," some from transmarine, German, Frankish, and Spanish councils, some from the decrees of the Roman pontiffs, some from the teaching of Truth itself, some from the Old Testament, some from the apostles, some from the sayings of Saint Gregory, the sayings of Saint Jerome, the sayings of Saint Augustine, the sayings of Saint Ambrose, the sayings of Saint Benedict, the sayings of Saint Isidore, and the sayings of Saint Basil, some from the Roman Penitential, some from the Penitential of Theodore, and some from the Penitential of Bede. If you find something of use among these things in this compilation, credit it to the gifts of God, but if you find something superfluous, ascribe it to my ignorance.

Be well, and I plead that in your sacred prayers you remember me, a sinner.

83. Burchard now uses the term *liber* ("book") and not the previous *libellus*.

4

The Era of Reform: 1050–1140

The works presented in this chapter mark a profound transition in the development of medieval canon law. The first text, the preface to Cardinal Atto's Breviary, differs little from the prologues of Halitgar or Burchard of Worms. The preface to the book On Mercy and Justice of Alger of Liège, the last item of the chapter, is a far different work, shaped by a new legal method which can be labeled "dialectical jurisprudence." The focus of jurisprudence has shifted decisively over the century treated here, from concerns about sources and their arrangement to the problem of harmonization of contradictions found in those sources. By the early twelfth century, canon law in Latin Christendom was in the process of becoming more systematized than it had been for nearly a thousand years.

These developments cannot be separated from the efforts on the part of eleventh-century reformers to eliminate such abuses in the Church as simoniacal appointments and clerical incontinence.[1] As noted in the last chapter, important reforming initiatives had emerged in the previous century in monasteries like Cluny, Gorze, and their daughter houses. These monasteries exemplified commitment to the religious life, and their demands

1. For the various reforming movements in the eleventh and twelfth centuries, with extensive bibliography, see Uta-Renate Blumenthal, *The Investiture Controversy: Church and Monarchy from the Ninth to the Twelfth Century* (Philadelphia, 1988); Colin Morris, *The Papal Monarchy: The Western Church from 1050 to 1250* (Oxford, 1989); and I. S. Robinson, *The Papacy 1073–1198: Continuity and Innovation* (Cambridge, 1990). Much of value also can be found in Tierney, *Crisis,* 24–95.

for autonomy and freedom from lay and episcopal interference echo in the preface to Abbo of Fleury's collection. Aspirations for reform and renewal also could be found among bishops, and in the middle of the eleventh century, beginning with Pope Leo IX (1049–1054), preeminently in the papacy. Details of the programs of the reforming popes from Leo onward cannot be discussed here and can be readily found elsewhere (see n. 1, above), but as in the Carolingian era, renewed study of canon law was an integral part of this ecclesiastical reform.

As churchmen turned "to the sources" of the canonical tradition for guidelines, and for models of holiness and discipline, they became increasingly aware of difficulties posed by the canons and how complicated it was to attempt to apply tradition to their world.[2] New collections of texts and new methods of interpretation were needed. A variety of works were produced, many of which, drawing on the Pseudo-Isidorian Decretals, presented ecclesiologies focused in one way or another

2. Little exists in English on the development of canon law during the eleventh- and twelfth-century reform era and the Investiture Contest. Fournier and LeBras, *Histoire,* vol. 2, remains invaluable, but it must be supplemented extensively with specific studies. In addition to Brundage, *Medieval Canon Law,* 35ff., and Blumenthal, *Investiture Controversy,* esp. chap. 3 (see n. 1, above), see John Gilchrist's introduction to his translation of an influential reforming collection, *The Collection in Seventy-four Titles: A Canon Law Manual of the Gregorian Reform* (Mediaeval Sources in Translation 22; Toronto, 1980), and Gilchrist's essay "Canon Law Aspects of the Eleventh-Century Gregorian Reform Programme," *Journal of Ecclesiastical History* 13 (1962): 21–38 (rpt. in Gilchrist, *Canon Law in the Age of Reform, 11th–12th Centuries* [Variorum Collected Studies Series CS406; Aldershot, 1993]). On the reformers' search of tradition, see Ronald Knox, "Finding the Law: Developments in Canon Law during the Gregorian Reform," *Studi Gregoriani* 9 (1972): 419–66. Canonical and polemical literature of the Investiture Contest is also discussed by I. S. Robinson, *Authority and Resistance in the Investiture Contest: The Polemical Literature of the Late Eleventh Century* (Manchester, 1978).

on the Roman Church as the source and arbiter of canonical tradition. Although there is no evidence that any collection was personally commissioned by a Roman pontiff, enthusiasm for papal leadership of the reform movement after the middle of the eleventh century clearly inspired writers to search tradition for evidence of the primacy and power of the Roman see. A number of these new collections have prefaces and prologues which reflect in varying degrees this renewed respect for the Roman Church and for the papacy. Not all of the compilations of this period contain prefaces; for example, the widespread *Diversorum patrum sententie* (known to modern scholars as the Collection in 74 Titles) and the pivotal collection from the early 1080s assembled by Bishop Anselm of Lucca do not.[3] Yet even in such cases, through selection and organization of texts, the Roman Church emerges as the standard by which the rest of the Church must be judged.

The translations presented here can be divided into two distinct groups.[4] The first is Roman in origin and dates from the

3. The 74 Titles is well known today, given its availability not only in a modern critical edition but also in translation by John Gilchrist (see n. 2, above).

4. Among collections compiled in the decades between Burchard of Worms and the second half of the eleventh century, the south-Italian Collection in Five Books may be the most significant. See two essays by Roger Reynolds, "The south-Italian Canon Law *Collection in Five Books* and Its Derivatives: New Evidence on Its Origins, Diffusion, and Use," *Mediaeval Studies* 52 (1990): 278–95, and "The south-Italian *Collection in Five Books* and Its Derivatives: The Collection of Vallicelliana Tome XXI," in *Proceedings of the Eighth International Congress of Medieval Canon Law,* ed. Stanley Chodorow (Monumenta iuris canonici, Subsidia 9; Vatican City, 1992), 77–91 (both rpt. in Reynolds, *Law and Liturgy in the Latin Church, 5th–12th Centuries* [Variorum Collected Studies Series CS457; Aldershot, 1994]). The Five Books contains a general preface and prefaces for each of the books. They are undoubtedly of interest, but

era of the Investiture Contest during the late eleventh and early twelfth centuries. Written over a period of three or four decades, these prefaces indicate how supporters of the papal cause of reform searched earlier collections for texts to back claims for an increasingly exclusive Roman control of canon law. The fact that all three of the works discussed under this rubric were compiled by cardinals indicates involvement with legal matters at high levels of Church administration but should not be interpreted to mean that these books represent official Roman canon law.[5]

The preface of Cardinal Atto of St. Mark's to his Breviary (*Breviarium,* below) reveals the state of interest in canon law at Rome early in Gregory VII's papacy (1073–85).[6] At an undetermined date Atto compiled a brief collection from various sources, preeminent among them the Pseudo-Isidorian Decretals, to replace the "Roman Penitential" in use at his church.[7]

---

lengthy, and derived in part from works already presented here, e.g., from Dionysius, the Spanish Collection, and the Pseudo-Isidorian Decretals, and hence will not be translated.

5. The best introduction to these issues remains Horst Fuhrmann's study, "Das Reformpapsttum und die Rechtswissenschaft," in *Investiturstreit und Reichsverfassung,* ed. J. Fleckenstein (Vorträge und Forschugen 17; Sigmaringen, 1973), 175–203.

6. For Atto and older bibliography, see Robert Somerville, "Pope Nicholas I and John Scottus Eriugena: JE 2833," *Zeitschrift der Savigny-Stiftung für Rechtsgeschichte,* Kanonistische Abteilung 83 (1997), and also Reynolds, "Law, Canon" 409; J. J. Ryan, "Atto of Milan," *New Catholic Encyclopedia* (New York, 1967), 1:1031ff.; and, in general, Fournier and LeBras, *Histoire,* 2:20–25. For the title of the work as *Breviarium* (instead of *Capitulare*), see Franz Pelster, S.I., "Das Dekret Burkhards von Worms in einer Redaktion aus dem Beginn der Gregorianischen Reform," *Studi Gregoriani* 1 (1947): 323, n. 4.

7. What Atto was referring to as the "Roman Penitential"—perhaps the sixth book of Halitgar's Penitential (see chap. 3)—remains unclear. See Raymund Kottje, *Die Bussbücher Halitgars von Cambrai und*

Atto made it clear in his preface that he felt compelled to create a useful, authentic compendium of law for the local church. The principal source and the judge of that law is the papacy, and thus Atto's preface captures the reorientation of canonistic jurisprudence toward the Roman Church that is central to the papal reform movement from the middle of the eleventh century onward. The Pseudo-Isidorian texts chosen for the collection reinforce this emphasis on Rome, as does Atto's somewhat ambivalent attitude expressed in his preface to canons found in Burchard of Worms's *Decretum.*

The second text, the introduction to the collection compiled by Cardinal Deusdedit, reveals a reformer enthusiastically devoted to the Roman Church.[8] Although he may have come originally from France—his contemporary, the discredited theologian Berengar of Tours, wrote that he came from Tulle—Deusdedit was in Rome by his thirties and eventually became cardinal priest of the church of St. Peter in Chains (also called Apostles in Glory). An ardent supporter of Gregory VII, he served as a papal legate in Germany during the height of the pope's struggle with Henry IV. Sometime before 1086, during the chaotic years surrounding Gregory VII's exile and death, Deusdedit assembled his collection of canons. Taken from a variety of sources, among them the Pseudo-Isidorian Decretals, the work attempts both to furnish a comprehensive review of canonical tradition, and also to buttress the power and authority of the Roman see. Presented as a dedicatory letter to Pope Victor III (1086–1087), the book's preface makes it clear

---

des Hrabanus Maurus: Ihre Überlieferung und ihre Quellen (Beiträge zur Geschichte und Quellenkunde des Mittelalters 8; Berlin, 1980), 159, n. 32.

8. See most recently Uta-Renate Blumenthal, "History and Tradition in Eleventh-Century Rome," *Catholic Historical Review* 79 (1993): 185–96, with references to earlier literature.

that the disastrous end of Gregory's pontificate in no way has diminished Deusdedit's faith in the unique authority of the Roman Church, "even while it lacked a bishop." Gregory had been deserted by many of the cardinals in the early 1080s and fled to Salerno with his Norman rescuers in the face of Henry IV's siege of Rome. Almost a year passed between his death at Salerno in May 1085 and the election by the Gregorian party of Abbot Desiderius of Monte Cassino as Pope Victor III. But Deusdedit lived through these dark days and to the year 1100, long enough to see his confidence rewarded when papal reform was renewed under Pope Urban II (1088–1099).

Deusdedit's preface is more elaborate than the introduction to Atto's collection. The unique position and power of the Roman Church is discussed at length. The author also takes particular care to delineate the organization of the collection by explaining his system for numbering the rulings in order to aid the reader searching for particular texts or topics. He even warns the scribe to be especially careful to preserve the proper numbering, lest the reader be "seriously vexed," since the *capitulatio*, or table of contents, which follows the preface is coordinated with these numbers.

The third and final preface in this group of Roman texts introduces the collection known as the *Polycarpus* (a title meaning an accumulation of many things), which was put together by a cleric named Gregory, appointed cardinal priest of S. Grisogono by Pope Paschal II sometime before April 1111.[9] Dedicated to Bishop Diego Gelmírez of Santiago de Compostela, the collection may have been a long time in preparation, with final composition sometime between 1111 and 1113, the year of

9. See Uwe Horst, *Die Kanonessammlung Polycarpus des Gregor von S. Grisogono. Quellen und Tendenzen* (Monumenta Germaniae Historica, Hilfsmittel 5; Munich, 1980), 1.

Cardinal Gregory's death. If so, then the *Polycarpus* reflects at least to a degree the sentiments of a papal supporter during the stormiest years of Paschal's pontificate, as he struggled not only with Emperor Henry V, but also with many of his own clergy over lay investiture. In the collection proper, which begins with a characteristic title, "On the principate of Peter" (*De principatu Petri*), Gregory's support of papal authority is unambiguous, although he does not explicitly elaborate this allegiance in the preface, which takes the typical form of a dedicatory letter to Bishop Diego. Nonetheless, compared to Deusdedit's perspective in the mid-1080s, with his exaltation of the Roman Church in general, the *Polycarpus* exemplifies the degree of success that Urban II and Paschal II had achieved in reattaching the cause of reform to the papal office, notwithstanding the disastrous end of Gregory VII's reign and the continued upheavals the papacy endured in the final decade of the eleventh and the early years of the twelfth century.

The second group of texts comes from northern France, and all of these relate in one way or another to Bishop Ivo of Chartres and his work. Ivo (c. 1040–1115) was one of the finest legal scholars of the reform era and one of the most significant figures in the history of medieval canon law—"a French canonist of massive learning," as Brian Tierney wrote.[10] He was bishop of Chartres from 1090 to his death—Urban II himself cham-

10. Tierney, *Crisis,* 75. Most scholarship on Ivo is in French, but two recent doctoral dissertations in English consider his life and works: Bruce C. Brasington, "The Prologue to the 'Decretum' and 'Panormia' of Ivo of Chartres: An Eleventh-Century Treatise on Ecclesiastical Jurisprudence" (Ph.D. diss., University of California at Los Angeles, 1990), and Lynn K. Barker, "History, Reform, and Law in the Works of Ivo of Chartres" (Ph.D. diss., University of North Carolina, 1988). The standard biography is by Rolf Sprandel, *Ivo von Chartres und seine Stellung in der Kirchengeschichte* (Pariser Historische Studien 1; Stuttgart, 1962). See also the recent assessment by Southern, *Scholastic Humanism,* 250–61.

pioned Ivo's election and consecrated him as bishop—and was a supporter of the reform movement, although at times not wholly in agreement with the papacy.[11] Ivo was educated at the monastery of Bec under the tutelage of Lanfranc, one of the most influential schoolmasters of his day, and served as a schoolmaster himself at the cathedral of his home city of Beauvais before becoming bishop of Chartres. Throughout his tenure in that see he struggled to maintain the rights of his church against kings and counts, to establish houses of regular canons against the protests of unwilling priests, and to balance the demands of distant papal authority with the daily realities of diocesan and pastoral life. Ivo was an advocate of ecclesiastical reform which centered on the diocese.

The first "Ivonian" work to be considered is called the Tripartite Collection (*Collectio Tripartita*) by modern scholars. Its title in manuscript varies, but often it is listed simply as Excerpts from the Decrees of the Roman Pontiffs (*Excerpta ex Decretis Romanorum Pontificum*), which, in fact, applies to only the first part of the work. The compilation is a product of the reform and the accompanying interest in canon law which flourished in northern France toward the end of the eleventh century. Tripartite Collection is a somewhat misleading title, for there are actually two—not three—main divisions, which have been labeled by modern investigators Collections A and B. The former is itself divided into two parts; the first containing papal decretals, and the second transmitting both conciliar canons and excerpts from Church Fathers. Part B is a reworked version of the *Decretum* of Bishop Ivo. Because of this, scholars have considered the Tripartite Collection to be an Ivonian compilation, although that view is currently under serious scrutiny.[12]

11. See, e.g., Tierney, *Crisis,* 75–76, for Ivo and the Investiture Conflict.
12. On the Tripartite Collection, see Martin Brett, "Urban II and the

Yet Ivo clearly knew Part A and used it in his *Decretum*. If he compiled it, this work would stand as the earliest of the Ivonian books of canon law. But regardless of his possible authorship, the book certainly stems from someone in a circle of like-minded clerics, and it is a valuable early witness to the reform movement as it was understood at a distance from Rome. Respect for the papacy is explicit in its introduction—not only from its reference to decretals and their unique authority, but also in its retrospective survey of ecclesiastical history, which is centered on the Roman pontiffs. The opening section of the collection continues this emphasis through its abundant use of the Pseudo-Isidorian Decretals. In both preface and compilation, therefore, the reader is reminded of the goal of striving to reform the Church back to, or at least according to, neglected standards, with the bishops of the Roman Church as leaders and guides par excellence.

In addition to numerous surviving letters and sermons—testimonies to a reputation for sound pastoral and legal counsel—and aside from whatever is made of the authorship of the Tripartite Collection, two other works seem to bear Ivo's imprint: the *Decretum* and the *Panormia* (a hybrid term created from Greek and loosely translated as "absolutely everything"), a book

---

Collections Attributed to Ivo of Chartres," in *Proceedings of the Eighth International Congress of Medieval Canon Law*, ed. Stanley Chodorow (Monumenta iuris canonici, Subsidia 7; Vatican City, 1992), 27–46, where previous literature is also discussed. As for virtually all collections of this period, the views of Paul Fournier have set the terms of debate (see Fournier and LeBras, *Histoire*, 2:55–114). A key source for material in this work is an equally misleadingly named contemporary collection, the *Collectio Britannica*, surviving in a single manuscript and taking its name from its current owner, the British Library. On this collection, see Robert Somerville (in collaboration with Stephan Kuttner), *Pope Urban II, the Collectio Britannica, and the Council of Melfi (1089)* (Oxford, 1996).

of Church law that is in large part, although not totally, derived from the *Decretum*. Although there is no evidence that either was composed solely by the bishop of Chartres, medieval audiences assumed that they had been. Whatever the extent of Ivo's involvement, the *Decretum* and the *Panormia*, like the Tripartite Collection, stem from the regional reform movement, and if not by Ivo and his followers at Chartres, they were produced by churchmen in northern France who were influenced by his writings. The *Decretum* survives in a handful of manuscripts; the *Panormia* is extant in well over one hundred, dating from the early twelfth century to early modern times. This extraordinary survival attests to the compilation's influence on succeeding generations of canonists and theologians and represents a diffusion which exceeds that of any canonical collection prior to Gratian's *Decretum* (see chap. 5).

Preceding manuscripts of both collections is an elaborate prologue. It is the longest document translated in this book and arguably the most remarkable, for it can be fairly called the first extended treatise on ecclesiastical jurisprudence. In length, scope of argument, and sensitivity to terminology and context, it is unlike anything that preceded it. The work may well have been composed independently of the two collections to which it invariably is attached.[13] At the heart of the text are the twin concerns of how to reconcile the apparent contradictions of sacred tradition, and deciding when a law could validly be abrogated through dispensation. Neither issue was new. Earlier

13. Bruce Brasington, "The Prologue of Ivo of Chartres: A Fresh Consideration from the Manuscripts," in *Proceedings of the Eighth International Congress of Medieval Canon Law*, ed. Stanley Chodorow (Monumenta iuris canonici, Subsidia 9; Vatican City, 1992), 3–22. Appearing too late to be used in this volume is a Latin text of the Prologue, with French translation and commentary, by Jean Werckmeister, *Yves de Chartres, Prologue* (Sources canoniques 1; Paris, 1997).

canonistic prefaces—for example, those of Cresconius and the Irish Collection of Canons (see chap. 2)—reveal that compilers were long sensitive to the changing demands which context made in ecclesiastical judgments, and in Ivo's day, Bernold of Constance, a monk of St. Blasien in southern Germany and an ardent supporter of Gregory VII, had addressed these questions in treatises written to define and defend papal supervision over canon law. Ivo, however, devoted his entire work to fashioning a jurisprudence that addressed the challenges of legal contradiction and context and found a solution in the concept of dispensation. Sensitivity to the contextual demands of necessity could permit the judge to choose a merciful instead of strict law. Dispensation, guided by Christian charity, thus became a jurisprudential aid to guide the ecclesiastical judge in interpreting and applying the canons.

Ivo's Prologue reflects its author's unusual position among his contemporaries interested in Church law and engaged in promoting reform. Many of his fellow reformers were more removed than he from the practical realities of pastoral care, either as figures at the papal court, or as theorists whose worlds were monastic cells. Ivo's study of the canons was guided, and tempered, by his responsibilities as pastor and judge. His jurisprudence reflects the necessary union of theory and practice in the episcopate. In this respect, he is reminiscent of such earlier authors as Burchard and Halitgar. Confronted with the challenges of interpreting and applying canon law, Ivo was especially sensitive to the quality of mercy. This emphasis on judicial responsibility driven by charity sets his jurisprudence apart from the arguments for authority and power that captivated a number of his contemporaries. To Ivo, charity alone links theory and practice and joins the precedents of history with the challenges of a living Church.

A variety of French churchmen, many anonymous, subsequently assembled collections at least partially derived from the *Panormia*. At times they paired Ivo's Prologue with their own prefaces. The so-called Collection in Ten Parts survives in greater numbers than any other of these derivative compilations.[14] On the basis of internal evidence, this work appears to have been put together some time before 1130, although both its author and patron remain unknown.[15] Like Cardinal Deusdedit, the compiler was particularly interested in helping readers navigate the internal organization of the collection, as evidenced by his use of a system of dots at the beginning of each title to designate the number of subdivisions found in that section. Another compilation, termed by modern scholars the Second Collection of Châlons,[16] was produced at Châlons-sur-Marne in the 1130s, one of several canonical works that demonstrate the vitality of canonistic study in that region during the

14. Robert Somerville, "The Councils of Pope Calixtus II and the Collection in Ten Parts," *Bulletin of Medieval Canon Law* 11 (1981): 80–86 (rpt. in Somerville, *Papacy, Councils, and Canon Law in the 11th and 12th Centuries* [Variorum Collected Studies, CS 312; Aldershot, 1990]). The medieval title of the work varies, sometimes being confused with the *Panormia* due to the presence of the Ivonian Prologue.

15. Ibid., 81–2, for the views of J. M. De Smet about the collection. De Smet never published his work, but it exercised considerable influence. He hypothesized that the Ten Parts were assembled shortly after the year 1123 by Archdeacon Walter of Thérouanne and were dedicated to his bishop, John of Thérouanne. See Van Hove, *Prolegomena*, 334, n. 2, and now L. Waelkens and D. Van den Auweele, "La collection de Thérouanne en ix livres à l'abbaye de Saint-Pierre-au-Mont-Blandins: le codex Gandavensis 235," *Sacris Erudiri* 24 (1980): 115–53.

16. The manuscript carries only the title *Collectio canonum*. Paul Fournier, "Les Collections canoniques attribuées à Yves de Chartres (Suite)," *Bibliothèque de l'Ecole des chartes* 58 (1897): 639 (rpt. in Fournier, *Mélanges de droit canonique*, 1:641), wrote that "La deuxième collection de Châlons (c'est la meilleure désignation qu'on puisse lui donner)."

third and fourth decades of the twelfth century.[17] It is largely based on the Ten Parts, mediated through a collection in eighteen sections termed the First Collection of Châlons. The Second Collection also transmits the widely disseminated Ivonian Prologue. In addition it contains the compiler's own preface, in which he illustrates how he took Ivo's jurisprudence in new directions, particularly in treating some of the implications of dispensation.

The preface to the book On Mercy and Justice (*De misericordia et iustitia*) of Alger of Liège concludes this chapter.[18] Slightly younger than Ivo, Alger, according to his contemporary Nicholas of Liège, was educated at the cathedral school of St. Lambert at Liège. He subsequently rose through the ranks of the local clergy to the dual positions of schoolmaster at St. Lambert and secretary to Bishop Otbert.[19] In this latter capacity he was responsible for the official correspondence of the diocese, a task that undoubtedly gave him much exposure to the daily workings of the Church, and hence to canon law. He composed his book Concerning Mercy and Justice sometime before the 1120s, when he retired to the monastery of Cluny to pass his final years.

Alger's work marks an important step in the technique of reconciling discordant canons. The dialectical form of textual analysis pioneered by earlier jurisprudents, such as Bernold of Constance and Bishop Ivo, emerged now as a consistent system

17. Fournier, "Les Collections," 648 (*Mélanges de droit canonique,* 1:650).

18. For Alger, see Robert Kretzschmar, *Alger von Lüttichs Traktat de misericordia et iustitia: Ein kanonistischer Konkordanzversuch aus der Zeit des Investiturstreits* (Quellen und Forschungen zum Recht im Mittlelater 2; Sigmaringen, 1985).

19. Ibid., 2–3.

of legal analysis. Unlike earlier collections, including even Ivo's, where theory was confined to the preface, Alger attempted to harmonize the canons throughout the body of his compilation by means of *dicta,* that is, interpretative comments interposed among the canons. This introduces the method that Gratian, who used both Ivo's and Alger's work, would employ in his *Decretum* a generation later. Concerning Mercy and Justice can thus be termed the first scholastic treatment of canon law, for it reveals the complementary activities of textual categorization and harmonization that is of fundamental importance in the schools of the High Middle Ages.

TRANSLATIONS

1. Preface to the Breviary of Cardinal Priest Atto of St. Mark's, 1073–early 1080s: dedicatory letter to the clergy of his church. Ed. Angelo Mai, *Scriptorum veterum nova collectio e Vaticanis codicibus edita* 6.2 (Rome, 1832), 60–61.

Atto, cardinal priest of the titular church of St. Mark, to the brethren of the same church, greetings.

I know, most beloved brothers, that there are two reasons for your ignorance. One is that the unhealthiness of the location does not permit strangers to live here who could teach you.[20] The second is that poverty does not let you depart for other places where you could learn. With reasons of that sort prompting, it happened that the apocryphal Roman Penitential was contrived, in an unlearned style, so that those who do

20. Paul Fournier, "Les Collections canoniques romaines de l'époque de Grégoire VII," *Mémoires de l'Institut nationale de France. Académie des inscriptions et belles-lettres* 41 (1920): 291 (rpt. in Fournier, *Mélanges de droit canonique,* 2:445), noted that in the Middle Ages the district of Rome around St. Mark's had a reputation of being unhealthy.

not know the authentic canons and do not know letters rely on these fables.[21] And so with such confidence they lay hold of the sacerdotal office which is not fitting for them, and being blind leaders they fall into a ditch with their followers.[22] And since among the texts copied therein scarcely any variation is found in rank, wisdom, or age, Jerome suffices in refuting something of the sort as apocryphal, saying that because it is not supported by divine authority "it is condemned with the same ease with which it is approved."[23] Hence Pope Leo says among other things concerning an apocryphal text: "If any bishop does not prohibit apocryphal texts from being used in his churches, he should know that he is to be judged a heretic."[24] And the Apostle says: "Do not be led astray by various and alien teachings."[25]

For just as, according to Job, there is a place where gold is refined, thus near to us is a place for minting this coinage: that what has not been confirmed by the Roman pontiff is not an authoritative writing.[26] Whence the venerable Pope Nicholas, who lived in the time of the Emperor Louis, thus said to certain men:[27] "It has been brought to the attention of our apostolic

21. For the Roman Penitential, see n. 7, above.

22. Cf. Matthew 15:14 and Luke 6:39.

23. See Jerome, *Commentariorum in Matheum libri IV* (Corpus Christianorum, Series Latina 77, ed. D. Hurst and M. Adriaen [Turnhout, 1969], 220, lines 304–6).

24. JK 412, c. 15.

25. Hebrews 13:9.

26. Cf. Job 28:1. For this passage in Atto's preface see Horst Fuhrmann, *Einfluss und Verbreitung der pseudoisidorischen Fälschungen von ihrem Auftauchen bis in die neuere Zeit,* (Monumenta Germaniae Historica, Schriften 24.2; Stuttgart, 1973), 2:530.

27. JE 2833, and see Monumenta Germaniae Historica, *Epistolae,* 6 (*Epistolae Karolini aevi,* 4), ed. E. Perels (Berlin, 1902–25), 651, and Somerville, "Pope Nicholas" (see n. 6, above).

office that a certain John the Scot has recently translated into Latin the work of the Blessed Dionysius, the Areopagite, which described in Greek the divine names and celestial hierarchies. According to custom this should have been sent to us to be approved or rejected by our judgment." For if, according to Pope Julius, no council is or will be valid which lacks the authority of this see,[28] then without the authority of this see the writings by which councils are accustomed to be constituted are not valid.[29] Indeed, Peter is the goldsmith's stone, testing the gold to see whether it is true or false.

It is, therefore, evident that the Roman Penitential is not valid, whether the man who composed it was a Roman, or another falsely titled that unlearned work with the authority of the Roman see. But the transalpine councils read in Burchard do obtain validity in the places where they were enacted, provided that they are contrary neither to reason nor to the regulations of the Roman Church. But otherwise, if they are not confirmed by this [Church] they are not valid except with the agreement of both parties.[30] Nevertheless, many things there,[31] though true, are attributed to an author falsely; others are plainly false; others are written in the foulest manner so as to be for holy men a disgrace to utter and a disgrace to hear.

Accordingly, with this confusion having arisen, and since you do not know what to reject and what to hold from among these things, I was urged by you to gather from the sacred canons a kind of breviary which would be pertinent for giving penances and settling cases. I obeyed you, beloved ones, and just as

28. Cf. JK +196 of Pope Julius I, c. 13.

29. This might be a reference to the liturgical orders by which councils traditionally were celebrated.

30. Presumably this is a reference to both parties in an action of whatever sort where such conciliar canons offer a ruling.

blessed Jerome excerpted certain things from the Psalter that were more suitable for prayer, thus I give you, in your unlearned state, a sort of bouquet from the decrees of the Roman pontiffs and from overseas councils—you who cannot understand that body of decrees, and even if you could understand, would not read it because of tedium. I have in this little work neither added anything to the words which I found there, nor changed anything; however, in certain places, because of abbreviating an opinion, I made a transition by interposing some words.

And because learned men, taking the Apostle as their model, do not cite the books from which they wrote,[32] do not be shocked if I do not mention my sources. Thus, like an innkeeper, I invite you, as it were travelers on the way, to taste the offered wine; yet I also beseech you to take your fuller hospitality inside, lest you be judged for your ignorance, as it is written: "He who ignores will be ignored."[33] As Pope Celestine says: "No priest shall be permitted to ignore the canons";[34] likewise, Pope Leo: "If ignorance seems hardly tolerable in the laity, how much more is it inexcusable and intolerable in those who rule."[35] Likewise the Lord, speaking through the prophet: "Since you rejected knowledge, I shall reject you, so that you may not perform for me the duty of the priesthood."[36]

31. In a note to this passage in the present edition, Mai said that this was a reference to the Roman Penitential; but it also could indicate Burchard.

32. Perhaps this is another slap at Burchard; see toward the end of his preface to the *Decretum* (chap. 3).

33. Cf. 1 Corinthians 14:38.

34. JK 371, c. 1; for this passage, see chap. 1.

35. JK 447 (near the beginning).

36. Hosea 4:6.

2. Preface to the Book of Canons of Cardinal Deusdedit,[37] 1086: dedicatory letter to Pope Victor III and the clergy of the Roman Church. Ed. Victor Wolf von Glanvell, *Die Kanonessammlung des Kardinals Deusdedit* (Paderborn, 1905; rpt. Aalen, 1967), 1–5.

Deusdedit *exiguus,*[38] priest of the title church of the Apostles in Glory, to the most blessed and apostolic man, the lord pontiff Pope Victor III, and to all the clergy of the holy Roman Church.

Your beatitude knows that the holy Roman Church is described as and believed to be the mother of all churches on this account: blessed Peter, its founder, initially gave the first pastors to the patriarchal sees in the East, and afterward, derivative from himself,[39] to all cities which are in the West. This ordination was especially appropriate for him to whom in the beginning Christ, the Son of God, having handed over the keys of the kingdom of heaven, had ordered to feed his sheep, and for whose faith he specially had prayed that it not fail, and whom he had commanded to confirm his brothers in the same faith.[40] Diligently giving heed to the extraordinary duties of this most excellent privilege, the 318 fathers who sat together in the Council of Nicaea stated, as Athanasius, bishop of Alexandria, writes to blessed Pope Felix,[41] that councils ought not to

37. For Deusdedit's work, which is usually designated as the Collection of Canons, titled as the Book of Canons (*Liber canonum*), see Victor Wolf von Glanvell, ed., *Die Kanonessammlung des Kardinals Deusdedit* (Paderborn, 1905; rpt. Aalen, 1967), x.

38. For the use of this adjective meaning "small" or "insignificant" by Dionysius and Cresconius in the sixth century, see the introduction to chap. 2.

39. The text reads *e latere suo,* literally "from his own side."

40. Cf. Matthew 16:18–19, Luke 22:32, and John 21:17.

41. Pseudo-Isidorian letter of Athanasius of Alexandria to Pope Felix II (antipope from 355 to 365); see Paul Hinschius, ed., *Decretales*

be celebrated nor bishops condemned without the decision of the Roman pontiff, and all major cases should be referred to his judgment.

And the Council of Sardica, which had 300 bishops as was attested by the universal synod which by its organizers is called the eighth,[42] stated the same things in canons 3, 4, 6, and 9, and among other things wrote thus to blessed Pope Julius: "It will seem to be best and indeed most proper if bishops of the Lord from every single province report to the head, that is to the see of blessed Peter the apostle."[43] It is read that even before that synod so much reverence was accorded to this see by the ancient Fathers that the eminent martyr Cyprian, primate of the African province, is seen in his letters humbly to have obeyed the statutes of the priests and deacons governing the Roman Church after the martyrdom of Fabian, and to have rendered an account in letters directed to them of what occurred in his province. In fact, in letters sent to Cyprian himself it is read that the same clergy directed letters both to Sicily and to different regions, and before Cornelius presided also to have convoked bishops, due to impending business of the time, for celebrating a synod at Rome.

This being the case, it seems sufficiently impious that anyone who boasts of the name Christian does not assent in Christian times to the admonitions of the Roman Church, which pontiffs worthy before God obeyed so devotedly under the cruelty of persecution, even while it lacked a bishop. Fathers filled with

---

Pseudo-Isidorianae et Capitula Angilramni (Leipzig, 1863), 478–83 (cf. 479, c. ii, lines 25ff.)

42. The Fourth Council of Constantinople, 869–70; for this reference to Sardica therein, see J. D. Mansi, *Sacrorum conciliorum nova et amplissima collectio,* 16 (Venice, 1771), 87B.

43. For Sardica, see chap. 2; for the various versions of the canons, see Mansi, *Anplissima collectio,* 3 (Florence, 1759), 1ff.

the spirit of God indeed testified that the blessed apostles Peter and Paul lived and presided in it with magnificent good works, and that the faith which it received from them, which was announced and extolled in the whole world, as the same blessed Paul bears witness,[44] did not fail in that same Church across the ages, but that, as it had been commanded to the same blessed Peter, they confirmed brothers everywhere based in the same faith. Even if this Church is sometimes oppressed by adverse breezes of the world, nevertheless by the merits of the princes of the apostles, who both live and preside in it, it is not overwhelmed. Even if at times, as a test, the gates of hell strive against it, nevertheless with the Lord Jesus praying for the faith of Peter that it not fail, in no way do they prevail.

Therefore, desiring to disclose to the ignorant the privilege of that authority by which they[45] are preeminent in all the Christian world, with the Lord giving me strength I culled the present little work, divided into four parts, from various authorities of the holy Fathers and Christian princes, each one being stronger having been assembled together. The first book contains the privilege of the authority of the same Roman Church. And since the Church is unable to exist without its clergy, nor the clergy without possessions by which it subsists in this world, to this book I added a second and a third concerning the clergy and the possessions of the same Church. But because the power of the world strives to subjugate the Church of God to itself, the liberty of that Church, both of its clergy and property, is clearly demonstrated in the third and especially in the fourth book.

I did not, however, arrange the individual excerpts inserted

44. Cf. Romans 1:8.

45. The edition has a plural at this point (*preminent*), which can only refer to the apostles Peter and Paul if it is not a misprint for the singular (*preminet*), referring to the Roman Church.

into this work according to the order of headings in the index,[46] because almost all treat sometimes two, sometimes many matters. And if they were cut up according to the number of issues which they handle, they would create a vast amount of work for me and a lessening of authority. I warn the scribe, therefore, lest a reader is seriously vexed, that he apply diligence not only in emending the codex, but also in copying accurately and in emending most cautiously each number, namely that which is placed after every heading in the index, and likewise that which throughout the entire book precedes the individual excerpts.

Furthermore, if any of the things inserted here, which often happens even with the evangelists, will seem to be contrary to one another, with discernment applied it will readily be evident that they are opposed neither to themselves nor to writings available outside. But if it turns out that they patently are opposed, the lesser authority ought to yield to the more powerful. I excerpted, therefore, in the first place, the best things from certain universal synods,[47] that is, Nicaea, first Ephesus, Chalcedon, and the sixth, seventh, and eighth synods, some of which by four or five patriarchs, some by their representatives, are known to have been convened as universal at different times. Concerning their authority, there is no one except a lunatic who would doubt. And I did not hesitate to borrow things which seemed appropriate to me from the rest of the Eastern councils, from which I saw that Roman pontiffs in their con-

46. This reference is to the index of topics for each book which Deus-dedit placed at the beginning of the collection.

47. The text is faulty at this point, reading *Itaque primum defloraui neque optima de quibusdam uniuersalibus sinodis*. Deusdedit obviously wanted to say that he collected the best texts, so emendation is required, e.g., *neque] necnon optima* ("and in fact the best things"); or, *neque] eaque optima* ("and those best things"). The authors are pleased to acknowledge assistance received from Stephan Kuttner on this troublesome passage.

stitutions accepted authority, which a reader who is curious can discover. Furthermore, I took certain things from the Council of Carthage, which was held by 217 bishops under Pope Zosimus, in the presence of his legates Bishop Faustinus and the priests Philip and Asellus, where, in the presence of the same men, African councils held at different times were confirmed and made part of the same synod, and from which Celestine, Symmachus, and Hadrian[48] seemed to insert certain things in their decrees.

And since an adversary denounces authority until he succumbs to reason, it ought to be known that all of the councils, either universal or provincial, which were held before the synod of Chalcedon subsequently were confirmed and corroborated in the same synod, in canon 1 which reads thus: "We decreed that the rules of the holy Fathers, constituted through individual councils up to now, maintain their own force." For the Council of Chalcedon, which was held by 630 fathers under Pope Leo, is of such authority and strength[49] that whoever does not adhere to its solidity, whatever his life and conduct, as blessed Gregory says,[50] even if he seems to be a precious stone, lies outside the building of God. But concerning the authority of the canons "of the apostles," which are said to be translated from Greek into Latin through Clement the Roman pontiff, the authority of which the seventh universal synod of 350 fathers[51] and the same Gregory in his register seem to use—concerning their authority, I repeat, and of any other canons at all,

48. Either Pope Hadrian I (772–95) or Hadrian II (867–72).
49. The text reads *sub Leone papa gestum est, eius auctoritatis et firmitudinis [est]*, and perhaps should be referred specifically to Pope Leo, i.e., "under Pope Leo, has his authority and strength so that."
50. Pope Gregory I, JE 1092 (near the end of the text).
51. The Second Council of Nicaea, in the year 787.

Anastasius, the librarian of the Roman Church, writes thus to Pope John VIII in the prologue of the same seventh universal synod which he translated from Greek into Latin: "With your predecessor, most blessed Pope Stephen, and you, in the apostolic office, decreeing, the Church receives not only fifty solitary canons 'of the apostles,' as from trumpets of the Holy Spirit, but also accepts from absolutely all of the worthy Fathers and holy councils rules and teachings, at least those which do not oppose right faith or good morals, do not conflict in any way with the decrees of the Roman see, but rather powerfully assail adversaries."[52] His [Clement] successors Anaclet,[53] Alexander, certain other pontiffs, and the father of monks, the one "blessed" by God,[54] show that the letters of Clement to James against which some people[55] seem to chatter are authentic, and they inserted in their writings many statements from them.

Concerning the authority of the apostolic see I assembled very many things here: some from the works of blessed Jerome,

52. Anastasius "Bibliothecarius," who died between 877 and 889, translated the acts of Nicaea II; see his preface to this translation in J. D. Mansi, *Sacrorum concilorum nova et amplissima collectio*, 12 (Florence, 1766), 982.

53. Deusdedit's chronology is confused, due to a forged text attributed to Pope Anaclet I in the Pseudo-Isidorian Decretals which seems to use the Pseudo-Clementine letters (see Wolf von Glanvell, *Kanonessammlung* [see n. 37, above], 4, n. 95). Anaclet is traditionally counted as the second, and Clement the third, bishop of Rome, after the Apostle Peter (see Kelly, *Dictionary*, 6–7).

54. The reference is to Saint Benedict of Nursia and is a play on words: *et a deo benedictus monachorum pater.*

55. The edition reads *quidem* ("indeed"), and the plural verb *uidentur* ("they seem") requires a plural subject. Perhaps it could be the adversaries of the previous sentence understood, but *quidem* emended to *quidam* ("certain ones") will be adopted here.

whose eloquence, as Augustine said of him in the work "Against Julian," brightly shines from East to West like the sun,[56] some from the works of blessed Cyprian, Ambrose, Augustine, and other Fathers. And I weighed carefully the works which I assembled here so that they would contain fullest authority, because I was not unaware that just as there are some to whom these things will be pleasing, certain men also will be at hand who will resent them. Moreover I was happy to insert in this work the ancient order of election and consecration of the Roman pontiff and his clergy.[57] For once upon a time certain men, in contempt of the sanctions of God and the holy Fathers, to be precise for showing off and for ascribing to themselves authority full of hot air which can stand on no canonical laws, wrote for themselves a new ordination [procedure] for the same Roman pontiff. How much they established therein which is nefarious and inimical to God I shudder to write; he who reads let him understand.

Few things are inserted here about the way to guide subordinates, since I judged it laborious and pertinent to another work to excerpt sacred writings for this purpose. The most important [sources] for a work to that end seem to me to be [the books] of the Gospels, the letters of the apostles and of Clement, the Pas-

56. This reference to Augustine's opinion of Jerome presents a problem. It does not occur in Augustine's writings against Julian of Eclanum, nor seemingly anywhere in his works (information based on searching the electronic database for Migne's *Patrologia Latina* and the CETEDOC database which covers modern editions of Augustine), and Deusdedit is the only author found who thus attributes it. But the image occurs in two anonymous lives of Jerome, printed in J.-P. Migne, *Patrologia Latina*, 22 (Paris, 1842), 200 and 209, and it is echoed by Cassiodorus, Migne, *Patrologia Latina*, 70 (Paris, 1847), 1135–36. (Thanks are due to Anders Winroth for investigating this question.)

57. For this disavowal of the papal election decree of 1059, see Blumenthal, "History," 195 (see n. 8, above).

toral Rule of Gregory, his forty homilies on the Gospels, and the eighth, ninth, and tenth homilies on Ezekiel. And since while zealous for brevity I grieve that I overlook very many useful items, I admonish the curious reader that when he has time he should devote study to those works from which these things were excerpted, not that he might add something to the excerpts, but that he can satisfy his curiosity. To you, father, I dedicated this work, which I thought will be useful not only to the holy apostolic see, but to every church and every cleric. I beg the reader in the Lord that he intercede with the Lord on behalf of my transgressions.

3. Preface to the *Polycarpus* of Cardinal Gregory of
S. Grisogono, 1111–1113: dedicatory letter to Bishop Diego
Gelmírez of Santiago de Compostela. Ed. Hermann
Hüffer, *Beiträge zur Geschichte des Quellen der Kirchenrechts
und des Römischen Rechts im Mittelalter*
(Münster, 1862), 75–76.

Here begins the prologue.
Gregory, most humble of priests, to the beloved lord Diego, worthily decorated with the pontifical chasuble[58] of the church of Santiago de Compostela, greetings.

You requested now for a long time, and often, that I undertake a work difficult and beyond my powers, namely, that I compile a canonical book selecting successively the more useful things from the decrees of Roman pontiffs, from the authorities of other holy Fathers, and from different authoritative councils. The decision to make that request of me, an unlearned man, was neither because your surpassing knowledge is insufficient for this work (or for one very much greater), nor because you

58. For the word *infula,* which also can mean "mitre," see Horst, *Kanonessammlung,* 4 (see n. 9, above).

lack many men more suitable and wiser for the task, willing to obey your command, but so that having been trained for a long time with this large work, I would be made more learned and more prepared for other, greater responsibilities. And even if my limited talent would fail in something, your wisdom could reach out your hands to me as master and helper. I assented to this request—even if it demanded greater talent and was not in line with my abilities, and if I feared that I would be judged foolhardy by certain people—lest by refusing I would offend so great and excellent a man. Thus in the end I obeyed your order with this confidence especially, that with your authority interposed I would be defended from the stings of detractors.

Indeed, just as in the past, daily in the Church business piles on business in a variety of ways, and so in the course of time the actions of many legal cases multiply. Thus I linked together under titles a great number of canons appropriate for each one [of them], attention having been paid to the circumstance of the authors, and with an eightfold division of books I concisely finished the volume. From the rationale of composition, with its authority drawn from you, I appropriately imparted to the work the name *Polycarpus*. But I vigorously entreat your diligence that you examine the content and form, and if in examining you see that something is missing, or that something therein exceeds what is proper, with careful consideration you should supply what is appropriate and should remove what is inappropriate. [The work] should be approved to your praise, and I should be credited with rendering obedience to your order with considered judgment. Moreover, lest in the course of the book something unclear troubles readers, it was decided to place the titles of this work at the beginning, so that a person can seek in the proper places what he sees to be predicted under an appropriate number.

4. Preface to the Tripartite Collection, end of the eleventh century. Ed. Augustin Theiner, *Disquisitiones criticae in praecipuas canonum et decretalium collectiones seu sylloges gallandianae dissertationum de vetustis canonum collectionibus continuatio* (Rome, 1836), 154–55, n. 25.

Since the decretals of some Roman pontiffs are older than synodal assemblies, it is not inappropriate that they win for themselves the first sections in our little work of excerpting. Indeed, from the episcopate of blessed Peter, prince of the apostles, up to the time of the most serene emperor Constantine, either none or in fact hardly any councils of bishops are believed to have been celebrated, either because of lack of bishops, or because of the rage of the persecutors. Furthermore, it happens that the canons "of the apostles" are held to be of less authority than those of Nicaea and very many other councils, inasmuch as they are read to be [considered] so by several of these [assemblies]. Thus because it had been more freely possible and also, as I would say, more suitably, the popes instructed their partners in the faith by means of letters, teaching them what they ought to seek, avoid, hold, and, finally, what they ought to reject.

But when the Christian religion, supported by the pious prince Constantine, began to spread far and wide throughout the world, then gatherings of bishops also began to be celebrated freely. And although they continue until now to be celebrated by prelates of the holy Church throughout the four corners of the world, nevertheless that one which is read to have been convened in the city of Nicaea in Bythnia by Saint Sylvester, and celebrated by 318 bishops, is considered to hold the preeminence of highest authority, though it is not first in chronological order.

But among these things it should be noted that although

from the pontificate of Peter, prince of the apostles, to the episcopate of Sylvester there are thirty-two pontiffs, excluding Linus and Cletus, who discharged the episcopal office while the Apostle Peter was still alive, none of them neglected to establish things by their decretals, with the exception only of Chrisogonus, numbered twenty-eighth from the Apostle Peter. Again, when from Saint Sylvester to the blessed Gregory thirty-two bishops are counted, all likewise are read to have produced decretals except Mercurius alone, who was the sixty-second to have discharged the episcopal office after the Apostle Peter.[59] We should also consider here what the word "decretal" signifies. "Decree," which is derived from the verb "I decide" and generates from itself another word, namely, "decretal"—plural *decretalia*—is understood as a regulation or a constitution. Thus decretals are able to be understood as regulations or constitutions. But now, finally, we should set forth on the page the requisite rulings of the same decretals.

Here ends the prologue. Here begin the canons.[60]

5. Prologue of Ivo of Chartres, late eleventh century. Ed. Bruce C. Brasington, "The Prologue to the 'Decretum' and 'Panormia' of Ivo of Chartres: An Eleventh-Century Treatise on Ecclesiastical Jurisprudence" (Ph.D. diss., University of California at Los Angeles, 1990), 232–53.

59. The source of this list of popes was the *Liber Pontificalis,* a widely transmitted capsule history of the papacy first compiled in the sixth century; see Raymond Davis, *The Book of Pontiffs (Liber Pontificalis)* (Translated Texts for Historians, Latin Series 5; Liverpool, 1989). For the pseudo Pope Chrisogonus and for Pope John II referred to by his pre-papal name of Mercurius, see Fournier and LeBras, *Histoire,* 2:59.

60. The word is *capitula,* which could also be translated as "chapters" or "chapter headings," but the Tripartite Collection does not have a complete index at the beginning, although it does give a list of headings before each group of papal decretals in the first part of the compilation.

Here begins the Prologue of the lord Bishop Ivo of Chartres concerning the excerpts of the ecclesiastical canons.

Excerpts of ecclesiastical rules, partly drawn from the letters of the Roman pontiffs, partly from the deeds of the councils of catholic bishops, partly from the treatises of the orthodox Fathers, partly from the institutes of catholic kings: these I have gathered into one body—and not without labor—so that anyone who might not be able to have at hand the works from which these have been drawn may simply take here what he judges advantageous for his case. Thus, from the foundation of the Christian religion, that is, beginning with faith, we have assembled, arranged under general titles, what pertains to the ecclesiastical sacraments, to the institution or correction of morals, to the investigation and resolution of every matter, so that it should not be necessary for the investigator to turn through the whole volume but simply to note the general title appropriate to his question, and then to run through the canons under it without pause. In this we have been led to caution the prudent reader that if perhaps he should read some things that he may not fully understand, or judge them to be contradictory, he should not immediately take offense but instead should diligently consider what pertains to rigor, to moderation, to judgment, or to mercy. For he did not perceive these things to disagree among themselves who said, "Mercy and judgment I will sing to you, O Lord,"[61] and elsewhere, "All the pathways of the Lord are mercy and truth."[62]

Concerning the intention of the divine page.

Indeed all ecclesiastical discipline chiefly has this intent: either to tear down every structure that raises itself up against

61. Psalm 101 (100):1.
62. Psalm 25 (24):10.

the knowledge of Christ, or to build up the enduring house of God in truth of faith and honesty of character, or if that house of God be defiled, to cleanse it with the remedies of penance. The mistress of this house is charity, which sees to the welfare of our neighbors, commanding that it be done for others what one wishes to be done for himself.[63]

That charity should be the mistress of every good thing.

Every ecclesiastical doctor should thus interpret or moderate ecclesiastical rules so that he may refer to the kingdom of charity those matters that he teaches; nor does he err or sin here, because, concerned for the welfare of his neighbors, he endeavors to achieve the required goal in the holy institutes. Whence the blessed Augustine says when considering ecclesiastical discipline: "Have charity and do whatever you will. If you correct, correct with charity. If you pardon, pardon with charity."[64] But in these matters the highest diligence must be exercised and the eye of the heart be cleansed as well, for sincere charity should aid the ills to be cured by punishing or pardoning. And no one should seek there something for himself, as is the case with venal doctors, lest he incur that reproach of the prophet, "Souls are perishing that were not dying, and souls are restored to life that were not alive."[65]

The purpose of bodily medicine is either to drive out diseases, or to cure wounds in order to preserve health, or to strive to improve it. Nor does it appear wrong that a doctor some-

63. Cf. Matthew 7:12.
64. This is a maxim with a long and complicated history. See, e.g., Augustine, *In epistolam Iohannis,* 7.8 (J.-P. Migne, *Patrologia Latina,* 35 [Paris, 1841], 2033), and Caesarius of Arles, *Sermo* 29 (Corpus Christianorum, Series Latina 103.1, ed. G. Morin [Turnhout, 1953], 128).
65. Ezekiel 13:19.

times applies harsh medicines to a patient and sometimes gentle medicines, according to the quality or degree of the patient's sickness. Sometimes he cuts with the knife that which cannot be healed with a poultice. Sometimes, conversely, he heals with a poultice what he dared not cut with the blade. Thus spiritual physicians, namely doctors of the holy Church, neither contradict themselves nor each other when they prohibit illicit things, order necessary things, exhort the highest things, permit milder things—when they impose severe laws of penance according to the hardness of heart of the delinquent for their correction or for the restraint of the rest, or when they lift these restrictions and apply the salves of indulgence according to the devotion of those repenting and desiring to change, having considered the frailty of the vessel they bear. For those who are lenient look to the removal of greater ills, those who prohibit illicit things deter from death, those who command necessary things wish to preserve health, and those who exhort the highest things strive to increase health. Considering these matters the diligent reader will understand, when he clearly determines the meaning of admonition, precept, prohibition, and remission, that there is only one form of holy eloquence, and that these categories do not oppose or stand apart from one another, but that they dispense the remedy of health to all, for their direction.

But now we must further distinguish what weight these individual things have or to whom they are appropriate, and which are remissible, which irremissible, and when or concerning which cases they may be remitted.

Concerning admonition.

And the first—admonition—does not bring punishment to someone who did not pursue it, but instead promises a reward to those acquiring it. As the Lord says in the Gospel, "If you wish to be perfect, go and sell all you possess and give it to the poor, and you will have treasure in heaven."[66] Behold, this Gospel lesson, placing perfection in the will of man, neither compels nor intends threats, just as that lesson does not which, praising eunuchs who have castrated themselves on account of the kingdom of heaven, adds, "Whoever is able to understand, let him understand."[67] Yet when someone binds himself by a vow to its fulfillment, or to a rank which no one without the virtue of continence is able to reach, it then becomes necessary and worthy of penalty if what was voluntary before this ascent is not maintained. Whence the Lord says, "No one who looks back after placing his hand on the plow is worthy of the kingdom of God."[68] What had been able before this ascent to be inferior but not wrong is now, afterward, both inferior and wrong. So much for admonition.

Concerning indulgence.

But it seems to us that indulgence, because it does not choose the better things, certainly offers a remedy not a reward, though if anyone should fall from this he should merit fatal judgment. For example, we know, just as we have learned from the Apostle, that in order to avoid fornication marriage is granted to the human race,[69] and that someone who violates it should merit eternal punishment, as the same Apostle testifies. Indeed he says, "God will judge fornicators and adulterers."[70] As we have said concerning admonition, this status compels no one except him who has earlier bound himself to it. It is voluntary, not necessary. Otherwise anyone who had not taken a wife would

66. Matthew 19:21.
67. Matthew 19:12.
68. Luke 9:62.
69. Cf. 1 Corinthians 7:2.
70. Hebrews 13:4.

be a transgressor. But after he has bound himself in marriage he should listen to the Apostle who says, "Are you bound to a wife? Do not seek divorce."[71] When speaking about marriage, the same Apostle also did not say that a woman should deserve a reward if she marries, but rather said that she would not sin if she did.[72] Again, if anyone should invite another to daily fasting, he urges something worthy to be gained and persisted in. Yet whoever would not gain it would not become inferior, for although remaining inferior to one doing it, he would not become worse in himself. But he who falls from a vow becomes inferior and worse. If anyone should restrain himself under a regimen of sobriety and frugal diet, he is not seeking the rewards of the highest things; but if he should fall thence into gluttony and drunkenness, it is shown that he has done something worthy of reprehension and rebuke.

Thus there are two conditions, one superior, the other inferior, which before a vow are both voluntary, but afterward are binding and have their modes and teachings which, when observed, as already mentioned, gain a remedy for some and reward for others, but when they are not observed merit instead eternal punishment. These things ought to be pondered before a vow is undertaken, but after a vow is made must be carried out. Having considered these things, we must now discuss other matters concerning precept and prohibition.

Concerning precept and prohibition.

Precepts and prohibitions: some are mutable, some immutable. Immutable precepts are those which eternal law sanctions and which, when observed, confer salvation, but remove it when not observed. These kind are: "You will love the Lord

71. 1 Corinthians 7:27.
72. Cf. 1 Corinthians 7:28.

God with all your heart and your neighbor as yourself," and "honor your father and mother," and others like them.[73] Mutable precepts, however, are those which eternal law does not sanction, but which the diligence of tradition has discovered by reason of utility, not principally for the acquisition of salvation but rather for guarding it more securely. An example of this comes from the words of the Apostle: "Shun the person who is a heretic after the first and second warning,"[74] not because conversation with him would by itself prevent salvation, but instead because frequency of contact might indirectly corrupt the simplicity of some. And you will find many examples of this sort in the canonical teachings. Similarly, immutable prohibitions are those which speak out against vices, such as "You shall not kill, you shall not lust, etc."[75] These are those minor precepts about which the Lord says, "Whosoever breaks these and teaches the same will be the least in the kingdom of heaven."[76] But whoever observes them will not immediately be worthy of the kingdom of God, since these are only basic precepts, not advanced ones.

Other things are interdicted in which neither would death be at work nor salvation endangered had they not been forbidden. But the sacred authority of the holy Fathers decreed them for this purpose, not that sincere charity should oppose things which are present, but rather it should provide for the restraint or avoidance of greater evils. For example, a cleric may neither remain a cleric after doing penance for some crime worthy of damnation, nor [may a penitent] gain entry to the clergy, which, as blessed Augustine says:

73. Cf. Deuteronomy 6:5, Leviticus 19:18, Exodus 20:12.
74. Titus 3:10.
75. Exodus 20:13-14.
76. Matthew 5:19.

has been spoken from the rigor of discipline, not the desperation of indulgence. Otherwise an argument is possible against the keys of the Church, about which it was said, 'Whatever you loose on earth will be loosed in heaven as well.' But lest perhaps a soul might do penance proudly, having been inflated in the hope of ecclesiastical honor, it is most strictly correct that no one may become a cleric or remain a cleric after completing penance. That diligence of our elders should not be judged superfluous. While nothing was withdrawn from salvation, they added something to humility so that salvation might be guarded more securely, knowing full well, I believe, that certain penances are falsely done in order to gain honors. Indeed, the experiences of many illnesses requires the discovery of many medicines.[77]

It is like that statement in the Gospel: "Let your word be 'yes, yes,' 'no, no,' for whatever exceeds this is evil"[78]—not because vowing is in itself wrong, but because compelling a vow is evil; not because it is wrong to vow out of necessity in certain human transactions, but rather because a person who never vows will be further away from perjury than someone who does vow on certain occasions. For it is said concerning the Lord, "The Lord vowed."[79] And the Apostle says, "The conclusion of all disputes is the vow."[80] And the same Apostle, vowing, says, "The

77. Cf. Augustine, *Ep.* 185, c. 45 (Corpus scriptorum ecclesiasticorum Latinorum 57, ed. Al. Goldbacher [Vienna, 1923], 39).

78. Matthew 5:37.
79. Psalm 110 (109):4.
80. Hebrews 6:16.

truth of Christ is in me";[81] and elsewhere, "Daily I perish for the sake of your glory, brethren."[82]

Therefore in these matters in which, when they are observed, salvation is gained, or, when neglected, death undoubtedly follows, no dispensation may be admitted, and thus all that has been mandated or interdicted ought to be preserved as sanctioned by eternal law. In those matters, however, which the diligence of tradition has sanctioned because of rigor of discipline, or for the protection of salvation, a considered dispensation can take precedence by the authority of those presiding, if an honest and useful compensation follows.

We read that many such things occurred in the Gospels, in the Acts of the Apostles, and in the deeds of councils, and later, were confirmed, we understand, by the authority of the popes. Let us, therefore, take a first example from the Gospel. When the Lord sent the disciples out to preach he forbade them wallet and sack.[83] And since the life of Jesus on earth is a model for behavior, when the time of his passion arrived he returned the wallet and sack,[84] thus giving in himself an example, in actions of this sort, of what should be conceded to the necessity of the moment. Similarly, when Paul had promised that he would visit the Corinthians on his way to Macedonia and then sensed that this would little benefit them, he altered his plan, not his word.[85]

81. 2 Corinthians 11:10.
82. 1 Corinthians 15:31.
83. Luke 10:4.
84. Luke 22:35-36.
85. Cf. Acts 20:1ff. and 2 Corinthians 1:15ff. See Bruce C. Brasington, "'Non veni Corinthum': Ivo of Chartres, Lanfranc, and 2 Corinthians 1.16-17, 23," *Bulletin of Medieval Canon Law* 21 (1991): 1-9. The citations from 2 Corinthians and the remainder of the paragraph may have been taken from the commentary on the Pauline Epistles written by Ivo's teacher at Bec, Lanfranc (see J.-P. Migne, *Patrologia Latina*, 150 [Paris, 1880], 219). Lanfranc's commentary transmits a version of this mixture

Thus he excused himself, saying, "When I wanted this, was I making a joke? Or what I thought, was it according to the flesh so that I could say both yes and no at the same time?"[86] He did not conceive that he had changed his word, for he sought their salvation both in coming and then not coming. Whence he says in the following words, "I call God as my witness, on my soul, that in order to spare you further I did not come to Corinth."[87] He also did not consider that he had changed his plan according to the flesh, since whoever thinks according to the flesh does not then fulfill his plans when he defers to greater persons, or is overcome by wealth or pomp. But a spiritual man does not fulfill his plans when, out of greater consideration, he provides something else for the salvation of those whom he wishes to benefit.

It was confirmed by the apostles through a common decision at Jerusalem, and spread through Paul and Barnabas to the brethren throughout Asia, that no one coming to the faith should be held liable to the circumcision of the law.[88] When writing to the Galatians, the Apostle himself says accordingly, "If you are circumcised, Christ will not help you at all."[89] And though he had resisted Peter face to face because the latter had given in to the pretense of certain Jews who considered circumcision necessary for salvation,[90] nevertheless, yielding to the necessity of the moment he circumcised Timothy at Lystria, so that he might avoid a scandal among the Jews dwelling

---

of citations and exegesis originally composed by the late antique exegete known as Ambrosiaster.

86. 2 Corinthians 1:17.

87. 2 Corinthians 1:23.

88. Cf. Acts. 15:19–22. For this passages and what follows, see Somerville (in collaboration with Kuttner), *Pope Urban II,* 104ff. (see n. 12, above), under JL 5383=*Collectio Britannica,* Urban, no. 30.

89. Galatians 5:2.

90. Cf. Galatians 2:11ff.

there.[91] Thus he demonstrated in action what elsewhere he says about himself, "I became as a Jew to the Jews so that I might win Jews."[92] He must be understood to have said this not out of lying deception but instead from the feeling of compassion, desiring to help those just as much as he himself would have wished to have been helped had he been thus affected.

Where dispensation can be allowed.

The princes of the churches also judge many matters more strictly on account of the tenor of the canons, tolerate many things due to the necessity of the moment, or dispense many things for the benefit of individuals or to avoid conflict among the people. Many things established by the testimonies of Scripture were altered by the holy Fathers, just as the holy pontiff of the holy Roman Church, Leo, allowed novices to rise to the rank of bishop, whom Paul in public preaching attempted to remove from the same office; similarly we read that even the Arians, after they converted, were received in their offices.[93] Whence the aforesaid Pope Leo wrote to Bishop Rusticus of Narbonne concerning stability regarding things that must not be changed, and discretion regarding those that should be moderated, saying: "Just as there are certain things that cannot be overthrown for any reason, so also there are many which either out of the necessity of the moment or out of consideration of age may be tempered, with the notion always preserved that in things uncertain or obscure we recognize that the solution must be followed that is found [to be] neither contrary to evangelical precepts nor against the decrees of the holy Fathers."[94]

91. Cf. Acts 16:3.
92. 1 Corinthians 9:20.
93. JK 410; 1 Timothy 3:6; JK 303, and JK 310.
94. JK 544.

Thus Augustine says in a letter to Boniface: "In cases of this kind where danger is present through grave rifts of dissension, not of this or that individual but instead, where conflicts of a great throng of people exist, some reduction should be made in severity so that sincere charity may aid in the healing of greater ills."[95] Likewise in the same letter, against heretics:

> "If it is necessary," he says, "that we who have been outside the Church should do penance so that we can be saved, how, after this penance, can we remain clerics or even bishops among you? This should not be so, since it must be admitted that it would not have been done unless for healing by the compassion of this peace." But let them say this to themselves; and then let those who lie in such a death of separation mourn with the greatest possible humility that they can be restored to life by such a wound of the catholic mother [Church]. For when a cut-off branch is grafted on another wound is made in the tree, where what was perishing without the life of a root can be received so that it lives. But when the grafted branch joins to the recipient both vigor and fruit will follow. If, however, it does not join, it will certainly wither, but the life of the tree will remain. For such is the method of grafting, that with no internal branch having been cut off, that which is external can be attached, not without some but with only the slightest wound to the tree. Thus neither the clerical nor the episcopal honor should be taken from those who, although following penance for their errors, come to the catholic

95. Augustine, *Ep.* 185, c. 44 (see n. 77, above).

root, as if, indeed, there is something in the bark of the mother tree against a fullness of severity. But because neither he who plants nor he who waters is of any importance, with prayers extended toward the mercy of God, and with the peace of the grafted branches increasing, charity covers a multitude of sins.[96]

Concerning this same dispensation of things to be corrected and qualified the same Augustine says in the second book against the letter of Parmenian: "When one of the Christian brothers in the society of the Church has been discovered in some sin where he might be considered worthy of anathema, let this be done only where there is no danger of schism."[97]

Concerning dispensation.

And below, the same man [says]: "When somebody's crime is known and seems to all worthy of condemnation so that he would have either no defenders at all, or none of the kind through whom schism might result, severity of discipline should not sleep." And further: "Neither can correction by many be beneficial, except when he who is being corrected does not have a large following. When, however, the same disease afflicts many, there is nothing left for good men to do but mourn and lament, so that through that sign which is revealed to holy Ezekiel the unharmed may merit to escape destruction with them." And below: "Truly, when the contagion of sinning infects a multitude, the severe mercy of divine discipline is necessary, for the counsels of separation are inane and pernicious

96. Ibid., c. 44.
97. The sequence of citations to follow comes from Augustine, *Contra epistulam Parmeniani* 3.2.13ff. (Corpus scriptorum ecclesiasticorum Latinorum 51, ed. M. Petschenig [Vienna, 1895], 115ff.).

as well as sacrilegious, since they become wicked and proud, and do more to disturb the good who are weak than to correct evil souls." And below: "When there is an opportunity of proclaiming a sermon to the people, the mob of evildoers ought to be struck by a general rebuke, especially if some scourge from God above presents an occasion and opportunity, by which he appears to whip them as they deserve." Again, in the letter to Marcellinus: "I am accustomed to hear that it is in the power of a judge to soften a judgment and to punish more gently than the laws."[98] Whence Innocent, writing to Rufus and Eusebius and the rest of the Macedonian bishops: "It is the law of our Church concerning those who come from the heretics, who were already baptized there, to grant them only the status of lay communion through the imposition of hands, and not to call anyone from them to either high or low clerical position. You, therefore, should be aware, beloved, that up to this point such things have happened, and, indeed, take care that what, as you say, necessity demanded, churches now constituted in peace do not presume. But, as frequently happens, as often as there are sins by the people or the crowd, since it cannot be punished in everyone because of the multitude, it is accustomed to pass unpunished."[99] And to the same men:

> This was the most important decision of the bishops, that those whom Bonosus had ordained, lest they remain with him and a significant scandal occur, ought to be received as ordained. We have overcome, I believe, the uncertain points. It is clear, therefore, that what now has been established as a remedy and for the necessity of the moment did

98. Augustine, *Ep.* 139 (Corpus scriptorum ecclesiasticorum Latinorum 44, ed. Al. Goldbacher [Vienna, 1895], 151).
99. JK 303.

not exist at first; and yet it is clear that there were ancient rules which, handed down by the apostles or the popes, the Roman Church maintains, and directs ought to be maintained by these who are accustomed to hear her. The necessity of the moment especially demanded that this be done. Therefore, what necessity discovers as remedy should accordingly cease when the necessity passes which compelled it, since one order is legitimate, the other a usurpation which the present moment compels to be introduced. The canons constituted at Nicaea concerning the Novatianists allowed this to be done. That earlier canon instituted by the Fathers should be set forth, so that we may regard what was considered and commanded by them and how. It says "concerning those who call themselves Cathars, that is to say the clean, and who at some time come over to the catholic Church, that it pleased the holy and great synod that, having received an imposition of hand, they thus should remain in the clergy."[100]

By means of a similar dispensation the blessed Pope Gregory ordered those clerics returning from the Nestorian heresy to be received in their orders, thus writing to the bishops of the catholic Church in Hiberia:

Therefore, whoever returns from the perverse error of Nestorius to the truth about Christ's nativity should confess before your holy assembly, brothers, anathematizing that same Nestorius with all his followers and the remaining heresies. Let them also

100. Council of Nicaea, 325, canon 8.

promise to accept and venerate the synods that must be venerated, which the universal Church accepts, and let your holiness accept them without any hesitation in your congregation, with their own orders preserved. With care you dispel the hidden things of their minds and teach them through true knowledge the right things which they ought to believe, and through gentleness you make no opposition or difficulty for them about their own orders, and thus you will snatch them away from the mouth of the ancient enemy.[101]

We have something similar from the letter of Cyril to Maximus, deacon at Antioch:

I have learned from my beloved monk Paul that your piety is still to this day reluctant to embrace the communion of the most reverend Bishop John, because certain ones in the Antiochene church may either, evilly, still be in agreement with Nestorius, or had been in agreement, though perchance now have rejected him. Therefore let your modesty investigate whether sometimes they agree to be united openly and irreverently with Nestorius and converse together, though sometimes they have had a troubled conscience. Let them now, however, be gathered together, with penance having been carried out for those things by which they deceived, though perhaps they may fear to confess the transgression.[102]

101. JE 1844: not to Spain, but to *Hiberia* near the Caucasus, i.e., Georgia.

102. These citations are from letters of Cyril of Alexandria which reached Ivo through a translation made by Anastasius Bibliothecarius

Below: "So that we may not be judged to love conflict, we embrace the communion of the most reverend Bishop John, indulging him; and on account of dispensation, this case involving his self-examination should not be carried out too minutely, strictly, or zealously. For, as I said, because of dispensation a great case is avoided." And the same author, writing to the presbyter and archimandrite Gennadius: "Dispensations in matters, reducing what is owed, sometimes compel that certain men perish on the outside, so that [others] can profit. Just as those sailing on the sea in fear cast off some cargo when a storm arises and the ship becomes endangered, so that the remainder might be preserved in safety, thus, when we do not have the clear certainty of saving all things, we eliminate some from them lest we suffer the loss of all." Below: "And I write these things, knowing that your piety is saddened about the most holy worshiper of God, our fellow minister Bishop Proclus, because he received Eugene of 'Heliensius,'[103] whom indeed the laws of the church of Palestine did not recognize as a prelate." And below: "Therefore your piety should not refuse the communion of the most holy and most amicable to God, Bishop Proclus, for my one concern was for his sanctity, and the mode of dispensation displeased no one among the wise."

With the same moderation of discretion the Roman pontiffs allowed translations of bishops, which had previously been strictly prohibited by apostolic and canonical sanctions, out of concern for the greater utility of the Church. And for the sake of honor of person and the necessity of the people, others even restored certain bishops who had been deposed by their prede-

---

in the ninth century; *Interpretatio synodi vii generalis,* in J.-P. Migne, *Patrologia Latina* 129 (Paris, 1853), 222–23

103. The Latin reads *Heliensium Eugennium,* and *Helienius* probably represents a place which remains to be identified (see n. 109, below).

cessors. These names will be found noted below. Also certain Roman pontiffs decreed that sons of presbyters should not be received into the priesthood, both for rebuke of the incontinence of certain priests, and for more secure preservation of the continence of others—not because respect of persons is of any importance with God,[104] or that nature, equally the mother of us all, could be censured by anyone, or that sons could be condemned for the iniquities of parents, for, as the prophet says, "The son will not bear the sin of a father";[105] and the Apostle, "If God justifies, who is there who will condemn?";[106] and blessed Augustine, "From wherever men are born, if they do not follow the sins of their parents they will be honorable and saved."[107]

But, since they recognized that certain persons from these were not only religious but also necessary for the Church of God, they tempered the decree, and thus permitted those sons whose lives have been tested in religious churches or in monasteries to be promoted not only to the priesthood but also to the episcopate. And while we are silent concerning our own time, we read thus in the acts of the Roman pontiffs: "Presbyter Felix III, Roman by birth, son of the presbyter Felix, was [pontiff] from the time of King Odogarus up to the time of King Theodoric. Likewise Agapitus, Roman by birth, son of the presbyter Gordianus, was supreme pontiff. Gelasius, African by birth, son of Bishop Valerius, sat for three years, eight months, and nineteen days. Silverius, Campanian by birth, son of Hormisdas, bishop of Rome, sat for one year, five months, and twenty-one days. Deusdedit, Roman by birth, son of the

104. Cf. Acts 10:34.
105. Ezekiel 18:20.
106. Romans 8:33.
107. Augustine, *De bono coniugali*, c. 16 (Corpus scriptorum ecclesiasticorum Latinorum 41, ed. J. Zycha [Vienna, 1900], 211).

subdeacon Stephen, sat for three years and twenty-three days. Theodorus, Greek by birth, son of Bishop Theodorus, sat for six years and twenty-four days."[108]

Concerning translation [of bishops].

That many bishops were translated from one city to another because of necessity, or utility of the times, is made clear from the following:

> Perigenes was ordained bishop at Petra, but since the citizens of his city did not want to receive him, the bishop of Rome ordered him to be enthroned in the metropolitan see of Corinth, since its bishop had died, and he governed that church for the rest of his life. Alexander, bishop of Antioch, translated Bishop Dosideus of Seleucia to Tarsus in Cilicia. Reverentius was translated from Archis of Phoenicia to Tyre. John of Gordolina was moved to Prochonixum, and he governed that church. Palladius was moved from Helinopolis to Aspona. From another city named Helinopolis, Alexander was moved to Hadrianopolis. Gregory Nazianzus was first bishop of the city of Cappadocia which is called Sasima and then, with the consent of the blessed Basil and the other bishops, was established at Nazianzus. Melenus first presided at the church of Sebaste and later was made bishop of Antioch. Eusebius was transferred from Apamea to Eudoxopolis, which was formerly called Salubria. Polycarpus was moved from the city of Antapristena in Mysia to Nicopolis in Thrace. Ierophilus was

108. As in the preface to the Tripartite Collection, this list is derived from the *Liber Pontificalis;* see Davis, *Book of Pontiffs* (see n. 59, above).

translated from Trebizond in Phrygia to Platinopolis in Thrace. Optimus was translated from Agardamia in Phrygia to Antioch in Pisidia. Silvanus was moved from Philopolis in Thrace to Troas.[109]

Concerning restored [bishops].

Examples also show that many deposed bishops have been restored by the apostolic see:

John Chrysostom was sentenced by two synods of orthodox bishops but was restored again. Marcellus, bishop of Ancyra in Galatia, was deposed, but afterward received back his bishopric. Asclepius was sentenced by a synod, and afterward received back his church. Lucian, bishop at Hadrianopolis, condemned by Pope Julius, received back the church of his episcopate. Cyril, bishop of Jerusalem, was [deposed],[110] but afterward was reconciled to his church. In a similar fashion Pope Sixtus condemned Polychronius, bishop of the same church of Jerusalem, and then reconciled him. Pope Innocent condemned Bishop Fortunus, but afterward

109. The following texts on episcopal translation and restitution have a complicated and obscure history. The exact source Ivo used is not certain, though they do appear in the *Decretum* of Burchard of Worms (bk. 1.233-34; J.-P. Migne, *Patrologia Latina*, 140 [Paris, 1880], 616-18), but in a reversed sequence from what is presented here. In the translation no effort has been made to provide modern equivalents for all the place names, although it was done in some obvious cases. This course of action can be criticized, yet some of these cities no longer exist, and in obscure cases confusion might arise by listing modern names for localities which are more often encountered in classical form.

110. Cf. the text in J.-P. Migne, *Patrologia Latina*, 161 (Paris, 1855), 56A.

restored him to his place in his church. Bishop Misenus, condemned by Pope Felix, was received again into communion by his successor, Pope Gelasius, and was restored to his church. While a priest, Leontius was deposed but afterward was patriarch in the church of Antioch. Pope Gregory IV consecrated Theodosius as bishop of the holy church of Segni, from whom his predecessor Eugene had taken the honor of priest. Bishop Ibas was sentenced, but a holy synod canonically restored his church to him. Pope Nicholas reconciled both Bishop Rothadus of the holy church of Soissons, condemned at a synod attended by King Charles, and Bishop Sofrenus of Piacenza, deservedly censured.

Also Pope John VIII restored the novice Photius, who had been deposed by Pope Nicholas, in the patriarchate of Constantinople with the intervention of august Basil, Leo, and Alexander, writing to them in these words:

> You wrote to us, most beloved sons, so that we, opening the apostolic depths of compassion, would receive all who lie under correction at your church, and so that we, striving for peace and unanimity, would restore that lord Archbishop Photius, in communion with us, to the highest dignity of priests and to the honor of the patriarchate, lest the Church of God remain longer disturbed by schism and scandal. We embraced your petition as just and pleasing to God, and, rejoicing that at last we found the appropriate time we long desired, we sent our emissaries to fulfill your will, although before they arrived your piety violently attempted to

restore that man, which we, nevertheless, willingly accept. And though we have the power to do this, nevertheless [we do not desire to restore him] [111] by our own power. [But] rather we offer proofs from the [apostolic] decrees and constitutions of the Fathers, not abrogating the laws of the Church granted of old, but with the diligence of grace incontrovertibly observed in them, the body of the Church tears out and destroys, desiring to restore all things for its benefit. And the synod of Nicaea says in the second canon that it frequently happens that men transgress the ecclesiastical canons, either out of necessity or in some other way. [112] And Pope Gelasius says that where there is no necessity, the decrees of the holy Fathers should remain unchallenged. [113] And speaking in the same spirit the most holy Pope Leo ordered: "Where there is no necessity, the statutes of the holy Fathers should in no way be violated. Where, however, there would be necessity, he who has the power should dispense them for the utility of the Church. For out of necessity comes change of the law." And Pope Felix: "It is necessary to consider that when necessity arises we often transgress the constitutions of the

111. For this and the other insertions here, see Migne, *Patrologia Latina,* 161:56D.

112. Council of Nicaea, 325, canon 2.

113. The passages which follow, attributed to Popes Gelasius, Leo, and Felix, present problems, for the texts given by Ivo have not been found in this form in the authentic writings of Gelasius I, Leo I, or Popes Felix I–IV (JK 636 of Gelasius I comes close). The authors are grateful to Karen Green for providing this information from the database for the *Patrologia Latina* at Columbia University's Electronic Text Service.

Fathers." And the synod of Carthage says in the thirty-fifth chapter: "We order that clerics should be received back into the Church, though they were previously deposed in a synod. One synod also dissolves another synod for the unity and peace of the Church."[114] And Pope Innocent says in the fifth chapter: "Those who were promoted by the heretic Bonosus should be once again received, lest scandals spread in the Church."[115] Not only did this apostolic see offer the hand of assistance, striving for ecclesiastical peace, to those deposed for heresy, but also aided with accustomed mercy both the orthodox bishops and the patriarchs fleeing to her, just as it did at the present time for Photius. For you know that the apostolic see restored to pristine honor the great Bishop Athanasius of Alexandria, and Cyril and Policronius of Jerusalem, and John, whom your charity calls Chrysostom, and Flavianus—all previously deposed by a synod. If, therefore, those ordained by Donatists and Bonosus and then completely cast from the bounds of the orthodox Church by a synod are received by an identical synod, and inscribed in the roll of the bishops lest the Church suffer loss or division, how much more is it necessary not to condemn men of orthodox faith and unstained life, but instead to recall them to pristine rank? So, this apostolic see, once receiving the keys of the kingdom of heaven from the first and great priest Jesus Christ, through the prince of the apostles Peter, to whom he said:

114. A source for this passage has not been located.
115. JK 303.

"I give you the keys of the kingdom of heaven, and whatever you bind on earth will be bound in heaven, etc."[116] has the power of universally binding and loosing, and, according to Jeremiah, of uprooting and planting.[117] Because of this, and employing the power of the same Peter, prince of the apostles, we with all our church command you and our holy brother patriarchs of Alexandria, Antioch, Jerusalem, and the remaining bishops and the entire church of Constantinople, according to your petition, to receive into communion Patriarch Photius, our brother and fellow bishop.

Likewise: "Receive him without excuse. No one can be excused [from so doing] because of the synods convened against him. Let no one accuse him with the judgments of my holy predecessors Nicholas and Hadrian; he is freed from these. No one should have your efforts against him as an occasion of schism. For we render all things as void and invalid, and place whatever things are against him in the hands of the prince of the apostles, and through him on the shoulders of Jesus Christ, the Lamb of God, who takes away the sin of the world." Likewise: "And we want you to confirm this, that after the death of our brother Photius, no one shall ascend from worldly dignity to the pontifical dignity, but [someone] from the cardinal priests of the same church, or from the deacons or the other priests who exist at the church of Constantinople." Again: "And since we have received our brother Photius out of concern for the peace of the Church, just as Pope Hadrian [received] Tarasius, no one should count this as canonical usage. For the privileges of the few do not make common law, and if anyone should pre-

116. Matthew 16:18-19.
117. Jeremiah 1:10.

sume to do something of this sort henceforth, he will be without pardon."[118]

Thus in addition, although it was determined in the ancient rules that no one who was in the clergy should have contact with "external women,"[119] but only with those who prevented all suspicion, the blessed Pope Gregory modified this rigor as follows for the English clergy, so that if any existed outside sacred orders who could not contain themselves, they could choose wives and receive their stipends externally. He understood that this lapse was less severe if, in tumbling, they were caught by the marriage bond, than if with a temporary liaison they were absorbed in the depth of unbounded desire.[120] Thus, other dispensations granted with healthful deliberation must cease when the necessity [that required them] ceases, nor should what either utility has recommended or necessity has commanded be considered as law. Whence it is read in the letter of blessed Pope Leo to the bishops of Africa: "What remains, therefore, brothers, is that in harmony you should lift up healthful exhortations, and, doing nothing through contention but united in full zeal of devotion, should submit to the divine and apostolic constitutions, and in no way allow the most provident decrees of the canons to be violated. And the things which we have remitted up to now in consideration of specific cases should henceforth be preserved with the ancient rules, lest what we conceded at the time with pious leniency we later punish by just penalty."[121]

118. The longest quotation in Ivo's treatise, divided into four sections, derives from JL 3271, from Pope John VIII, dated August 16, 879. Its textual tradition is complicated by various recensions, among them a forged version drafted by Photius himself.
119. *extranearum consorcium mulierum*
120. Cf. JE 1843.
121. JK 410.

Not only should this be observed in ecclesiastical rules, but it also is read in those laws concerning the veneration of Roman laws: "Whatever the emperor constituted by letter or ordered by edict stands as law. These are what are called constitutions. Clearly some of them are termed 'personal,' which cannot be taken as precedents, since the prince does not wish this.[122] For what he granted to someone on account of merit, or if he inflicted[123] a penalty on him, or if he has aided him without precedent, does not pass beyond [the case] of the individuals."[124] We could gather a great many rules and a great many examples of this sort, but these few should be sufficient for the prudent reader, and to him who knows how to learn many things from a few.

But what we warned before we warn again: If anyone refers to charity, "which is the fullness of law,"[125] what he has read concerning ecclesiastical sanctions or dispensations, he will neither err nor sin. And when he avoids supreme rigor for some plausible reason, charity will excuse him, if he has employed nothing against the Gospel, nothing against the apostles. But if some judgments from secular laws which contain capital punishment have been inserted, they have not been included so that by means of them an ecclesiastical judge should condemn someone, but rather so that he might make from them an argument of canonical decrees, considering hence how much penance that

---

122. *quoniam nec hec princeps uult,* but with the more feasible form *hoc,* which will be followed here, as a frequent variant for *hec* (see Brasington, ed., "Prologue to the 'Decretum,'" 288; cf. Migne, *Patrologia Latina,* 161.58D [as in n. 110, above]).

123. See Brasington, ed. "Prologue to the 'Decretum,'" 289 for *irrogauerit,* and Migne, *Patrologia Latina,* 161.58D.

124. Justinian, *Institutes* 1.2.6: in *Institutiones,* ed. T. Mommsen and P. Krueger (Corpus Iuris Civilis 1; Berlin, 1928), 1–2.

125. Romans 13:10.

crime or disgrace requires as punishment which secular judges sentence with death or mutilation of members. Indeed the Roman pontiffs frequently employ this reasoning in the argument of their decrees. For if secular laws contain these things, should not divine laws all the more? [126]

But enough of these matters. Next we have briefly brought together the plan of the individual parts of the whole work, so that from here a prudent reader can see what, indispensable to him, he ought to seek in each part.[127]

6. Preface to the Collection in Ten Parts, perhaps compiled shortly after 1123 by Archdeacon Walter of Thérouanne: dedicatory letter to an unknown patron, perhaps to Bishop John of Thérouanne. Ed. Valentin Rose, *Verzeichniss der Lateinischen Handschriften: Die Lateinischen Meerman-Handschriften des Sir Thomas Phillipps,* 1 (Die Handschriften-Verzeichnisse der Königlichen Bibliothek zu Berlin 12; Berlin, 1893), 209–10.[128]

As far as I was able, most reverend father, I obeyed your will, and having surveyed with diligent curiosity libraries of many churches, at different points I collected decisions of the holy Fathers from the acts of councils, the decrees of the Roman

126. Cf. 1 Corinthians 6:3.

127. In manuscripts of Ivo's *Panormia* a summary of the contexts of the eight books follows. That extensive list will not be given here, both in consideration of space, but also to reiterate the possibility that the Prologue was written as an independent treatise on harmonizing the canons and then adapted (e.g., the final sentence added) as a preface to canonical collections (see Brasington, "Prologue of Ivo," at n. 13, above).

128. An earlier printing of a text of this preface can be found in Augustin Theiner, *Disquisitiones criticae in praecipuas canonum et decretalium collectiones seu sylloges gallandianae dissertationum de vetustis canonum collectionibus continuatio* (Rome, 1836), 166–68, n. 8.

pontiffs, and also from the treatises of illustrious and orthodox men. I brought that same collection together in this volume, in an ordered arrangement, so that anyone who has difficulty obtaining or reading all those works from which these things have been gathered can find more easily here what he judges useful for himself.

Following a list of the names and dates of the Roman pontiffs, I prefaced to this collection the treatise of the venerable man lord Ivo, bishop of Chartres, which he drafted in very brilliant language concerning the concordance of canons, so that a diligent reader may find these things, as it were akin to a lamp in the vestibule of a house which he intends to enter, and should read and understand. He thus can traverse with deft steps the innermost recesses and all that is hidden in the subsequent work. For I labored to arrange the total structure of this same work so that it [the Ivonian prologue] seems to fit in every respect as a preface. And in order that the same book also matches the tenfold numbering of the sacred law, I separated the whole volume into ten parts and then added, following the treatise of the aforesaid man, a suitably brief description of the full contents of these parts, so that what should be sought in which part appears more clearly.

At the beginning of each part, moreover, I took care to present in order the titles covered therein, so that it is not necessary for a reader to run through the whole volume for the sake of some opinion, but only to note the heading appropriate to his business, with the prefixed number, and to investigate successively the decisions placed under it. Lest among these [decisions the rubrics] "Likewise" and "About the Same Thing," repeatedly inserted, constitute an obstacle for an investigator and monotony for a reader, I condensed things, annoying prolixity for the most part being avoided, in that I did not give separate rubrics to individual canons but assembled a number of canons under each title.[129] In many places I even designated subtopics within these same titles and indicated the number of subtopics by the number of dots affixed both in the [list of] titles and in the canons under titles.[130]

I also inserted some decisions that are dissonant and for the most part less suitable for our times. I did not do so because either I would adjudicate or would suggest that adjudication be given by others according to them. But I thought that it should be pointed out that different men have different views, and that it should be left to the judgment of a prudent reader which of them ought to be followed. Thus I ask through the mercy of God that you repay my labors especially in this way: that you

129. The words *Item* and *De eodem* are often repeated in collections as rubrics for texts, indicating either the same source as the preceding canon or coverage of the same topic. The compiler of Ten Parts aimed to eliminate such repetition by copying appropriate canons under one title.

130. The list of numbered titles at the beginning of each part carried a system of dots over certain words to designate subtopics within titles. In manuscripts of the collection which have been examined, the titles themselves are not reproduced within the separate parts, but their numbers occur in the margin (note the comment just above about the numbering of titles). Dots also appear in the margin, opposite the canon which treats the subtopic indicated by that number of dots in the title. This system can be grasped fully only from examining the collection (which remains unedited), but it is described briefly in Fournier and LeBras, *Histoire,* 2:297, and better in Fournier, "Les Collections," 434–35 (in *Mélanges de droit canonique,* 1:615-16; see n. 16, above). Here Fournier took as an example title 1 of part 7—"Concerning marriages: when and by whom they should be celebrated, and that they should not be celebrated clandestinely or without a gift."—where two dots appear over "when," three over "by whom," four over "clandestinely," and five over "without a gift." This complex schema is, of course, found in manuscripts of the work with varying degrees of accuracy.

deign to intervene for my sins with [Him] who takes away the sins of the world.[131]

The first part deals with the faith; certain heresies; baptism, and the ministry[132] of those about to be baptized; preparation and distribution of chrism; confirmation; the sacrament of the body and blood of the Lord; offering and reception of the Eucharist; reverence for the sacred vessels.

The second part deals with the operation of a church; offerings of the faithful; dedication of churches; burial; consecration of altars and how churches are held by priests; tithes; legitimate ownership;[133] those seeking sanctuary in a church; sacrilege; the free tenants and goods of a church and their alienation; authentic and apocryphal writings and councils; customs; fasting and alms.

The third part deals with the election and consecration of the pope and bishops; examination and ordination; certain men who, for various reasons, should or should not be ordained; the relocation of those ordained, and that those ordained are not to be reordained; their continence; symoniacs; heretics; those lapsed in sacred orders; murderous and usurious clerics; serfs

131. The list of the content of the ten parts which follows is given by both Rose and Theiner (see n. 128, above), immediately after the collection's preface. Yet in manuscripts of the work this list does not follow the preface, but is inserted after the Ivonian Prologue (see above in the text, and Fournier and LeBras, *Histoire*, 2:297, more clearly in Fournier, "Les Collections," 435, [rpt. in *Mélanges de droit canonique*, 1:616; see n. 16, above]). As the preface notes, and as is verified in the manuscripts, the preface to Ten Parts is followed by a list of popes in turn followed by the Ivonian Prologue and the list of content. Rich in information and printed by Rose, the latter will be included here, but with the caveat that the topics at times are designated epigrammatically, and translation is not always a straightforward matter.

132. See the preface to Burchard's *Decretum* (chap. 3).

133. That is, of the property of a church.

ordained unwittingly; corrupt clerics; abbots and monks; veiled virgins and widows, and abbesses.

The fourth part deals with the Rule of blessed Augustine and its observance; archbishops and bishops about to be consecrated; what [bishops] should do in churches and throughout dioceses about banished, ignorant, and discordant [clerics]; their [bishops'] ministries and how they should be in harmony with princes and restrain evil men; their goods, sobriety, moderate circumstances, and liberty; witnesses about bishops; dead bishops; episcopal and ecclesiastical goods; priests and clerics: where and how they should live and teach others; possessions of dead clerics.

The fifth part deals with the primacy and dignity of the Roman Church; convoking councils; establishing a province; the power of primates and metropolitans; where cases involving clerics ought to be handled; reinvesting those despoiled; accusations:[134] by what procedure and by which and against which persons they ought and ought not to be made; witnesses: who, how many, in which case, and how they ought or ought not to testify; postponements:[135] when, and for how long they should be given; those using delaying tactics: for how long and for what reason they should be tolerated; judges: what sort of men they should be, and when they should render judgment; appeal: when and how it should be made, and those appealing incorrectly; choosing judges; condemning bishops and clerics; sentences.

The sixth part deals with how clerics, only accused of infamy, are cleared; business and cases of the laity; the power of binding

134. The word appears in the singular (*accusatione*), but the verbs which follow are plural.

135. The text reads *de iuditiis* ("concerning judgments"), but *de induciis,* as found in Theiner's edition (see n. 128, above), seems to be what is required.

and loosing; summoning those who ought to be excommunicated; excommunication; absolution; those who are bound by fealty or oath to those excommunicated; heretics who ought to be excommunicated after death, and that one should not associate with those excommunicated by name; illicit, unjust, and rash excommunication.

The seventh part deals with marriages: when, among which persons, and for what reason they ought to be made; three things which make a complete marriage; complete and incomplete marriage; concubines; spouses, one of whom without the other vows continence or takes the habit; wives who marry others when their husbands have been captured; that marriage exists among persons of the same status, that is, among the heathen and among Jews; for what reasons marriage should not be dissolved; what sort of union does not make a marriage; separation in a marriage for reasons other than fornication.

The eighth part deals with marriage, not to be dissolved except for fornication; fornication with sisters and relatives, and that no one should marry her whom he previously defiled; murderers of their spouses; adultery; concerning Lothar and Theutberga;[136] fornication in spirit;[137] reconciliation of spouses; processes of accusation,[138] separation, and reconciliation, and the subjugation which should be exhibited by wives to husbands; who should be prohibited from being or ordered to be married and why; consanguinity: its enumeration, regulation, and

136. The reference is to the proposed divorce of King Lothar II of Lotharingia and Queen Theutberga in the 860s.

137. The text reads *de fornicatione spirituali;* see Gratian, *Decretum,* C. 32, q. 7, c. 15, where the same term occurs in reference to the prohibition in Matthew 5:28.

138. The text reads *excusationis,* but Theiner's text (see n. 128, above) has *accusationis,* which seems to make more sense and will be followed here.

demonstration, as well as accusation, computation, and investigation; its degrees calculated both vertically and laterally.[139]

The ninth part deals with murders; those who kill themselves, bishops, or other ecclesiastics; parricides and killers of spouses and penitents; murders committed voluntarily, non-voluntarily, and in premeditated fashion; he who strikes a pregnant wife causing an abortion; that certain homicides are done without sin; incantations, divinations, and diverse forms of magic; the nature of demons; auguries; [superstition] associated with days and months; eight types of lies;[140] oaths which should or should not be observed, and illegitimate oaths; requiring an oath and deceitful oaths; specific oaths and partners in an oath; every sort of falsehood.

The tenth part deals with penance, those doing penance, and the differentiation which should be kept in mind regarding them; how clerics should do penance; confession of sins,[141] satisfaction, and reconciliation; greater and lesser faults and deathbed penance; correction of all wrongdoing, and satisfaction through fasts.

7. Preface to the Second Collection of Châlons-sur-Marne, c. 1130. Ed. Paul Fournier, "Les Collections canoniques attribuées à Yves de Chartres," *Bibliothèque de l'Ecole des chartes* 58 (1897), 639 n. 1 (rpt. in *Mélanges de droit canonique,* 1:641, n. 1).

139. That is, calculation of degrees of both consanguinity, strictly speaking, and affinity.

140. See Gratian, *Decretum,* C. 22, q. 2, c. 8.

141. Three words are used in this section, *peccata, culpe,* and *crimina.* All can mean "sin," but they are translated as "sin," "fault," and "wrongdoing," to show the shift in terminology. Only an analysis of the canons can show the distinctions, if any, which were intended.

The little volume of this collection is divided in thirteen parts, according to what the thickness or number of the quires seems to require. Anyone, of course, should realize that this division into so large a number of parts was done so an investigator can more easily determine what he needs, and in which part he can find what he seeks. Whence at the beginning of each part the titles covered therein are listed, announcing to those wishing to know what is treated in each section, so that one need not run through the whole work for the sake of some opinion, but only note the part appropriate to his business and by investigating the decisions of the same with a retentive mind to remember them.[142] Yet not all the decisions inserted here appear suitable for establishing something in these times, but because different men have different views, it was decided to point out to a sagacious investigator what he could consider worth following or worth rejecting. Indeed different regions establish many things because of places, persons, and the times, but which, when necessity does not require them, can be changed if utility urges. Now, therefore, what is contained in the parts [of this work] should briefly be revealed.[143]

8. Preface to the book On Mercy and Justice of Alger of Liège, early twelfth century: preface in the form of a letter "to all catholics." Ed. Robert Kretzschmar, *Alger von Lüttichs Traktat "De misericordia et iustitia." Ein kanonistischer Konkordanzversuch aus der Zeit des Investiturstreits. Untersuchungen und Edition* (Quellen und Forschungen zum Recht im Mittelalter 2; Sigmaringen, 1985), 187–189.

142. For this and what follows, cf. the preface to the Collection in Ten Parts (above).
143. The list of contents is not provided by Fournier.

Whoever I may be [I send] to all catholics, each according to his own measure, what Jethro [sent] to Moses, not a burden or something fleeting.[144]

Pondering the fact that the state of the holy Church is shaken by various errors and schisms—since the precepts of the canons are either unknown to or neglected by the corrupt, while the simple grasp them neither in their meaning nor in their discretion—to the extent that omnipotent grace answered my prayers, I thus have brought the matter to prominence for everyone, so that the devotion of good men might be aided by discernment of truth, and the contention of the corrupt might be overcome by the evidence of canonical authority. Some canonical precepts are for mercy, others are for justice, differentiated by diverse circumstances, persons, and times, so that now mercy may totally remit justice, now justice may totally disguise mercy. Those who do not know how to apply such diverse things through discernment think them to clash in contradiction, not considering that the method of ecclesiastical guidance is this: whether by indulging or by punishing, to preserve the same intention of charity, the same operation of salvation. Hence those using canonical rules noncanonically so impugn and assail precepts with precepts that at times they remove justice from its place through unwarranted grace, at times they remove grace from its place through untempered justice.

Because canonical precepts should be adapted to different persons, events, and times by varying procedure and varying application—so that a heretic ought to be handled in one way, a sinner in another, a prelate in another, a subordinate in another, each appropriately, each singled out by separate intention, or action, or circumstance—I thus labored, however much God

144. Cf. Exodus 18.13–27.

granted discernment, to this end, namely, that a unity of intention, utility, and truth might shine forth in the canons, and that any diversity in them would not yield a cacophony of contradiction. For since "all the pathways of the Lord are mercy and truth,"[145] I tried to set forth with these authorities of the sacred canons, as far as I was able, how indulgence is owed to penitents and punishment to those who are obdurate, how the one with its own discretion is not prejudicial to the other, thus establishing that what is pious ought to be dispensed only justly and what is just only piously, and not in mutual confusion. I would allocate to each individual his own measure, to judgment or to grace, according to heresy or sin, person or circumstance, and not according to confused law or procedure.

In proof of such a position I have presented with equal authority the deeds and the sayings of the saints, because just as their precepts should be obeyed, so also their deeds should be imitated, for since even the Lord Jesus began to act before he began to teach,[146] who would believe the saints to have taught other than they acted? I have, therefore, divided [this work] into three parts. In the first I shall treat grace, namely, how and for how long it ought to be extended in tolerating sinners. In the second I shall treat justice, namely, in what circumstance, with what procedure, and with what discernment it should be exercised against those same individuals. In the third I shall treat various heresies, namely, how they differ in their damnable teaching or in their sacraments, on the one hand, from Catholics and, on the other hand, from one another.

Yet because, as Augustine said to Jerome, "It is possible that something could appear to you to be other than what is true,

145. Psalm 25 (24):10.
146. Cf. Acts 1:1.

while something done by you could not be other than what is charitable,"[147] if by chance I seem clumsily to have distorted the sayings of the saints so that for my error, if it is an error, I can allege no authority, I, nevertheless, demand reciprocity of charity. Because I composed this little work for the sake of brotherly utility, if what I did negligently is neglected, at least let it not be neglected if I, insignificant as I am, was able beneficially to add something to the decrees of the saints. For as Augustine said in his letter to Boniface: "We ought not to regard the arguments of any men, however catholic and praiseworthy, as we regard the canonical scriptures, and thus we should not be restricted from condemning or rejecting something in their writings, the honor which is owed to them being preserved, if perchance we find that they believed differently than the truth which has been grasped by us or others with divine assistance. I am of this view about the writings of others; thus I desire those acquainted with mine to be."[148] Likewise, Isidore to Bishop Massona, in chapter 10: "But at the end of this letter I thought this should be added, that however often a discordant ruling is found in the acts of the councils, let the ruling of that council rather be held whose authority stands as older and stronger."[149]

Since, therefore, such great men left their own writings, those of others, and even the rulings of councils to the judgment of others for examining and correcting, who am I that I

147. Augustine, *Ep.* 73, c. 2.3 (Corpus scriptorum ecclesiasticorum Latinorum 34, ed. Al. Goldbacher [Vienna, 1898], 266, lines 12–14).

148. Augustine, *Ep.* 148, c. 4.15 (Corpus scriptorum ecclesiasticorum Latinorum) 44, ed. Al. Goldbacher [Vienna, 1904], 344–45).

149. Isidore of Seville, *Ep.* 4, c. 13, to Bishop Massona of Mérida, in J.-P. Migne, *Patrologia Latina*, 83 (Paris, 1850), 901D–2A. It is uncertain whether this is an authentic letter. According to Kretzschmar's note it was transmitted to Alger through the Collection in 74 Titles (see introduction to this chapter).

should dare to be incensed by my correctors, provided that they do not harm themselves on account of me by rejecting my good points, if there are any. I have, therefore, taken care to preface each and every ruling with its own heading, so that they might be both easier for the studious to find and clearer for the slow to understand. I also mixed in among them, generously as it were, some things which not only can serve here as if on the flank, but also in their places defend their own position straight on.

5

Gratian and the Decretists

The prefaces in this chapter reflect the maturation of medieval canon law during the "Renaissance of the Twelfth Century"—a phenomenon that in reality encompasses about a century and a half, from around the year 1050 to the end of the twelfth century.[1] The political and cultural dynamics of the ongoing papal reform and the appearance of vibrant urban schools demanded —and enabled—this transformation of canon law, from a heterogenous tradition to an increasingly rational legal science.[2] Many contributed to this achievement, but one figure stands above the rest: Master Gratian of Bologna. Around 1140, Gratian completed his Concordance of Discordant Canons (*Con-*

1. See Charles Homer Haskins, *The Renaissance of the Twelfth Century* (Cambridge, Mass., 1927), and *Renaissance and Renewal in the Twelfth Century,* ed. Robert L. Benson and Giles Constable, with Carol D. Lanham (Cambridge, Mass., 1982), including essays by Stephan Kuttner and Knut Wolfgang Nörr, on canon and civil law, respectively. For the developments covered in this chapter see also Southern, *Scholastic Humanism,* chaps. 8–9. Appearing too late to be used in this volume is the excellent work of R. H. Helmholz, *The Spirit of Classical Canon Law* (Athens, Ga., 1996).

2. For wide-ranging essays on theology, philosophy, historiography, and other aspects of the intellectual life of the twelfth century, see M. D. Chenu, *Nature, Man, and Society in the Twelfth Century,* trans. Jerome Taylor and Lester K. Little (Chicago, 1968). For more on the transformation of canon law and on earlier collections, see Martin Brett, "Canon Law and Litigation: The Century before Gratian," in *Medieval Ecclesiastical Studies in Honour of Dorothy M. Owen,* ed. M. J. Franklin and Christopher Harper-Bill (Woodbridge, Suffolk, 1995), 21–40.

cordia discordantium canonum), commonly called the *Decretum*.[3] During the remainder of the twelfth century it gradually came to replace its predecessors, and by the early thirteenth century it was in almost universal use in the classrooms of the West (although the evidence from manuscripts shows that earlier collections continued to be transcribed).

Gratian furnished his readers with a detailed review of canonical tradition, whose range far exceeded that of any previous compilation, including the large systematic works of Ivo of Chartres and Burchard of Worms. The *Decretum's* distinctions (*distinctiones*) and cases (*causae*) examined a vast array of subjects. The 101 distinctions of the work's first section presented texts under general categories, from the sources of law itself to the intricacies of Church-state relations. The second part of the collection, 36 *causae,* or short statements of hypothetical cases, gave the reader an opportunity to analyze discrete topics through a series of questions raised about these legal situations. Among the *causae* is a body of texts that seems to function as an independent treatise on penance—the Tractate on Penance (*Tractatus de penitentia*)—and following the last *causa* there is another book that treats ritual and sacramental theology— the Tractate on Consecration (*Tractatus de consecratione,* i.e.,

3. For a recent survey, including a select bibliography on the *Decretum,* see *Gratian: The Treatise on Laws (Decretum DD 1–20) with the Ordinary Gloss,* trans. Augustine Thompson, O.P., and James Gordley, with an introduction by Katherine Christensen (Studies in Medieval and Early Modern Canon Law 2; Washington, D.C., 1993). See also Brundage, *Medieval Canon Law,* 44ff., and 190–94; Chodorow, "Law, Canon"; and the discussions and translations in Tierney, *Crisis,* 116–26. Earlier views on Gratian and his collection must now be reconsidered in light of the research of Anders Winroth. A summary of his findings can be found in, "The Two Recensions of Gratian's *Decretum," Zeitschrift der Savigny-Stiftung für Rechtsgeschichte,* Kanonistische Abteilung 83 (1997).

on sacred things). The origins and function of these two treatises have been subjects of discussion and disagreement among scholars, and it is unclear whether they come from Gratian's own hand or were added by early students of his work.

Gratian did not compose a preface for his book,[4] but interwoven with the *distinctiones* and *causae* were the author's own *dicta,* a running commentary that attempted to organize and harmonize the canons. This commentary, anticipated by such works as Alger of Liège's On Mercy and Justice and Ivo of Chartres's Prologue (see chap. 4), covered much of the *Decretum.* Although at times the *dicta* merely summarize the texts or pass over in silence a contradiction—the prefaces translated in this chapter are not totally complimentary about Gratian's analysis—often they reduce inconsistencies and contradictions to agreement through the dialectical method of laying out contextual, categorical, and etymological distinctions.

A single generation lay between Ivo and Gratian, yet the difference between their collections and their jurisprudence is striking and fundamental. For all the fame of his teacher, Lanfranc of Bec, Ivo's education had differed little from that afforded earlier canonists like Burchard and Regino. Gratian's world was different.[5] While his obscure background makes his

4. Some commentators took it upon themselves to remedy this omission by writing such introductions: see Kalb, *Studien,* 26.

5. See, in general, the *Cambridge History of Later Medieval Philosophy: From the Rediscovery of Aristotle to the Disintegration of Scholasticism,* ed. Norman Kretzmann et al. (Cambridge, 1982). There is also an extensive bibliography in Charles M. Radding and William W. Clark, *Medieval Architecture, Medieval Learning: Builders and Masters in the Age of Romanesque and Gothic* (New Haven, 1992), 151–64. A compact survey of a vast subject is provided by John W. Baldwin, *The Scholastic Culture of the Middle Ages, 1000–1300* (Lexington, Mass., 1971), and Kuttner, *Harmony from Dissonance,* is a short but classic study of the development of canonistic jurisprudence during early scholasticism.

own legal education impossible to determine, the *Decretum* as used from the middle of the twelfth century was a product of Bologna, where the formal study of Roman law had been revived at the turn of the century. Gratian's attitude to Roman law was not a simple matter. He included excerpts when he found them in the earlier canonical collections that served as his sources, such as in works of Ivo. Yet it is very likely that he did not incorporate texts directly from the Roman law books themselves, although his acquaintance with that law is clearly revealed in the *dicta*. If it was Gratian's task not only to resolve the contradictions of canonical tradition—an ongoing concern since the beginning of the Investiture Contest—it was the early commentators who set about effecting an assimilation of civil law into canon law, thus linking the legal traditions of the ancient emperors with canonistic tradition and placing both in the service of the papacy and the intellectual world of the High and Late Middle Ages. What Manlio Bellomo and others have called the "common law" (*ius commune*) of the Latin West was taking shape.[6]

Legal study helped to create the university in the early twelfth century. School-trained jurisprudents who were called Decretists, that is, students of Gratian's *Decretum,* extended, modified, and questioned Gratian and one another.[7] Scattered

6. See Bellomo, *Legal Past;* Kenneth Pennington, "Learned Law, Droit Savant, Gelehrtes Recht: The Tyranny of a Concept," *Rivista internazionale di Diritto Comune* 5 (1994): 197–209; and James A. Brundage, "The Rise of Professional Canonists and the Development of the Ius Commune," *Zeitschrift der Savigny-Stiftung für Rechtsgeschichte,* Kanonistische Abteilung 81 (1995): 26–63.

7. A fundamental work on the Decretists is Kuttner, *Repertorium.* See also Gabriel LeBras, Ch. Lefebvre, and J. Rambaud, *L'Age classique 1140–1378: Sources et théorie du droit* (Histoire du droit et des institutions de l'Eglise en occident 7; Paris, 1965); and, more recently, Brundage, *Medieval Canon Law,* 49ff., and Rudolf Weigand, "Frühe Kanonisten."

glosses on selected texts soon became layers of sustained analysis and commentaries, and schools of interpretation identified with particular masters and their disciples arose. Over time, these commentaries were detached from the margins of the *Decretum* to circulate as *summae*—self-standing, organized treatises that increasingly did far more than merely "sum up" Gratian's texts. Like similar contemporary works in theology, for example the *Sentences* of Peter Lombard, these treatises summarized and analyzed the textbook Gratian had created. They also drew freely from one another, as the prefaces in this chapter will show. At first glance, the Decretists, like Gratian himself, appear to be a wholly new intellectual phenomenon. To an extent they were, as a comparison of any of their prefaces with earlier texts will quickly demonstrate. Yet they did not perceive their work as standing in opposition to tradition, but rather as preserving continuity with the past in their exposition of the canons. Indeed, traces of older canon law which Gratian did not use, for example, texts from Burchard of Worm's *Decretum* and excerpts from Ivo's Prologue, appear in their *summae*.

Historians customarily divide the decretists into two main "schools"—Bolognese and French—although these categories are hardly precise given the large number and variety of commentaries, most of which are anonymous, and their frequent interdependence. At best, one can say that each "school" had certain jurisprudential tendencies in its reading of the *Decretum*. From Bologna came such masters as Paucapalea, Rolandus, and Rufinus, jurisprudents sensitive not only to apparent contradictions among the canons but also to the challenge of

---

Much useful information, despite idiosyncrasies, also can be found in J. A. Clarence Smith, *Medieval Law Teachers and Writers, Civilian and Canonist* (Collection des travaux de la Faculté de droit de l'Université d'Ottawa, Monographies juridiques 9; Ottawa, 1975).

understanding canon law in light of Roman law. The "French school" was influenced as much by contemporary theology and rhetorical theory as by Roman law. This approach to Gratian, seen in the prefaces to Stephan of Tournai's *Summa,* the *Summa "Parisiensis,"* and the *Summa "Antiquitate et tempore,"* was less inclined toward the more strictly juridical hermeneutics characteristic of the Bolognese masters.

Like Gratian, little is known of Paucapalea, who probably was Gratian's student and is certainly one of the earliest commentator on the *Decretum.*[8] His name is attached to glosses in early manuscripts of the *Decretum,* and sometime around the year 1150 he composed his *Summa.*[9] Although Paucapalea's commentary lacks the scope and sophistication of later Bolognese products, its preface defines the distinctive jurisprudence of the school. After placing the origins of law in Adam's pleading in the Garden of Eden, Paucapalea pays careful attention to defining key terms and concepts. Like other authors of *summae,* he lays out the schematic analysis known as the *accessus* ("access, approach"), for the work under consideration, discussing Gratian's choice of title, subject matter, intent, and method of proceeding[10]—in short, providing a framework which in essence

8. Specific studies on Paucapalea include John T. Noonan, "The True Paucapalea?" in *Proceedings of the Fifth International Congress of Medieval Canon Law,* ed. Stephan Kuttner and Kenneth Pennington (Monumenta iuris canonici, Subsidia 6; Vatican City, 1980) 157–86, and Rudolf Weigand, "Paucapalea und die frühe Kanonistik," *Archiv für katholisches Kirchenrecht* 150 (1981): 137–63.

9. Brundage suggests a date before 1148 (*Medieval Canon Law,* 49); Weigand, "Frühe Kanonisten," 136, dates Paucapalea's work around the year 1150 or a bit later.

10. On the development of the *accessus,* see Edwin A. Quain, "The Medieval accessus ad auctores," *Traditio* 3 (1945): 215–64, and R. B. C. Huygens, *Accessus ad auctores* (Leiden, 1970). For a discussion of the *accessus* in Decretists' prologues to their *summae,* see Kalb, *Studien,* 21–28.

gave the introduction that the *Decretum* lacked. Rufinus, Rolandus, and others echo Paucapalea in this regard.

Until fairly recently, scholars believed that the author of the work known as the *Stroma* was the same Rolandus who later became Pope Alexander III. Now it appears that canonist and pope were different men, with the former likely an obscure teacher at Bologna in the mid-twelfth century. Professor Weigand has shown that his *Stroma* was revised repeatedly in the 1150s.[11] It summarizes Gratian's distinctions and then presents a more detailed treatment of the *causae*. Both of the long tractates—*De penitentia* and *De consecratione*—are omitted, possibly signs of the *Stroma's* early composition. The preface shows Rolandus's debt to Paucapalea, although he added distinctive elements of his own.

Rufinus was the most influential early representative of the Bolognese school.[12] His fame was established by the *Summa* assembled from his many earlier glosses at Bologna in the year 1164.[13] This work reflects how quickly and how far jurisprudence had advanced since the work of Paucapalea a generation earlier, for Rufinus provides a comprehensive, well-organized commentary drawing on both Roman and canon law.

11. For Rolandus, see John T. Noonan, "Who Was Rolandus?," *Law, Church, and Society: Essays in Honor of Stephen Kuttner,* ed. Kenneth Pennington and Robert Somerville (Philadelphia, 1977), 21–48; Rudolph Weigand, "Magister Rolandus und Papst Alexander III," *Archiv für katholisches Kirchenrecht* 149 (1980): 3–44 (rpt. in *Diritto, persona e vita sociale, Scritti in memoria di Orio Giacchi* [Vita e pensiero, Sciente giuridiche 6; Milan, 1984], 178–213); and Weigand, "Frühe Kanonisten," 136–37, with further bibliography.

12. Stephen C. Ferruolo, "Rufinus," *Dictionary of the Middle Ages,* 10 (New York, 1988), 545–46. For more extensive treatment, see Robert L. Benson, "Rufin," *Dictionnaire de droit canonique,* 7 (Paris, 1961), 779–84.

13. Gouron, "Sources," 68, and see Weigand, "Frühe Kanonisten," 138.

The French school traces its origins to Stephen of Tournai.[14] He was a student at Bologna in the early 1150s, perhaps studying canon law with Rufinus and Roman law with Bulgarus (one of the famous so-called Four Doctors of Roman law who flourished in the mid-twelfth century).[15] Around the middle of that decade Stephen was back in Orléans as a regular canon at St.-Euverte and after spending a few years at Chartres, was abbot at St.-Euverte by 1167.[16] Shortly after the appearance of the *Summa* of Rufinus he composed his own *Summa* on the *Decretum*.[17] Scholars have long recognized its important contributions to jurisprudence, political theory, and ecclesiology, and its influence on subsequent *summae*. Through Stephen, French canonists not only learned of the Bolognese school, above all Rufinus, but also were motivated to undertake their own commentaries.

14. Stephan Kuttner, "Les Débuts de l'école canoniste français," *Studia et documenta historiae et iuris* 4 (1938): 193–204 (rpt. in Kuttner, *Gratian and the Schools of Law, 1140–1234* [Variorum Reprint CS185; London, 1983]), and, more recently, André Gouron, "Une école ou des écoles: Sur les canonistes français (vers 1150–1210)," in *Proceedings of the Sixth International Congress of Medieval Canon Law,* ed. Stephan Kuttner and Kenneth Pennington (Monumenta iuris canonici, Subsidia 7; Vatican City, 1985), 223–40, and George Conklin, "Stephan of Tournai and the Development of *aequitas canonica:* The Theory and Practice of Law after Gratian," in *Proceedings of the Eighth International Congress of Medieval Canon Law,* ed. Stanley Chodorow (Monumenta iuris canonici, Subsidia 9; Vatican City, 1992), 369–86.

15. On Bulgarus, see Bellomo, *Legal Past,* 112–13. On Rufinus and Stephen, see Ronald Knox, "The Problem of Academic Language in Rufinus and Stephan," in *Proceedings of the Sixth International Congress of Medieval Canon Law,* 109–23, who analyzes their divergent use of identical terms.

16. Weigand, "Frühe Kanonisten," 140.

17. Weigand (ibid.), following Kalb, *Studien,* 112, dates this around 1166–69; Gouron, "Sources," 68–69, points to the years 1165–66.

Stephen's prologue opens with a memorable scene where he likens his task to that of a host who has invited two guests with dissimilar tastes to a banquet.[18] They are a canonist and a theologian, both of whom Stephen hopes to satisfy with his work. In the remainder of his prologue, Stephen elaborates on a number of diverse themes. He spent a good bit of time considering the sources and categories of law, and with the latter reveals his knowledge of Ivo's Prologue. But while his treatment of legal categories was inspired by Ivo's work, Stephen's approach is original. Like other authors of *summae* he deals with Gratian's book within the framework of the *accessus,* another sign of his familiarity with the formulaic structure of Bolognese commentary.

During the late 1160s and throughout the 1170s other northern canonists followed Stephen's lead in composing *summae* on the *Decretum.* Another early example is the *Summa "Parisiensis."* Composed around 1170, perhaps at Paris (hence the title), this work cites Paucapalea and other opinions from unnamed Bolognese masters, and it also contains traces of influence not only from Rufinus and Stephen, but also from Peter Lombard's *Sentences.*[19] The *Summa "Antiquitate et tempore"* is an anonymous, fragmentary work treating only the distinctiones, and even here the commentary is incomplete. Composed in the 1170s, it was possibly written at Paris by someone who had earlier spent time at the cathedral school of Cologne.[20] The author drew upon

18. Kuttner, *Harmony from Dissonance,* begins by evoking this scene. See also Kalb, *Studien,* 29ff.

19. Terence P. McLaughlin, C.S.B., *The Summa Parisiensis on the Decretum Gratiani* (Toronto, 1952), xxxi–xxxiii, discussed the date of composition of the work and opted for around 1160, in opposition to Kuttner, *Repertorium,* 177, who placed it about a decade later. Brundage, *Medieval Canon Law,* 51, gives "shortly before 1170."

20. *Summae,* as in this case, can take their name from the work's open-

several works, including the *summae* of Rufinus, Stephen, and the *Summa "Parisiensis."* As in the latter, the preface to *Antiquitate et tempore* depends heavily on Stephen of Tournai's introduction to his *Summa.* It is, nevertheless, more than mere copying, for the writer offers his own distinctive view of canonistic jurisprudence, mixing older theory, such as material from Ivo's Prologue, with new insights.[21]

The Decretists helped in a significant way to define an evolving legal renaissance of the twelfth century. They were leaders in dealing with the great intellectual and religious issue of the day, that is, confronting problems of how to maintain, organize, and systematically interpret sacred tradition by accommodating disparate elements which are sometimes useful but often potentially disruptive. In an endeavor that paralleled the work of contemporary theologians like Peter Lombard, who struggled to systematize and interpret orthodox faith amidst the contradictions of inherited tradition, the Decretists worked to maintain harmony and achieve clarity in the canons. Yet this was no mere academic exercise. The Investiture Contest had made it clear how easily a variegated canonical tradition could contribute to fundamental disagreements about the nature of authority and power in the Christian world. The study of Roman law in the late eleventh and early twelfth centuries, facilitated by the

---

ing line or "incipit." On the date and place of the *Antiquitate et tempore,* see Stephan Kuttner and Eleanor Rathbone, "Anglo-Norman Canonists of the Twelfth Century," *Traditio* 7 (1949–51): 298–99, esp. n. 21 (rpt. in Kuttner, *Gratian and the Schools of Law* [see n. 14, above]), and S. Kuttner, "Gratian and Plato," in *Church and Government in the Middle Ages: Essays Presented to C. R. Cheney,* ed. C. N. L. Brooke et al. (Cambridge, 1976), 95ff. (rpt. in Kuttner, *The History of Ideas and Doctrines of Canon Law in the Middle Ages* [Variorum Reprint CS113; London, 1980]).

21. For the use of Cresconius's *Concordia* in the *Antiquitate et tempore,* although not in the preface, see n. 15 to chap. 2 (above).

recovery of the full corpus of the books inspired and commissioned by the Emperor Justinian in the sixth century, revealed a legal system based on ancient imperial authority, which assumed state supervision of the Church and hence could render the Church's own law vulnerable.[22] Within the vigorous intellectual environment of legal study in the twelfth century, the canons thus had to be interpreted, with contradictions eliminated and with the ancient texts of Roman law integrated into an ecclesiastical framework. Harmonization of the canons had to be achieved not at the expense of Roman law, but along with its assimilation, and the preface to the *Summa "Antiquitate et tempore"* offers a window onto an intellectual scene where that blending is very much in process.

The prefaces written by the Decretists not only introduce, in different ways, an ecclesiastical tradition of nearly a thousand years as mediated through Gratian, they also represent a variety of competing styles of legal interpretation. Behind their occasionally dense and repetitive terminology lies the ferment of new ideas. Out of the world which created the Decretists' *summae* — the world in which the medieval Romano-canonical "common law" was born — would come the sophisticated jurisprudence of their successors, the decretalists.

TRANSLATIONS

1. Preface to the *Summa* of Paucapalea on Gratian's *Decretum*, c. 1150. Ed. Johann Friedrich von Schulte, *Summa über das Decretum Gratiani* (Giessen, 1890; rpt. Graz, 1965), 1–3.

22. See Bellomo, *Legal Past,* esp. 37ff., and 58 ff.; Brundage, *Medieval Canon Law,* 202ff.; and Southern, *Scholastic Humanism,* 274–82.

Since it is known that in everything a finished product is made up of all its component parts but that the beginning of anything is the most important part,[23] it thus seems to me that it is not useless to reveal to those ignorant [of these matters] the procedure for conducting cases, the origin of ecclesiastical law, and its development. Indeed, a mind that is enthusiastic [to know] about the decrees of the holy Fathers and the statutes of councils will more easily understand their rulings. The procedure of pleading[24] seems to have been found initially in paradise, when the first man, questioned by the Lord about the sin of disobedience, used a counteraccusation and a shift of responsibility for the sin, and alleges that the guilt was placed on [his] wife saying, "The woman, whom you gave, gave to me and I ate."[25] Then it was handed down to us in the old law when Moses in his law says, "In the mouth of two or three witnesses, every word will stand."[26] In the New Testament, too, the Apostle Paul seems to have referred to cases and the process of settling them when he says in the letter to the Corinthians, "If, therefore, you have worldly judgments, constitute those of low esteem in the Church for the purpose of judging."[27] Thus it is clear from the text of each Testament that both secular laws and the decrees took the procedure of pleading from canonical scripture.

It remains to discuss the origin of law, but since some ecclesiastical laws are called natural, some written, some customary,

23. See Justinian, *Digest* 1.2.1; *Digesta,* ed. T. Mommsen and P. Krueger (Corpus Iuris Civilis 1; Berlin, 1928), 30.

24. For the equivalence of the term *Placitandi forma,* used here, to *litigandi forma,* see the preface to the *Summa* of Stephen of Tournai (below).

25. Genesis 3:12.

26. Deuteronomy 19:15.

27. 1 Corinthians 6:4.

it properly is asked when each one of these originated. Natural law, which is contained in the law and the Gospel, by which each is prohibited to inflict on another what he does not wish to be done to himself and is ordered to do to another what he wishes to be done to himself, began with the origin of the rational creature and obtains primacy among all laws. Indeed at no time does it vary, but remains immutable. The law of custom came into being after natural law,[28] when men, coming together in one place, started to dwell together, which is believed to have happened from that time when it is read that Cain built a city.[29] Although because of the small number of people, this law seems almost to have been snuffed out in the flood, it is thought rather, afterward, in the time of Nimrod, to have been changed and revived, since he together with some men began to overpower other men, and others in their own feebleness began to be subject to their authority. Whence in Genesis it is said about him, "Nimrod began to be a mighty hunter," that is, an oppressor and suppressor of people, whom he enticed to building the tower.[30]

But written constitution originated with the teachings which the Lord gave to Moses saying: "If your kin, a Hebrew man or a Hebrew woman, was sold to you and serves you for six years, in the seventh year you will set him free. And you never should allow him to depart empty-handed, but you will give a viaticum from your flocks, your threshing floor, and your winepress, with which the Lord your God blessed you. If, however, he is unwilling to go since he loves you and your house, taking an awl you will pierce his ear onto the door of your house, and he

28. To this point the word *ius* was being used for "law," but a switch now is made to *lex: post naturalem legem.*
29. Genesis 4:17.
30. Cf. Genesis 10:8–9 and 11:1ff.

will serve you forever. And you also will do likewise to a maid-servant."[31] Moses, before all others, spelled out this and other divine teachings in sacred writ to the Hebrew people.

Having shown the origin of divine constitutions, custom, and also of natural law,[32] decrees should now be considered, because first the decrees of the holy Fathers began to be formulated and then the statutes of councils. For after the apostles, the supreme pontiffs and holy Fathers, in whose power was the authority of formulating canons, succeeded one another without interruption. They did not have freedom, nonetheless, for convoking councils, until this was granted in the days of blessed Pope Sylvester. When, under the Emperor Constantine, Sylvester was hiding in the remote reaches of Mount Sirape, he was recalled by that emperor, who, thus converted through him and made most Christian, granted freedom of opening churches and of assembling Christians therein. And from that time bishops began to gather together to celebrate councils and to formulate decrees of councils. For under him [i.e., Constantine],[33] the holy Fathers assembling from the whole world in the Council of Nicaea condemned the perfidious Arian blasphemy, which the same Arius had asserted concerning the inequality of the Holy Trinity, namely, that different substances exist in the Trinity. The same holy synod defined through a confession that the Son of God is consubstantial to God the Father.

All decrees, both of councils and of the holy Fathers, have common subject matter—namely, ecclesiastical orders and offices, and legal cases about them. They also have a common intention, namely, to show what the ecclesiastical orders are, who ought to be promoted to them, what the duty of each is, what

31. Deuteronomy 15:12–17.
32. The word *ius* returns here; see n. 28, above.
33. Cf. for what follows the preface to the *Spanish Collection* (chap. 2).

the ecclesiastical offices are, to whom and through whom they should be conferred, and what way of life is proper in them. Concerning ecclesiastical cases, [they show] also in the presence of whom and through whom they should be handled. See then what the subject matter and the general intention of the decrees is.

The decrees themselves, however, are the subject matter of the Master producing this work.[34] For just as in the arts there is one subject matter of the art itself and another of the person occupied with it—for instance, the subject matter of the art of rhetoric is the question proposed for debate, but the subject matter of Cicero is that very art—even so the decrees have one subject matter, and the person setting them in order another, namely, that which already was indicated. His intention was to set the decrees in order and on the surface to reduce those which are dissonant to harmony. The method of proceeding is as follows. Setting out to compose this work he begins in the first part with the division of law[35] and custom, and then adding in a detailed manner their species, he probes each and every one. He continues with the purpose of making laws[36] and their function, then treats the number and order of the councils and which of their decrees ought to take precedence over others. Finally he comes to orders and to ecclesiastical offices, teaching to whom and through whom they ought to be conferred. Then he moves on to cases, of which he gives a large and varied number. With questions having been formulated about them, he alleges authorities on this side and that, in affirmation and negation, and always strives to reduce to harmony those things which seem at first glance to be opposed. In the end he treats fully the dedica-

34. I.e., Gratian.
35. The term is *ius*.
36. The term is *lex*.

tion of churches, the body and blood of the Lord, baptism, and also confirmation, and with these things concludes his treatise.

2. Preface to the *Stroma* of Rolandus on Gratian's *Decretum*, c. 1150, but after Paucapalea. Ed. Friedrich Thaner, *Summa Magistri Rolandi* (Innsbruck, 1874; rpt. Aalen, 1973), 1–4.

Here begins the extraordinary, very beautiful *Stroma* of Rolandus, culled from the corpus of decrees.

The merciful Father, desiring to satisfy the tripartite genus of humans with the fourfold genus of nourishment on the table of presentation, arranged, by means of the service of Moses, to make square a ternary. For he instructed Moses, saying:[37]

> You will make a table from acacia wood, of two cubits in length, one in width, and one and a half in height, covered with purest gold. And you will make for it four legs, and also four gold rings attached to the legs; and you will make two poles from acacia wood covered with purest gold, which will always be in the rings at the top of the table. You will make also a gold lip around it, and a polished gold crown of four fingers' height; and you will make a small gold cap which you will place on the crown. You will also place the twelve loaves of presentation, of finest wheat flour, on the table,

37. See Exodus 25 for the basis of the complicated if not opaque imagery with which Rolandus begins his text. Exploiting the rich Christian symbolism surrounding the numbers three and four, he uses God's instructions to Moses for the construction of the table in the tabernacle to exemplify how mysteries of sacred scripture can be interpreted. The central exegetical motif of "making square a ternary" is a motif of harmony and resolution, which Rolandus links to the work of the canonist. The authors are grateful to Kären Sorensen for her insights into this text.

with twelve gold covers over them, upon which the
purest frankincense will be placed. These loaves will
be on the table from Sabbath to Sabbath, and none
may be removed unless another is freshly added.

This table signifies sacred scripture, which is well called a table,
for just as a physical table holds bodily refreshment, a spiritual table serves spiritual nourishment. Likewise it is said to be
made of acacia wood, because it is constructed out of the strong
sayings and actions of the holy Fathers. And not undeservedly
it is called gilded, that is, adorned with the wisdom of heaven.
The length of two cubits signifies perseverance of action, which
is appropriately designated in two cubits, because it is chiefly
based in two virtues, namely, innocence and purity. This table
is also one cubit in length, because sacred scripture teaches perfection in charity, and one and a half cubits in height, because it
introduces the unity of the hope of heaven toward which it in-
doctrinates us, that is, the less perfect "halves." Further, it has
a gold lip around it, because the teaching of the sacred word is
furnished through the pure mouths of preachers.[38]

Through the crown, which is appropriately enjoined to be
made four fingers high, since one comes to it by the teaching of
the four evangelists and by the good work of the four principal
virtues, the merit of eternal reward is indicated; and in [this]
quaternary we understand faith in the Trinity, with purity of
works, through which we trust we are going to gain the prize
of eternal reward at last. This crown is worthily said to be polished, because there will be a variety of rewards for the merits of
diverse individuals, whence the Lord in the Gospel says: "In my
father's house, there are many mansions."[39] Through the gold

38. The wordplay cannot be adequately translated, i.e., *aureum* =
"gold," *ora* = "mouths."
39. John 14:2.

cap placed on top of the polished crown is understood the special quality of those who, it is not doubted, excel among others. Paul recognized this when he said: "It is better for me to die than that anyone should deprive me of my glory."[40] To this cap pertains that song which virgins alone can sing.[41]

Through the four legs the four senses of divine scripture are understood, namely, the historical, the allegorical, the moral, and the anagogical. By these four legs the table is supported, because by the above-mentioned four modes divine scripture is expounded. Through the four rings the books of the Gospels are signified. A ring lacks beginning and end, and for this reason the books of the Gospels are signified by the term rings, because they concern principally that which utterly lacks beginning and end. Through the two poles, we understand those preaching about two peoples.[42] They [the poles] are appropriately covered with purest gold, because they [the preachers] are adorned with the splendor of wisdom both in word and in deed. They ought always to be inserted into the rings, for it is necessary that their mind adhere closely to the lesson of the Scriptures, so that according to blessed Peter they may be always ready to render an account concerning that faith and hope which is in them.[43]

The twelve loaves designate the apostles and "apostolic men,"[44] who are rightly said to abide at the table, that is, in the contemplation and teaching of the Scriptures; [it is said] "from

40. 1 Corinthians 9:15.

41. Cf. Revelation 14:1–5.

42. The text reads *praedicationes,* which means "sermons," but what follows seems better served by translating the word essentially as "preachers," i.e., as if it were *predicatores.* For "two peoples," see the preface of Stephen of Tournai, below.

43. Cf. 1 Peter 3:15.

44. The words are *apostolicos viros,* which normally is translated as "popes," although here that rendering seems a bit forced, and probably the term could just as easily mean "bishops."

Sabbath to Sabbath," because from the Sabbath of hope, which happens now, until the Sabbath of splendor, which is hoped for in eternal life. No one is taken up, that is, removed, by judgment or by death unless another is immediately set in his place. Gold covers are placed on these loaves. In the gold covers are signified the hearts of preachers, lifted up through charity, in which the purest frankincense, that is, prayers, ought always to be contained. Indeed with the word frankincense prayer is understood, according to that verse: "Let my prayer be directed, etc."[45]

In this table, therefore, a ternary is clearly made square by sacred Scripture, that is, the faith of the holy Trinity is taught and fixed by the books of the four Gospels. Alternatively the ternary of the law, the prophets, and the psalms is made square, that is, it is expounded in four modes, namely, historically, allegorically, morally, and anagogically. Or again, through the ternary three types of people are understood: the righteous, the ordinary, and the evil, and through the quaternary we understand four ways of speaking of divine law. For all law consists in precepts, prohibitions, permissions, and counsels, and in fact the ternary, that is, the triple genus of people, is made square, that is, fully instructed, by the quaternary of counsel, permission, prohibition, and precept. Counsel is for the righteous, permission for the weak, and precepts and prohibitions for all, for there are precepts of things to be done, prohibitions of things to be avoided, permissions of things to be tolerated, counsels of nonobligatory or most excellent things. For this reason some, considering this fourfold character [of law], wondering especially at its dissonance and hindered by the weakness of their perceptions, believed that the statutes of the holy Fathers very often are mutually contradictory. For since certain things sometimes are tolerated which at other times are utterly prohibited,

45. Psalm 141 (140):2.

and other things are advised which are never commanded, they seem to have rational excuses for their doubt.

Master Gratian, therefore, considering the doubts of these men and desiring to advise those present and future, composed this work. In introducing it, the title, the reason for writing, for whom he wrote, the subject matter, the intention, [and] the method of composition are sought. This work received its title from the compiler, not because he was the author of the decrees, but because he collected them from diverse places into one location. The reason for writing was to demonstrate the concord of the canons, to reduce their difference to concord. We believe he wrote it particularly for his companions, or we may say he wrote it, as if providing for the whole world, for all who wish to apply themselves to the reading of the sacred canons. The subject matter consist of the things which it treats. Since, therefore, a concord of canons treats the business of churches by settling questions, by establishing concord in the canons, by reducing dissonance among them to harmony, these same things comprise its subject matter. The method of composition is this. He begins with a twofold law, namely, of nature and of customs, showing what the law of nature is and in what things it is contained. He continues with the similarity and difference of the same, adds the definition and the cause of legislation, [and] provides categorization and etymologies of terms. After this he treats the canons by setting out their differences, and so that this can be clarified in a better way, he treats councils. The remainder the prudent and solicitous reader should endeavor to discover for himself.

3. Preface to the *Summa* of Rufinus on Gratian's *Decretum*,
1164. Ed. Heinrich Singer, *Rufinus von Bologna,
Summa decretorum* (Paderborn, 1902; rpt. Aalen
and Paderborn, 1963), 3–5.

The canonical instruction of the sacrosanct Church is distributed commonly to all, but not equally to everyone. Just as in the house of the paterfamilias [46] all things are governed with one disposition, but individual duties are arranged in different ways, thus it was fitting that the host of the celestial Israelites set up camp with ordered watches, so that in the army of God even the least were useful, and in admiration of this strangers were made devout in a certain way and filled with awe.[47] Furthermore, that [example] of ancient times lives in memory, when King Solomon so governed the affairs of his house with the clearest organization that the Queen of Sheba, who had come from the ends of the earth to hear Solomon's wisdom, thought that, among other things, especially the cupbearers and the rest of the officials in the royal court should be admired.[48] This clearly was a prefiguration of the present time, when, with Christ who is our peace reigning, making both times one, the bedchamber of the bridegroom is so peacefully fruitful and so adorned with manifold splendor that even the pagans are amazed that the ranks and orders of the Church harmoniously differ, and differently harmonize, under so much rigor of justice and so much rectitude of discipline.

Constantly observing these arrangements of the celestial family, therefore, and admiring them as if we were one of the heathen, we tried to show, not in hands-on fashion from within, but through a latticework of canons as with a finger hover-

46. In Roman law the eldest male in the extended family, the *paterfamilias,* exercised ultimate legal authority over all members of the family: see Berger, *Encyclopedic Dictionary of Roman Law,* 620.

47. The imagery is obscure and cannot be tied to a biblical reference. "The celestial Israelites" seem to refer not to Israel but to the Church. David Weiss-Halivni kindly suggested that a combination of verses such as Exodus 33:7ff. and Numbers 1:52 may have been in Rufinus's mind.

48. Cf. 1 Kings 10.1ff.

ing at a distance, how the status of churches are determined, [and] how the dignities and offices of clerics are established and changed, hurrying along the long and spacious path of the decrees with giant steps. We do not desire to copy here inane conceptions of certain of our predecessors, but rather to create sufficiently useful and practical distinctions and expositions, which especially are supported by the very convincing reasons which predominate in the words of divine law. Yet we will not do this because, consumed with envy toward other clever men who labor in perhaps the same studies, we wish [their] rewards of praise to be impeded, but so that we can accommodate the various desires of readers, who, although they shuddered sometimes to consume the honeyed new wine of others, will taste our vintage with pleasure.

The dignity of the human creature before sin was conspicuous, as if suspended from threads, in these two things, namely, rectitude of justice and clarity of knowledge. Through the first it presided over human affairs; through the second it approached heavenly things. But as the envy of the Devil increased, the rectitude of justice was oppressed by the weight of perverted evil, and the light of knowledge was obscured by the gloom of error. Because, therefore, through the lameness of evil comes the blindness of ignorance, with the natural order as a reminder, it was necessary that through the practices of justice soundness of knowledge be restored. Thus since natural capacity was not completely extinguished in man, he began indeed to be concerned about how he stood apart from brute animals, as with the privilege of knowing and hence of living by law. And when man decided to gather with his neighbors and to take thought for things of mutual benefit, immediately, as if from within dead ashes, the sparks of justice produced honest and, to be sure, venerable precepts, which taught reduction of the savage and wild customs of men to graceful and honest ways, submission to convenants of concord, and establishment of secure pacts. These are called the laws of nations,[49] because nearly all nations practice them inasmuch as there are sales, contracts, exchanges, and similar things.

But since through these our infirmity was incapable of being restored to the fullness of good, merciful God, helping that law of living which he had written from the beginning in the heart of man, pronounced in ten written mandates a law received and presented through Moses, which we call the old law or the law of the synagogue. Yet because, as the Apostle witnesses, the law led no one to perfection,[50] when the fullness of time came God sent his Son, through whom he established for us the law of life, a perfect law converting souls,[51] which we designate with a joyous word, the Gospel. Then, God granting, when the Church grew and ranks and orders were set up in it, the Gospel seemed insufficient for those things which needed to be decided, and for disputes emerging among ecclesiastical persons which needed to be settled. Many things were added both by the apostles, by their vicars, and by other ministers of the Church —many things which, though they may be designated individually in a multitude of ways, nevertheless are all called by a single general word, that is, "canons."

All these Gratian included in this book as the subject matter for his work. His intention is to collect the canons, scattered far and wide in so many places, into an orderly arrangement, and to unify their contradictions through interspersed distinctions. The method of proceeding is this: he divides his book into three

49. The text is a mixture of singular and plural (*que quidem ius gentium appellantur*), translated as plural.

50. Cf. Hebrews 7:19.

51. Psalm 19 (18):8.

parts, the first of which he devotes to ecclesiastical ministries, the second to [ecclesiastical] business, and the third to ecclesiastical sacraments. In the first part he proceeds in the following way. First of all, describing the multiple forms and divisions of laws, he demonstrates the difference between natural law and other laws, and he explains clearly enough the origin, arrangement, and name of canon law. Afterward, running through the individual ecclesiastical orders up to the highest pinnacle of the pontifical office, he adequately treats who can be promoted into which orders, the entire treatise having been completed in one hundred distinctions.[52]

In the second part he works in this way. He divides it into thirty-six sections, which we call "cases." In these he considers first how crimes should be made known and judged. Then he treats the state of the Church and of clerics, considering immunity and privileges of the Church, its tithes and oblations, and also the special status of clerics, the vocation of monks, and how heretics, schismatics, and astrologers should be punished. Finally, he considers marriages: which are legitimate and which are polluted, designating how some married couples could or should be separated.

The order running through the last part is as follows. It is divided it into five distinctions, treating in the first the consecration of churches, in the second the sacrament of the Eucharist, in the third feasts, in the fourth baptism and confirmation, in the fifth fasts. With two chapters concerning the Holy Spirit, the work, having been completed, ends. How useful this book is will be apparent to those who read it studiously and with perseverance.

52. In the *textus receptus* of Gratian's work the first part comprises 101 distinctions.

4. Preface to the *Summa* of Stephen of Tournai on Gratian's *Decretum*, second half of the 1160s. Ed. Kalb, *Studien*, 113–20.

If you invite two guests to dinner, you will not serve the same fare to those who demand opposite things. With the one asking for what the other scorns, will you not vary the dishes, lest either you throw the dining room into confusion or offend the diners? A Latin embraces unleavened bread, a Greek leavened. If they approach the altar together neither despises the sacrifice of the other. I invited two men to a banquet, a theologian and a lawyer, whose tastes diverge toward different desires, since this one is delighted by tart things, and that one longs for sweets. Which of these should we offer, which should we withhold? Do you refuse what either one requests?

If I propose to discuss the laws which appear in the present work, one skilled in law will endure it with difficulty. He will wrinkle his nose, shake his head, thrust out his lip, and what he deems to be known to himself he believes to be unnecessary for others. If I shall have begun to narrate the sacred deeds of the Fathers of the Old and New Testaments, a theologian will consider these remarks as useless and will both charge our little work with prolixity and accuse it of ingratitude. Let them mutually come down a peg; let them join together in healthy agreement; let them pay the costs for something useful; let the theologian not reject the laws under the pretext of sacred history, nor should one skilled in law dismiss with the haughtiness of the laws[53] what is included in sacred history. I seek pardon for prolixity, although I would be unable to traverse the sea in the brief space of an hour, or to go around the lengthy span of the earth with a small step. With these things briefly having

---

53. The Latin reads *legum fastidio*, which also can mean "by the monotony of the laws."

been poured forth for washing the hands, let us serve the promised feast to the diners.

In the same city there are two peoples under the same king, and with the two peoples two ways of life, and with two ways of life two dominions, and with two dominions a double order of jurisdiction emerges. The city is the Church; the king of the city is Christ; the two peoples are the two orders in the Church, of clerics and of lay people. The two ways of life are the spiritual and the physical; the two dominions are the institutional Church and secular government; the double order of jurisdiction is divine and human law. Render to each its own and all will be in accord.

Many things are read variously and diffusely about human law in the constitutions of emperors and in the responses of legal experts. Consideration, however, should be given to divine law, and to its origin and development. Certain men say that divine law had its origin with the beginning of the world.[54] For when Adam was charged by the Lord with disobedience, hurling a counteraccusation against [his] wife, just as a defense in a suit, he turned rather into a prosecutor of [his] wife saying, "The woman whom you gave to me as a companion deceived me, and I ate."[55] And thus the process of litigating, or as we commonly say of pleading, seems to have arisen in paradise. Others say that procedure for judgments had its beginning with the old law. For in the law Moses says, "In the mouth of two or three witnesses every word should stand."[56] In the New Testament, too, the Apostle Paul says, "If, therefore, you have worldly judgments, constitute those of low esteem in the Church for the purpose of judging."[57] Others, beginning in a

54. For what follows cf. the preface to the *Summa* of Paucapalea, above.
55. Cf. Genesis 3:12.
56. Cf. Deuteronomy 19:15.
57. 1 Corinthians 6:4.

more circumscribed manner, take the origin of divine law from the primitive Church. For when the Church began to catch its breath under the Emperor Constantine, the persecution of the martyrs having ceased, the Fathers began to assemble safely to celebrate councils, and, due to a variety of ecclesiastical business, enacted therein and published diverse canons.

Some councils are general, some provincial. Those are called general which are celebrated in the presence of the lord pope, or his legate acting as his deputy, with bishops and other prelates of the Church convoked from everywhere. Provincial councils are those which are held in a province by its primate or any archbishop, with only his suffragan bishops convoked to it. The canons enacted in general councils extend their force universally to all churches, and those who do not observe them are held as transgressors. But those canons which are enacted in provincial councils do not go beyond the province, and do not bind people other than those who are subject to the jurisdiction of the comprovincial bishops. Whence it is the case even that some canons are called general, that is, those issued in a general council, others provincial, that is, those promulgated in a provincial synod. But among the general councils there are four principal ones which almost compare with the Gospels: Nicaea, Ephesus, Chalcedon, and Constantinople.

Properly, therefore, canons are what are promulgated in councils by the authority of many bishops. Decrees are what the lord pope constitutes and puts in writing about any ecclesiastical matter, with the cardinals being present and furnishing their authority. A decretal letter is what the lord pope writes as a response and transmits to any bishop, or to some other ecclesiastical judge, who is doubtful about some case and consults the Roman Church. Canons, nonetheless, indifferently are called decrees and, conversely, decrees canons. They are what exist both for handling and settling ecclesiastical business. In deciding ecclesiastical cases, nevertheless, this care ought to be taken, that evangelical precepts should indeed hold first place, and when they are inapplicable the dicta of the apostles, and then the four councils previously mentioned, after them the rest of the councils, and finally decrees and decretal letters. In last place come the words of the holy Fathers Ambrose, Augustine, Jerome, and others.

And these all make up the common subject matter of everyone dealing with divine law, but since sometimes they seem to be opposed to each other, this fourfold examination ought to be undertaken with regard to them. For some ecclesiastical constitutions are issued according to counsel, some according to precept, some according to permission or indulgence, some according to prohibition.[58] Those four [categories] relate to the four types of humans, since some are righteous, some are to be made righteous, some are weak, and some are reprobate. The [constitutions] which involve counsel are given for the righteous, those which involve precept for the ones to be made righteous, those which involve permission for the weak, those which involve prohibition for the reprobate. It is a counsel to sell everything and to give to the poor. To love God is a precept, to marry a permission; a prohibition is not to kill, not to commit adultery. Counsel is higher, permission lower, precept and prohibition are in the middle, as if, indeed, precept is based on counsel, but prohibition restrains permission. Counsel does not threaten punishment, but promises a reward. Permission does not promise a reward, but grants a remedy. The higher and the lower are voluntary, the two in the middle are necessary. For if you are so inclined you will not assent to a counsel nor accept a permission, but you will not resist a precept and a prohibition without punishment. For the things which we said were volun-

58. Cf. the Prologue of Ivo of Chartres (chap. 4).

tary, understand, nonetheless, [that this is so] before acceptance or vow. For after a vow of continence, which pertains to counsel, you are compelled to observe it, and after marriage, which pertains to permission, you are unable to divorce a wife.

Some precepts and prohibitions are, however, mutable, some immutable. Immutable precepts are those which, observed, confer salvation, but not observed rescind it, and which also were in place in every age, for example, "You will love the Lord your God, etc." Those which sometimes are observed, sometimes not, are mutable, for example, regarding circumcision and the Sabbath, or even those which the law never decreed but the diligence of later men discovered by reason of utility, such as this: "Shun the person who is a heretic after the first and second warning."[59] Likewise, immutable prohibitions are those against which it never was or will be permitted to act, just as: "You will not kill, you will not commit adultery." Mutable ones are of the sort which are altered with the quality of persons, and the necessity of the times or cases, for example, that a cleric after a lapse is not to be restored, and that the son of a priest is not to be ordained. But some permissions also are mutable. For it was sometimes permitted for a daughter to be married to an uncle, and for relatives in the fourth or fifth degree of consanguinity to be wed, which today is not allowed. The things which pertain to counsel at times also were otherwise. For although today it is a counsel of perfection to be a virgin, it seemed to be prohibited in the Old Testament, where it is read, "Cursed is the sterile woman and she who does not give birth," and again, "Cursed is he who does not leave his seed upon the earth."[60]

59. Titus 3:10.
60. These passages are not found in the Old Testament. For a conflation of the two by Gratian, see C. 32, q. 4, *dict. p.* c. 2, and on that text see the notes of the sixteenth-century Correctores Romani to Gratian (printed in Freidberg's edition, col. 1128).

Both in this work and in others, therefore, the rulings of the Fathers ought to be examined so that in them the reasoning of counsel, precept, permission, and prohibition is grasped. Likewise, attention should be paid to which rulings exist as judgments given, which as judgments which ought to be given. Those are called "judgments given" which announce that their transgressor already is excommunicated, and "judgments which ought to be given" which declare that he should be excommunicated. This is similar to those who are infamous, some of whom are infamous ipso facto by the law itself, some through a judgment.[61] Likewise certain rulings are given out of rigor, some out of dispensation or equity. Some, in addition, are given on account of time, some on account of place, some of person, some of necessity, that is, some are temporary, some local, some personal, some circumstantial. Whoever does not diligently pay attention to all these things will run into knots of perplexities. And, indeed, these aforesaid things concern all who are dealing with divine law.

About the book which we have at hand,[62] however, these things ought to be considered, namely, what is the subject matter of the compiler, what is his intention, what is the result of the intention, what is the cause of the work, what is the method of presentation, what is the internal division of the book? I should properly say that Gratian is the compiler of this work, not the author, for he brought together in this volume—that is, he arranged—rulings enacted by the holy Fathers. He was not their author or framer, unless perchance someone wishes to

61. The text reads *ad similitudinem infamiam, quorum quidam sunt infames ipso iure, quidam per sententiam,* where *infamiam* seems to be a misprint for *infamium;* see the edition by Johann Friedrich von Schulte, *Stephan von Doornick, Die Summa über das Decretum Gratiani* (Giessen, 1891; rpt. Aalen 1965), 4.

62. That is, Gratian's *Decretum.*

say that he is thus the author since he offered on his own in his dicta many things for clarifying and explicating the opinions of the holy [Fathers].

The canons are his subject matter: decrees and decretal letters, the difference of which you read above, and also the authorities of the holy Fathers who, although they did not have the right and power of making canons, have, nevertheless, a not unimportant place in the Church. His intention is to collect together different rules of different Fathers, which are called canons, and to reduce to harmony the contradictions which appear in them. The result, that is the utility: to know how to treat ecclesiastical cases according to the law of the canons, and how to settle canonically those which have been treated. The cause of the work is this: since through ignorance divine law had now fallen into disuse, and individual churches were governed by customs rather than by canons, Gratian, reflecting on that danger, collected diverse manuscripts containing rulings of the councils and the Fathers, and included in this volume the ones which seemed to him more serviceable for deciding cases.

The method of proceeding is as follows. First he sets out distinctions and differences of law, then the origins of constitution, laws, and canons, and afterward he moves to the order and number of councils, pointing out which of their decrees ought to take precedence over others. After this he comes to ecclesiastical offices and orders, teaching to whom they ought to be conferred and what way of life is proper in them. And also about orders: at what intervals of time they ought to be bestowed, and even how those who lapse can be restored. Finally he moves to cases, where he first points out what procedure ought to be followed about accusations, witnesses, and judicial proceeding in diverse ecclesiastical matters, finally coming to cases of marriage and dealing with them as needed. At the end he adds [things] about the consecration of churches, the sacrament of the body and blood of the Lord, baptism, and confirmation.

This book sometimes is divided according to the perspective of readers, sometimes according to the custom of scribes. Readers divide it into three parts, which is what Gratian seems to have wanted. The first part, which Gratian divided into 101 distinctions, extends up to the case treating simoniacs. The second, which is divided into 36 cases, each cut up into questions, goes from the first case to the treatise "on consecration"; the third, which they cut into 5 distinctions, from the treatise "on consecration" to the end. The first of these parts is devoted to ecclesiastical ministries, the second to ecclesiastical problems, the third to ecclesiastical sacraments. The custom of scribes divides the book into four sections, each fourth of which they call a part. They set up the first from the beginning to the first case, which is about simoniacs, the second from the first case to the thirteenth, which begins thus, "Parishioners,"[63] the third from there to C. 27, which is the first on marriage, the fourth from C. 27 to the end of the book. With these things as an introduction, let us come to the text.

5. Preface to the *Summa "Parisiensis"* on Gratian's *Decretum*, c. 1170. Ed. Terence P. McLaughlin, C.S.B., *The Summa Parisiensis on the Decretum Gratiani* (Toronto, 1952), 1.

Master Gratian, antonomastically called in this work "the Master," in place of an introduction prefaced his book with the following title, *Concord of discordant canons,* by which he concisely sets forth subject matter and intention. As an authority maintains, unless it would be changed by some distinction, nothing contradictory, nothing repetitive, nothing of

63. *Diocesani,* i.e., *dict. ante* C. 13.

similarity is found in the laws,[64] whence how much less should this have occurred in the canons? Thus we explicate "of discordant canons" not as those which are, but as those which seem to be. Certain canons, nonetheless, are similar if they would be changed by a distinction, that is, if something is added in one which never is found in the other. Likewise certain canons in no way agree, for example, that of Jerome and that of Augustine, one of which, namely Jerome, says that a man is not monogamous who chose one wife before baptism and another after baptism, but Augustine affirms the opposite. *Solution:* Even if orthodox Fathers are opposed, yet the canons are not. For what Jerome says here is not received as a canon. Indeed the opinion of Augustine prevails, confirmed by Pope Leo.[65]

6. Preface to the *Summa "Antiquitate et tempore"* on Gratian's *Decretum,* 1170s. Ed. Johann Friedrich von Schulte, *Die Geschichte der Quellen und Literatur des canonischen Rechts von Gratian bis auf die Gegenwart,* 1 (Stuttgart, 1875; rpt. Graz, 1956), 245–50.[66]

In ancient days and over the course of time, public and human law exists before ecclesiastical and divine law. Whence the voice of imperial majesty thundered: "Our laws do not disdain to copy the sacred canons."[67] First, therefore, it should be seen what public law, and afterward what ecclesiastical law, treats, and whether they treat the same things or not, and what

64. This "authority" has not been found.

65. These texts are found in Gratian, D. 26, cc. 1–3, although c. 3 is from Pope Innocent I, not Leo.

66. The work is erroneously ascribed there to Rufinus, but see Kuttner, *Repertorium,* 178.

67. Justinian, *Novella* 83.1 (= Auth. 84; Coll. VI, tit. 11): *Iustiniani Novellae,* ed. R. Schoell and W. Kroll (Corpus Iuris Civilis 3; Hildesheim, 1988), 410.

the difference between them is. Then: what is the intention of those who have the power of establishing public law, and what utility exists in so doing? Likewise, what is the intention of those who have the power of making ecclesiastical law, and what utility exists in doing this? Finally, we will state what Gratian's subject matter is in this work, what [his] intention is, what [his] method of proceeding is, what the utility of the work is, and other things pertinent to these.

Public law treats three matters: persons, things, and actions. Persons acquire and are acquired. Free persons, children under paternal power,[68] and even serfs, acquire; servile persons are acquired. Likewise, some persons are free, some freed, some servile, [that is] serfs of servile condition. Further, some persons are under [someone's] power, others are not. Therefore all laws which deal with these matters treat persons.

Things are acquired and do not acquire. Sometimes they are acquired as a totality, as all the possessions of someone through a will, sometimes in parts, for example, through a legacy or trust, or through purchase or sale. Even in natural law things are acquired, for example, wild animals, fish, birds, gems on the seashore, and things of this sort, which are granted to those taking possession of them. Things acquired are kept, lost, or alienated. Not only someone who loses [something] is said to lose [it], but [also] he who releases a thing from himself. Therefore all laws which speak about acquiring, keeping, or losing things or possessions treat things.

A third category of law concerns actions. For repeatedly it happens that what is ours is denied to us; thus by divine command actions were born, by which we can wrest away from the unwilling those things which are ours or are owed to us. Those

68. In Roman law the term *Filii familias* designates children under paternal power; see Berger, *Encyclopedic Dictionary of Roman Law,* 472.

who do not obey a constitution are compelled to obey by the sentence of a judge. Therefore all laws which concern actions to be pursued, namely, about the process of judgments, examination by a judge, [and] promulgation of a decision, pertain to actions. From these comments one can understand what public law concerns.

Similarly, ecclesiastical law concerns persons to the extent that they are subject to religious obligations, to ecclesiastical lordship, or are under ecclesiastical jurisdiction. But if it sometimes concerns other persons, this is done in consideration of piety, as when a priest admonishes an emperor who is under neither his lordship nor his jurisdiction, nor subject to religious obligations. Likewise, it concerns the movable and immovable possessions[69] of the persons just mentioned, and if it concerns other things, it does so in consideration of piety, for example, in regard to alms that should be given. Ecclesiastical law does not concern actions, since these are fully and sufficiently treated in secular laws. But the sacred canons certainly embrace those things contained in secular laws, unless [such items] are contrary to them.

Divine law specifically concerns articles of faith, ecclesiastical persons and their possessions, and the sacraments—which are seven in number, namely, baptism, confirmation, extreme unction, the Eucharist, marriage, ordination, and penance. But is human law concerned with these things which specifically and chiefly divine law treats? Indeed it is, though neither with great dignity nor thoroughness. It says that there must be no dispute about the doctrine of the Trinity, but this should be understood as meaning "on the street" or with some heretic. For these matters ought to be handled with great reverence

69. For this distinction between *res mobiles* and *res immobiles,* see Berger, *Encyclopedic Dictionary of Roman Law,* 678-79.

and fear or otherwise not at all. It thus prohibits public dispute about the Trinity and imposes penalties on disputants according to the condition of the person. The most sacred emperors also deal with churches, oratories, and houses of religious, both their privileges and their community, that is, the congregation of the faithful. For they say: no one unwilling can be dragged away if he fled to a place of religion; no one should be buried or entombed in that church, that is, unless he has a special privilege of status or piety. Further: the goods of a church can neither be sold nor alienated, except in great necessity and with a clearly determined purpose, nor should guests be received there, and other things in this vein. And it is conceded and granted by the most sacred emperors that anyone is able to confer his goods on churches.

In acquiring, the Church also enjoys a privilege. No private person acquires dominion by purchase or donation unless the object has been handed over to him, but the Church, if it buys something, or if it receives a donation, acquires dominion even if no delivery follows. It also has the right to mortgage.[70] In retaining its possessions the Church enjoys a privilege too, for it holds them immune from any extraordinary and humble obligations.[71] Extraordinary obligations are things like payments which are made for building roads and bridges; humble obligation: that is, the burden of compulsory service,[72] such as to serve in transporting dung, and things of this sort. The Church is completely free from any extraordinary and humble obligations, unless they would pertain to what is beneficial and pious, to the distribution and collection of alms, and similar things.

70. For the term used here, *actio hypothecaria*, see Berger, *Encyclopedic Dictionary of Roman Law*, 490.
71. *Sordida munera;* see Berger, *Encyclopedic Dictionary of Roman Law*, 589.
72. *Angaria;* see Berger, *Encyclopedic Dictionary of Roman Law*, 362.

Likewise, the Church was privileged by imperial grant in that a private person is excluded by prescription after ten, twenty, or thirty years [from reclaiming a thing held by another],[73] or five years or some other period for a minor; the Church only is excluded by prescription after forty years. The Roman Church alone enjoys a time of one hundred years.

Public law also concerns ecclesiastical persons, for example, bishops and other clerics. For it is said that a bishop by his consecration is liberated completely from servile condition, and that he has the power to alienate possessions which came to him before his episcopacy. But he is in every way compelled to preserve the other things of the Church or to expend them in pious causes. It speaks of clerics who can take wives, namely, doorkeepers, lectors, exorcists, but not acolytes and any higher order. Yet divine law permits an acolyte to take a wife. Here, therefore, divine and human law disagree, and likewise in this, that human law, speaking about marriage, says that a nobleman is not able to contract marriage with the daughter of an inn-keeper. From these [examples] one can note which things this or that law treats, and in which respects they differ.

It remains to see what the intention is of those who have the power of making human law, and what the utility is in doing this, and similarly for divine law. The intention of the former is to impose law on subjects, to enjoin what ought to be observed, to supply what is lacking, to remove what is superfluous, to interpret what is obscure, and to deal legally with things which wreck transactions. Their utility is to teach the ignorant [and] to restrain the rebellious and the negligent, so that thus they can be made good men both by the promise of rewards and by fear of penalties. The intention of the canons is this. To show

73. For *praescriptio* in Roman Law, see Berger, *Encyclopedic Dictionary of Roman Law,* 645.

which person should rule over whom, and to whose jurisdiction one should submit. Regarding the faith, to show what should be believed, and how heretical evils should be eliminated. Regarding possessions, to show how one acquires, and how they can be retained and alienated. Regarding the sacraments, to show who can confer baptism, to whom, and how; similarly concerning confirmation, unction, and the Eucharist; to show which persons can contract marriage, when, and how; to show for what, how, and by whom penance should be done; to show to whom, and through whom, which order should be conferred; to show through whom, in whose presence, for which crime, who should be demoted from which order. The utility of the canons is to know these things and to settle canonically questions which arise.

Thus with these as a prelude, it ought to be considered what the subject matter, intention, method of proceeding, utility, and title of Master Gratian are. The subject matter is twofold, both what he selects and what he treats. He selects from the writings of the Old and New Testaments, from the acts of councils, from the writings of orthodox Fathers, from the letters of the supreme pontiffs, and from the laws of the emperors. Likewise he selects precepts, prohibitions, admonitions, and indulgences or permissions.[74]

Admonitions concern the highest matters, precepts and prohibitions things that are necessary, indulgences lesser goods and venial sins. Admonitions promise a reward to the obedient; they should not bring punishment on one who does not obey, for example: "If you wish to be perfect, go and sell all you possess."[75] See, this is left to the will of the individual. Precepts and prohibitions, such as "You will love God," "You will love

74. Cf. the influence of the Prologue of Ivo of Chartres (chap. 4).
75. Matthew 19.21.

your neighbor," "You will not kill or commit adultery," declare eternal glory for those who observe, and eternal punishment for those who disregard. Indulgences agree with admonitions in this respect, that they do not promise punishment to the one not observing nor a reward to the one observing. But they differ in this: indulgences are about lesser goods such as marriage, and about venial sins such as intercourse in place of incontinence, which is excused through the benefits of marriage so that it is not sinful.

Some precepts and prohibitions are mutable, some immutable, or, if I may use the language of civil law, some have a perpetual reason for prohibition, others do not. Concerning precepts, you will say that some have a perpetual reason for immutability, others do not. Admonitions and indulgences, therefore, are not necessary; but the law, promising eternal life to those observing and eternal death to those disregarding, decreed immutable precepts, nor do they admit any dispensation by which they could be changed. Mutable precepts are those which later diligence and not the eternal law decreed, such as: "Shun a heretic after a second and a third warning."[76] Such things have been instituted not for the purpose of gaining eternal life, but rather for holding onto this life more securely. For it is not evil in itself to speak with a heretic, but he should be avoided because evil conversations corrupt good morals. Dispensations allow things. For example: he who does public penance should not remain a cleric, nor be made one if he was not already. This was instituted because of certain men who feigned penance in order to be promoted more quickly to great dignities; but it can be changed through dispensation. Likewise, the sons of clerics are prohibited from advancing to orders so that their parents might be kept from sins, yet if they lived

76. Titus 3:10.

as professed religious, they are permitted by dispensation to advance. Therefore precepts which are decreed by eternal law, and prohibitions which prohibit vices, do not admit of dispensation in any way; others do. One should note some examples. In the Gospel, the Lord prohibited the disciples from having a wallet and a staff, but later conceded [them].[77] The Apostle planned to visit the Corinthians, but then changed his mind.[78] Out of prudence the supreme pontiffs also sometimes interdict, sometimes concede, the same things.

Thus is described whence Gratian selects, and which things, and how they agree and disagree among themselves. These items, therefore, from which he selects, are Gratian's subject matter, that is, the body of material [i.e., the canons] from which derive those which he picks from the rest. For[79] other men treated persons, things, and sacraments. He, however, treats the canons, by establishing a threefold teaching: moral, judicial, and sacramental. The moral [is that] by which he teaches mores, for example, about the distribution of alms, about penance, about confession, and things of this sort. The judicial shows how judgments should begin, proceed, and conclude. Finally, the sacramental concerns baptism, marriage, and the like.

Gratian's intention is this: to remove unjust discord from the canons, if it appears. For he first presents those things which seem contradictory in the canons and the writings of orthodox [Fathers]. Then, by presenting his dicta he reduces them to harmony.

77. Cf. Luke 10:4 and 22:35-36. The *sacculum* ("sack") of the Gospel has become *baculum* ("staff") in the *Summa*.

78. Cf. Acts 20:1ff., and 2 Corinthians 1:15ff.

79. The transition is rough, but the author is now moving, briefly, to the second part of the twofold characterization given above of Gratian's subject matter, i.e., the things treated.

After the aforesaid, it remains to explain the method of proceeding and the order which Master Gratian uses in order to determine the utility of that book and to show what its title means. First, therefore, it is a question of the origins of human and divine law. Both are categorized according to their particular forms, and similarities and differences are variously designated among the general categories and particular forms. Then ranks, offices, and dignities are classified: which rank should be conferred to whom, through whom; and also who can be removed, where, when, from what, through whom, for what crime, and how; and what should pertain to what office. Similarly: which dignity should be conferred to whom, by which electors, by conferral of whom, in which place, and in whose presence. It also is shown who is able to move up, and from what to what. Then Master Gratian treats judgments, whether actions or accusations, by showing how they should be instituted, examined, and concluded. Finally, he treats the sacraments. We are able even to explain his method of proceeding more distinctly because Master Gratian divided his book into three parts. In the first part, which is divided into different distinctions, he treats persons. In the second, which is [divided] into cases [he treats] judgments, transactions, and also possessions; in the third, the sacraments. But how he would treat this or that has become clear from the foregoing.

From these it is also clear which part pertains to which category of teaching. The first pertains to the moral category, in which it is shown how one should live and who is fit for which order. The second pertains to the judicial category, the third to the sacramental. Yet in the third section it is not a question of all the sacraments. On the contrary ordination, which is divided into seven [ranks] and is one of the sacraments, is treated in the first part, and similarly, in the second, penance and marriage. For since dispute frequently occurs about this [i.e. marriage], in treating it Master Gratian sets forth a topic, formulates questions, brings forward on each side conflicting arguments, and then brings them into harmony, and thus adequately handles marriage. In the final part it is a question of the remaining sacraments, namely, baptism, confirmation, unction, and the body of the Lord. Whence it is clear that a kind of summary of the content of all theology is contained in this book, and for one knowing this book completely, knowledge of the entirety of "the sacred page" cannot be lacking.

The book is useful for knowing how mores should be taught, how judgments should be concluded, and what should be thought concerning the sacraments. Likewise utility is able to be assigned from intention. For if the intention of the Master is to remove discord from the canons if it appears, the utility of this book is to know how to reduce to harmony canons which appear to disagree.

The title is of this sort. Just as he prefaces each and every canon with a title or rubric by which he opens up the purpose and meaning of the full canon, thus even he prefaces the whole work with the title "Concord of Discordant Canons," that is to say: "I intend to show, elucidate, and point out [the concord of discordant canons]." He speaks of discordant canons, not because they really are discordant, but because they seem to be. For since some things are said according to precept, some according to admonition, some according to indulgence, considered according to the shell and surface of the text they seem contradictory, but when examined more deeply although diverse, they are not adverse.

Behold, the things which we proposed to be considered as an introduction have reached their conclusion. For we spoke about what human and divine laws treat and whether or not they treat the same things, the difference between them, the intention of those making public law, the utility in doing this, and, similarly, the intention of those making divine law and the utility in doing that. Then we spoke of Gratian's subject matter in this work, the intention, method of proceeding, utility, and the title. Finally, before we come to the text itself, it should be known that Master Gratian [made] a compilation, and those things which he places here he selected by compiling them from other writings. Nevertheless he frequently inserts his dicta, either for summarizing things said diffusely, or for providing a transition for things to be said later, or for proposing a new question, or for offering some solution. It should be known, nonetheless, that after this work was composed another man, Paucapalea by name, applying no less diligence for understanding the canons, so that the distribution of contradictions and harmonizations could be made clearer, divided the first part into one hundred and one or two distinctions. He did not divide the second part, since it was already adequately divided into cases, topics, and questions by Master Gratian, but he divided the third part into five distinctions. Furthermore, he also appended certain canons which, although not of less authority than others placed here, are, nevertheless, not studied, since they were not included by the principal author of this book.[80]

80. This reference must be to the texts designated as *paleae* found scattered throughout Gratian's *Decretum,* which are additions to the original work, perhaps as noted here by Paucapalea; see Brundage, *Medieval Canon Law,* 190–91.

6

Papal Decretals and Their Collectors:
1190–1245

The great collection of canon law promulgated in 1234 by Pope
Gregory IX (1227–41) is the last work discussed in this volume.
The Gregorian Decretals were compiled at the pope's request,
and in the bull *Rex pacificus* he authorized their use in schools
and courts, to the exclusion of all other compilations of decretals.[1] This work forms the second part of what came to be
termed the Corpus of Canon Law (*Corpus iuris canonici*)[2] and
is an official papal compilation.

Decretal letters were not new vehicles of papal authority.
They were sent out by popes at least as early as the fourth century, were prominent in such works as the collections of Dionysius Exiguus and the Spanish Collection, and offered a form
of law which was exploited in the ninth century by the forg-

1. Reference to papal bulls is according to the "incipit," that is, the
opening Latin words. For a general survey of the decretal collections, see
Chodorow, "Law, Canon."

2. In the fifteenth and sixteenth centuries the term *Corpus iuris canonici*
came to designate a set of published works, i.e., Gratian's *Decretum,* the
three official compilations—the Gregorian Decretals, the Decretals of
Boniface VIII (the *Liber sextus*), the Clementine Decretals promulgated
by John XXII—private collections of decretals called *extravagantes* (those
outside the three major compilations), and sometimes other material as
well (see Stickler, *Historia,* 274). This body of law was analogous to the
early printings of Justinian's compilations of Roman law titled the Corpus
of Civil Law (*Corpus iuris civilis*): see Brundage, *Medieval Canon Law,* 56,
199–200.

ers known as Pseudo-Isidore. The predominance of decretals in Latin canon law after the middle of the twelfth century depends on both the evolution of canonical jurisprudence as sketched in chapter 5, and the success of the papacy in moving its claims as head of the Church from theory into practice. Questions increasingly came to papal attention from litigants and judges who realized the advantage of having disputes heard in a central court, removed (and even distant) from the local scene. The popes readily offered solutions to such cases and assigned ad hoc juridical responsibility to specified judges. These delegated judges might or might not be from the litigants' district, but they were armed with decretals providing instructions on what to do. The work of Gratian could be a starting point for treating cases, but the "old" laws compiled therein, even with Gratian's commentary, often were inadequate for the needs of the Church in the later twelfth century.[3] New cases required new laws, and although synods—including papal councils—legislated on many issues throughout this period, it was by means of decretal letters especially that the papacy took control of and transformed canon law in the High Middle Ages.

Not all churchmen applauded an increasing papal occupation with legal issues. Bernard of Clairvaux, in his admonitions to his fellow Cistercian, Pope Eugene III, is but one critic of that trend, and not the most vociferous.[4] Furthermore, the grow-

---

3. For the notion of the decretals as "new law," see the discussion below of the preface to Bernard of Pavia's compilation of decretals.

4. See Bernard of Clairvaux, *Five Books on Consideration: Advice to a Pope,* trans. John D. Anderson and Elizabeth T. Kennan (Cistercian Fathers Series 37; Kalamazoo, 1976), 29–32. See also Duggan, *Decretal Collections,* 26. For Stephen of Tournai's reference to the "unmanageable forest" (*silva intractabilis*) of decretals see Duggan, *Decretal Collections,* nn. 1 and 4 (the text is in J.-P. Migne, *Patrologia Latina,* 211 [Paris, 1855], 516–18, *ep.* 251). Fransen, *Les Décrétales,* 14, n. 4, noted that Stephen cited

ing volume of correspondence, the political tensions of Alexander III's pontificate and his lengthy absences from Rome, and the omnipresent danger of forged or tampered documents contributed to a situation in which the papal chancery could barely keep up with the torrent of lawsuits and with its own paperwork.[5] New law did not automatically bring with it mechanisms for keeping track of legal activity.

Questions as to what constituted a decretal, and how widely it was applicable, were important topics of discussion among canonists.[6] As long as a given decretal letter did not circulate beyond its destination, it remained an ad hoc statement. But letters often bore multiple addressees, and copies of decretals could readily travel elsewhere. Such texts could be added as supplements to existing law books, especially to Gratian, and in the second half of the twelfth century papal decretals were being organized into compilations made up overwhelmingly of decisions from recent popes. The earliest were unsystematic accumulations of the letters in their entirety, transcribed in chronological order or simply haphazardly. But even as collections became systematic they remained, without papal authorization, private books of juridical guidelines—Gérard Fransen

---

no recent decretal in his *Summa*. See also the *Gospel According to the Mark of Silver*, and other satirical texts, in John A. Yunck, "Economic Conservatism, Papal Finance, and the Medieval Satires on Rome," in *Change in Medieval Society*, ed. Sylvia L. Thrupp (New York, 1964), 73–74.

5. For problems engendered by the increased activity in papal courts in the twelfth century, see Stanley Chodorow, "Dishonest Litigants in the Church Courts, 1140–98," in *Law, Church, and Society: Essays in Honor of Stephan Kuttner*, ed. Kenneth Pennington and Robert Somerville (Philadelphia, 1977), 187–206.

6. See Duggan, *Decretal Collections*, 32ff. Fransen, *Les Décrétales*, 7 and 12, noted that anything found in collections of decretal letters came to be called a decretal.

termed them compilations of "selected jurisprudence"[7]—and their import depended on diffusion and, especially, reception in the schools, where they could be communicated to students, debated, and glossed.

Early collections of decretals can be seen as analogous, in form if not in size, to the great chronological works of Church law from earlier centuries. The need for more ready access, in both cases, led to rearrangement of contents into systematic works. From late in the pontificate of Alexander III compilers began to arrange decretals under titles, which were then grouped into books. Concomitant with this shift in organization were editorial developments which complicate the use of these texts as historical sources by modern scholars. The canonists were interested in legal content and hence pared decretals to eliminate what was not of canonical significance. In so doing, historical context often was lost, proper names dropped or mangled, circumstances of a case truncated, and complex decretals dealing with several subjects cut up and distributed under different titles, with little or no obvious connection remaining among the severed parts.

In compiling the Decretals of Pope Gregory IX, Raymond of Peñafort used five systematic collections for texts before the time of Gregory. These five works are called the the Five Old Compilations (*Quinque compilationes antiquae*), characterized thus in respect to the Gregorian Decretals which superseded them.[8] They originated between the years 1190 and 1226

7. "recueils de jurisprudence choisie": Fransen, *Les Décrétales,* 35.

8. These five collections had numbers by the mid-thirteenth century at latest: Stephan Kuttner, "Johannes Teutonicus, das vierte Laterankonzil und die Compilatio quarta," in *Miscellanea Giovanni Mercati* (Studi e testi 125; Vatican City, 1946), 5.630ff. (rpt. in Kuttner, *Medieval Councils, Decretals, and Collections of Canon Law* [Variorum Collected Studies Series

and predominantly transmit decretals promulgated from Alexander III to Honorius III (1216–1227), although a smattering of texts from before Gratian also can be found, primarily in Comp. I. Canons from the Lateran councils of 1179 and 1215 are also included in Comp. I and Comp. IV, respectively. Two of these five collections—Comp. III and Comp. V—were officially approved papal works, and as far as is known the former is the first collection in the Church's history accorded such recognition.

These five compilations were not the only such works made during these years, nor are they the only significant ones. With one exception, however, the seven prefaces translated in this chapter focus on them and the Gregorian Decretals.[9] Comp. II and Comp. IV contain no introductions, nor were they authorized by papal bulls, but Bernard of Pavia composed a preface both to Comp. I and for his own *Summa* on that work. Comp. III and Comp. V circulated with bulls of authorization from Innocent III and Honorius III, respectively. The bull

---

CS126; London, 1980; 2d ed. 1992]). In general, see Brundage, *Medieval Canon Law,* 194–96.

9. Other items could fit here, e.g., the *Collectio Romana* of decretals of Innocent III compiled by Bernardus Compostellanus (see below) ends with a somewhat technical epilogue, with references to specific decretals: Heinrich Singer, *Die Dekretalensammlung des Bernardus Compostellanus antiquus* (Sitzungsberichte der Kais. Akademie der Wissenschaften in Wien, Philosophisch-Historische Klasse 171.2; Vienna, 1914), 114–15. The corpus of decretal collections is vast and still being sorted and analyzed: see Fransen, *Les Décrétales,* esp. 37ff.; Walther Holtzmann, C. R. Cheney, and Mary G. Cheney, *Studies in the Collections of Twelfth-Century Decretals* (Monumenta iuris canonici, Corpus collectionum 3; Vatican City, 1979); and esp. Duggan, *Decretal Collections,* 2ff., who warns of forming a distorted picture of the scope of medieval canon law by looking only at "a small number of well-known compilations" (p. 3).

Rex pacificus by Gregory IX has already been mentioned; and the preface of Bartholomew of Brescia to his revision of the standard (or "ordinary") gloss (*glossa ordinaria*) on Gratian's *Decretum* depends on the Gregorian Decretals, revision of the gloss being necessary after 1234 when *Rex pacificus* made earlier books of decretals obsolete. Added to this set of closely interrelated material is the preface to the collection of Innocent III's decretals assembled by Rainier of Pomposa, which offers a remarkable perspective on Pope Innocent and his legislation.

Comp. I was not the first systematic assembly of decretals, but its organization established a pattern for many later collections, certainly for the remaining four "old compilations" as well as for the Gregorian Decretals. Surviving in different versions made between 1190 and 1198, the work contained decretals of popes through Clement III (1188–91).[10] It was organized into five books whose themes were summarized, very broadly, by the following mnemonic snippet:[11] *Iudex* ("Judge"), *Iudicium* ("Judgment" — the first two books primarily treat sources of law, offices, and canonical procedure); *Clerus* ("Clergy"), *Connubium* ("Marriage"), and *Crimen* ("Crime," i.e., offenses and canonical penalties). Each book was subdivided into titles. Some details are known of the life of the author, Bernard of Pavia. He studied and taught at Bologna, was for a time at the papal curia, and was subsequently named provost at Pavia in 1187, where, as indicated in the preface to Comp. I, he assembled his collection (at least its first redaction). In his later career Bernard succeeded the canonist Johannes Faventinus in the episcopacy at Faenza in 1191 and in 1198 returned to Pavia as bishop, where he died in 1213.[12]

10. For dating see Fransen, *Les Décrétales*, 23.

11. Duggan, *Decretal Collections*, 22.

12. See F. Liotta, "Bernardo da Pavia," *Dizionario Biografico Italiano*, 9 (Rome, 1967), 279–84; Weigand, "Frühe Kanonisten," 143–44; and

The preface to Comp. I is noteworthy for its wealth of biblical citations; the collection itself includes material from the Bible, especially Exodus and Leviticus.[13] Bernard clearly stated his purpose: he hoped to provide, especially for students, a "richer supply" of both allegations (i.e., "prooftexts" to be cited on specific points) and judgments—"richer," presumably, than anything else which was available. He also expressed his desire to honor God and the Roman Church with his work. Assembling a book of papal decretals is an obvious sign of the latter intention, and perhaps his use of the Bible as a source of law was a specific aspect of Bernard's hope to accomplish the former.

From the perspective of the Gregorian Decretals, the Five Old Compilations gave parameters to decretalist history, but Bernard in his preface to Comp. I employed another chronological division which also was fundamental for medieval canon law: a division between the "old" and the "new" law. Bernard was referring to the demarcation which was created by Gratian's work. The new law is the law of papal decretals; the old law is what preceded and what was sifted and preserved by Gratian. This perspective also is clear in the title of Bernard's work. The collection came to be called the First Compilation, but the author's title was Breviary of Extravagant [Decrees] (*Breviarium extravagantium*). That is to say, Bernard assembled a collection of "vagrant texts" which were "wandering around outside of" Gratian (*extra vagantia*).[14]

Some of the same considerations apply to the introduction to Bernard's commentary on the Breviary, composed, as he revealed therein, during his episcopate at Faenza. Biblical allu-

---

Brundage, *Medieval Canon Law,* 210–11 (where "1178" is a misprint for "1187").

13. Gaudemet, *Les Sources,* 125.

14. See Fransen, *Les Décrétales,* 19, n. 10, on the term *extra.*

sions again are prominent, as is the intention to provide a work useful for study, for locating allegations, and for settling cases. The notion of extravagant canons reappears, with specific references to items contained in the register of Pope Gregory I, in Burchard of Worms, and in the "corpus of canons,"[15] which were excluded by Gratian. Using the schematic headings of "subject matter," "intention," "utility," and "order of proceeding" (see in the preceding chapter for the *accessus* employed by Paucapalea and other Decretists), Bernard reflected briefly on the goals and the format of Comp. I.

The pontificate of the aged Celestine III (1191–98) did not produce many decretals of interest to canonists, and although unsystematic compilations were made of texts from both Clement III and Celestine III, there were no new systematic books of decretals until the reign of Innocent III (1198–1216).[16] Innocent's pivotal role in the history of the medieval Church is well known, but important disagreements persist about his education, aims, and the bases on which he devised his policies.[17] However those issues are viewed, Innocent's reign marked a new departure in papal administration and in the history of canon law. From the beginning, he was responsible for innovative decisions which commanded the attention of canonists, and important new collections of decretals appeared in the first

15. See section on format in chap. 1.

16. The authors are grateful to Kenneth Pennington for his kindness in allowing them to see portions of his unpublished chapter on decretal collections for the *History of Medieval Canon Law* (ed. Wilfried Hartmann and Kenneth Pennington [Catholic University of America Press, forthcoming]), on which parts of this discussion are based. Pennington also called our attention to the preface for Rainier of Pomposa's collection of decretals.

17. Many of these questions are treated, with reference to current literature, in Jane Sayers, *Pope Innocent III* (London, 1994).

decade of the thirteenth century. The first was by Rainier of Pomposa, another figure about whom little is known.[18] The monastery of St. Maria de Pomposa is located in the diocese of Comacchio, and it is uncertain whether or not Rainier taught in the law schools. He had, nevertheless, contacts at the papal court, for his collection was dedicated to a monk named John who was papal chaplain, and he used Innocent's registers in assembling decretals.

In his preface, Rainier stated that he selected material from the first three years of the register, although in fact his selections extended into the fourth year, to May or June of 1201. His work probably can thus be dated in the second half of that year. He extolled Innocent's legal reputation and noted, as is also recorded in the contemporary Deeds of Pope Innocent III (*Gesta Innocentii papae tercii*), that people journeyed to the papal court to experience firsthand this legal acumen.[19] Rainier did not follow Bernard of Pavia's model of organization; his work is not divided into books, and although Rainier placed his texts under titles, he did not use the ones which, following Bernard, had become common in the schools.[20] He made it clear that his work was an anthology—a selection of items which he considered the best from both the "judgments" and the "letters"

18. See Stephan Kuttner, "Rénier de Pompose ou Rainerius Pomposanus ou de Pomposa," *Dictionnaire de droit canonique*, 7 (Paris, 1965), 83–84.

19. The relevant passage of the *Gesta* can be read in J.-P. Migne, *Patrologia Latina*, 214 (Paris, 1855), 81, c. 41; see also Kenneth Pennington, "The Legal Education of Pope Innocent III," in Pennington, *Popes, Canonists and Texts, 1150–1550* (Variorum Collected Studies Series CS412; Aldershot, 1993), 4–5 (and p. 6 for the *Gesta* written c. 1210). This is a revised version of Pennington's early study with the same title (*Bulletin of Medieval Canon Law* 4 [1974]).

20. Kuttner, "Rénier," 584 (see n. 18, above) sees this as evidence that Rainier had no contact with the Bolognese school of canon law.

and which possessed "fullest authority" as canons, presumably due to inclusion in Innocent's register. Rainier also acknowledged that he cut up texts and arranged the pieces under different titles according to content; and at the end of the preface he borrowed language from Dionysius Exiguus to introduce his index, perhaps another hint that Rainier was not working within the context of the late twelfth-century schools, where Dionysius's compilations from the early sixth century probably received scant attention.

Rainier's collection did not have the influence of Bernard's Breviary, but the Bolognese canonists seem to have considered it a reliable source for Innocent's texts—a matter of no small significance given the traffic in forgeries at the time.[21] A few years later another collection of Innocent's decretals appeared—the so-called Roman Collection (*Collectio Romana*) by Bernard of Compostella (the elder).[22] But with some dubious texts therein, plus Bernard's zeal in editing his material, the canonists felt the need to have another compilation for Pope Innocent, and thus Peter Collivacina from Benevento assembled a new collection covering the first dozen years of the

21. See C. R. Cheney and Mary G. Cheney, *The Letters of Pope Innocent III (1198–1216) Concerning England and Wales* (Oxford, 1967), xxii–xxiii.

22. Bernard's title was *Breviarium decretalium domini pape Innocentii III.:* Singer, *Dekretalensammlung,* 37 (see n. 9, above). For what follows, see two articles by Kenneth Pennington, "The French Recension of Compilatio tertia" (rev. in Pennington, *Popes, Canonists and Texts* [see n. 19, above], from the version which originally appeared in *Bulletin of Medieval Canon Law* 5 [1975]: 53–71), and "The Making of a Decretal Collection: The Genesis of Compilatio tertia" (rev. in *Popes, Canonists and Texts* from the version in *Proceedings of the Fifth International Congress of Medieval Canon Law,* ed. Stephan Kuttner and Kenneth Pennington [Monumenta iuris canonici, Subsidia 6; Vatican City, 1980], 67–92). For Bernard, see Pennington, "Making of a Decretal Collection," 69–70.

pontificate.[23] Peter's work, titled Decretals of the Lord Pope Innocent (*Decretales domini Innocentii papae*), was promulgated in 1209/1210 with a papal bull of authorization (*Devotioni vestrae*), was addressed to the students and masters at Bologna, and came to be known as the Third Compilation.[24] The destination of Innocent's bull indicates the influence of Bologna. Clerics from throughout Europe studied there, and the glosses and commentaries from the Bolognese masters of canon law were prime instruments for the evolution of canonical jurisprudence.

Perusal of *Devotioni vestrae* could prompt the conclusion that Peter of Benevento worked on commission from Innocent III and employed the pope's registers. Yet the matter is not straightforward, for it has been demonstrated that Peter relied to some extent on earlier, private compilations. In what way then does it make sense to speak of Comp. III as an official collection? *Devotioni vestrae* stated that the texts which Peter collected were authentic, were found in the registers, and could be used without worry. The pope thus authenticated the book, although Pennington's research makes it an open question whether or not Innocent was involved in its conception and composition. He suggests that the pope wished to honor Peter's effort and to resolve problems surrounding the *Collectio Romana* by guaranteeing the authenticity of the texts in a compilation which had been conceived and executed privately.

Comp. III, despite the name, was the second of the Five Old Compilations to be assembled. It derives its number from the dates of the texts therein: between 1198 and 1210. Comp. II,

23. On Peter, made cardinal bishop of Sabina under Honorius III, see Brundage, *Medieval Canon Law*, 195, and Weigand, "Frühe Kanonisten," 151.
24. For the date, see Pennington, "Making of a Decretal Collection," 67 (see n. 22, above).

made between 1210 and 1215 by John of Wales, presents decretals from the 1190s before Innocent's reign. Comp. IV, like Comp. II, was a private work, assembled early in 1216 by the famous canonist Johannes Teutonicus. Johannes gathered the legislation of the Lateran Council of 1215 together with Innocentian decretals dating after Comp. III, perhaps in the hope of gaining papal approval for his book. If that was his goal it was never realized, for Innocent gave no such endorsement.

Ten years later, in 1226, the Bolognese canonist Tancred published what came to be termed the Fifth Collection, prefaced by a bull of authorization by Pope Honorius III, *Novae causarum*, addressed to Tancred, who now held the important position of archdeacon of Bologna.[25] Honorius instructed Tancred both to use the decretals included in Comp. V and to arrange for their circulation to others. The same covering letter—note that *Novae causarum* does not identify the person who compiled the collection—has been found addressed to Master Marcoaldus and all the scholars at Padua, revealing Honorius's intention to diffuse the work widely. Leonard Boyle has shown that the registers of Honorius were Tancred's exclusive source and has suggested that in the final stages of redaction Tancred had the services of scribes from the papal court. These two factors, coupled with the fact that *Novae causarum* designated the pope's role in initiating the project, distinguish Comp. V from what is known

25. For what follows see Leonard E. Boyle, O.P., "The Compilatio Quinta and the Registers of Honorius III," *Bulletin of Medieval Canon Law* 8 (1978): 9–19 (rpt. in Boyle, *Pastoral Care, Clerical Education and Canon Law, 1200–1400* [Variorum Reprints CS135; London, 1981]), and Jane E. Sayers, *Papal Government and England during the Pontificate of Honorius III (1216–1227)* (Cambridge Studies in Medieval Life and Thought, 3d ser., 21; Cambridge, 1984), 133ff. See Brundage, *Medieval Canon Law*, 227–28, for Tancred; and for the importance of the archdeacon of Bologna, see Bellomo, *Legal Past*, 119.

of Comp. III. Honorius and not Innocent III seems to have been the first Roman pontiff who influenced the direction of the Church's law by commissioning a collection.

A short thirteenth-century history of canon law which Stephan Kuttner found in a Borghese manuscript from the Vatican Library relates an amusing anecdote.[26] Early in his pontificate, Pope Gregory IX was confronted with a decretal that could not be found in any of the collections, including the Five Old Compilations. In anger, the pope ordered that "the book of decretals" should be destroyed.[27] The cardinals directed their friends and nephews at Bologna not to study the decretals, but only Roman law and Gratian, until a papal decision was made "about the compilation of that book."[28] The result was a commission to Raymond of Peñafort to make a new collection. The truth of this story cannot be determined, but the point is clear enough: how could a path be found through the forest of decretals and collections of decretals which engulfed canonists by the end of the pontificate of Honorius III?

Raymond of Peñafort was active at Bologna in the second decade of the thirteenth century, joined the Dominican Order in 1222, and in 1230 came to the court of Gregory IX as papal penitentiary. He had a long, distinguished, and prolific career, including a period as master general of his order, and died in 1275,

26. Kuttner, "Johannes Teutonicus," 633 (see n. 8, above); see also Pennington, "Making of a Decretal Collection," 73–74 (see n. 22, above).

27. Kuttner, "Johannes Teutonicus," 633: *quia destruerent librum decretalium*. Presumably this refers to the unspecified book whence the troublesome text was alleged, and not to the accumulation of decretal collections which was at hand. The item in question actually is found in Comp. IV (1.3.1), whence it was taken into the Decretals of Gregory IX (1.6.35). See Kuttner, "Johannes Teutonicus," n. 19.

28. See the previous note. The text reads *quousque ipse idem dominus greg. disponeret de conpillatione ipsius libri*. Presumably this again designates the particular book where the troublesome decretal occurred.

at nearly one hundred years of age.[29] The bull of promulgation for the Gregorian Decretals, often termed the *Liber extravagantium* (Book of "Extravagant" [Decretals]), or simply the *Liber extra* for short, is a concise masterpiece of both jurisprudential philosophy and information about the collection. As with *Devotioni vestrae* preceding Comp. III, it is addressed to the masters and scholars at Bologna, but as with Comp. V, the collection also was transmitted elsewhere, in this case to Paris and perhaps to other universities as well.[30] In organization the Decretals followed the format initiated by Bernard of Pavia, and *Rex pacificus* presented ideas which were not new, for example, the need for new laws to meet new situations and the confusion engendered by the proliferation of decretals. Even Gregory's instructions to Raymond to excise "superfluous" material from the texts which he assembled could be taken as parallel to the editorial practice the decretalists had used for decades, although Raymond's numerous "excisions, interpolations, or alterations of words or phrases" are on an unparalleled scale.[31]

In others ways, too, the Decretals represent a clear leap beyond any previously existing collection of canon law. Gregory instructed Raymond to insert his papal rulings in order to clarify uncertainties in older texts.[32] The pope intended, furthermore, that this compilation alone be used in Church courts and in teaching canon law, and he prohibited anyone to make

29. See Brundage, *Medieval Canon Law,* 150.

30. See Ch. Lefebvre's comments in G. LeBras, Ch. Lefebvre, and J. Rambaud, *L'Age classique 1140–1378: Sources et théorie du droit* (Histoire du droit et des institutions de l'Eglise en occident 7; Paris, 1965), 240.

31. See Stephan Kuttner, "Raymond of Peñafort as Editor: The 'Decretales' and 'Constitutiones' of Gregory IX," *Bulletin of Medieval Canon Law* 12 (1982): 66 (rpt. in Kuttner, *Studies in the History of Medieval Canon Law* [Variorum Collected Studies CS325; Aldershot, 1990]).

32. On these supplements, see Kuttner, "Raymond of Peñafort as Editor."

another one without the explicit permission of the papacy. These regulations transcend anything which either Innocent III or Honorius III prescribed for Comp. III or Comp. V, and they establish the *Liber extra* as both authoritative and exclusive.

Applying those two adjectives to the *Liber extra* is easier than being precise about their meaning, which was debated among medieval decretalists and still commands the attention of scholars. Some of the questions which thus are raised will be obvious to readers who have worked through the present anthology up to this point. Can texts which are not found in compilations still be used? What of Gratian, or, indeed, what of earlier canons which were omitted in the *Decretum?* *Rex pacificus* makes no mention of Gratian, and his work seems to have been excluded from its prohibition, but thirteenth-century canonists debated the extent to which previous collections were now off limits.[33] Other questions raised by *Rex pacificus* might be less obvious: for example, how are the Gregorian Decretals as a unit to be viewed as legislation? The parallel has been made between this work and the collections of Roman law ordered by the Emperor Justinian in the sixth century, with their conscious effort to shape and define an inviolate law. Others see that comparison as less apt, stressing Pope Gregory's concern with establishing a firm basis for decretal law but not insisting that his book encompass all canon law.[34]

33. For an introduction to those issues see Pennington, "French Recension," 65–67 (see n. 22, above); LeBras, et al., *L'Age classique,* 241–42 (see n. 30, above); Stephan Kuttner, "The Code of Canon Law in Historical Perspective," *The Jurist* 28 (1968): 142–43; and P. Torquebiau, "Les Décrétales de Grégoire IX," *Dictionnaire de droit canonique,* 4 (Paris, 1949), 629–30.

34. This is the view of Stephan Kuttner, "Quelques observations sur l'autorité des collections canoniques dans le droit classique de l'Eglise," *Actes du Congrès de droit canonique, Paris 22–26 Avril* (Paris, 1950), 310–11

One thirteenth-century canonist who took the prohibition of *Rex pacificus* literally was Bartholomew of Brescia. Around the year 1245, Bartholomew completed a revision of the standard (ordinary) gloss on Gratian's *Decretum*, which had been assembled toward the end of Innocent III's pontificate by Johannes Teutonicus.[35] This revision became the accepted form, and it appears in manuscripts from the thirteenth century onward and in the early modern printings of Gratian which contain the gloss. It is introduced by a short preface which repeats some old themes but also provides insight about the impact of the *Liber extra*.[36] In the first recension of the gloss Johannes Teutonicus, in the manner of scholastic discourse, often alleged texts to confirm a point, provide a contrary opinion, and so on, and when papal decretals were employed they were cited according to the collections at hand in the second decade of the thirteenth century. The Gregorian Decretals superseded such compilations, and *Rex pacificus* asked that only the Decretals be used in schools and courts. A great part of Bartholomew's work of revision was spent, consequently, in correlating Johannes's older allegations with the texts as now found in the *Liber extra*.

(rpt. in Kuttner, *Medieval Councils* [see n. 8, above]), and of Pennington, "Making of a Decretal Collection," 70–72 (see n. 22, above); but see Pennington, "French Recension," 64, nn. 15–16 (see n. 22, above), for citation of contrary opinion from Walter Ullmann, *Law and Politics in the Middle Ages* (Ithaca, 1975), 142–43, and LeBras, et al., *L'Age classique*, 240–41 (see n. 30, above). See also Bellomo, *Legal Past*, 71–72, who perhaps under estimates the degree of authority which the Decretals possessed throughout the Church.

35. For Bartholomew, see Brundage, *Medieval Canon Law*, 201 and 207.

36. Bartholomew writes, as did Bernard of Pavia in his preface to Comp. I, that he labored for the honor of God and the Roman Church. How this might relate to his use of the Bible (see the comment above on Bernard) remains to be studied.

In some cases Raymond of Peñafort excluded or trimmed a text which Johannes had alleged, thus Bartholomew could write in his preface that his revision also was necessary "due to the omission or shortening of decretals."

The Decretals of Gregory IX mark the end of this book, although they are not the end of the story. The Five Old Compilations and the Gregorian Decretals were glossed and commented on by canonists, and these expositions could open with prefaces, as did the *Summa* of Bernard of Pavia to Comp. I and Bartholomew of Brescia's revision of the ordinary gloss to Gratian. Yet with or without introductions, these works were fundamental for the development of canonical doctrine in the thirteenth century and later. Furthermore, other papal collections were promulgated in the course of the thirteenth and early in the fourteenth centuries, including the extensive *Liber Sextus* of Boniface VIII in 1294 — a collection of five books, although presented as a "sixth book" of the *Liber extra* — which formed the third part of the *Corpus iuris canonici*.

In his study of Comp. V, Leonard Boyle made a series of important observations, "none of them entirely new," concerning papal registers and decretal collections, and it is useful, at the end of this chapter, to reiterate some of them.[37] It is well known that the registers are incomplete, and that not all or in some cases not even the most interesting decretals were enregistered. Principles of selection are unclear, but not everything was thus preserved. Tancred probably did not go beyond Honorius's registers in making Comp. V, and he took no texts from the last thirteen months of the pontificate. As with Comp. V, so Comps. I–IV represented only a selection of what their authors had available either in papal registers or in earlier, private com-

37. Boyle, "Compilatio quinta," 18–19 (see n. 25, above).

pilations. Thus the law in the *Liber extra*, which was officially promulgated by Gregory IX, was chosen by Raymond of Peñafort predominantly from the Five Old Compilations and stands at the end of a chain of selection processes whose mechanisms are opaque. It is important to differentiate what is included in these books, on the one hand, and the full array of what the popes said, on the other. Notwithstanding the wealth of information which the decretal collections offer about Church and society in the High Middle Ages, the full corpus of papal enactments tells a story richer still.

1. Preface to the Breviary of *Extravagantia,* or the First Compilation, compiled by Bernard of Pavia, c. 1191. Ed. Aemilius Friedberg, *Quinque compilationes antiquae* (Leipzig, 1882), 1.

Judge justly sons of men[38] and do not judge according to appearance, but render a just judgment[39] in order to show that you love justice, you who judge the earth,[40] having before the eyes of the heart him who will render to each and every one according to his works.[41] For with what measure you measure out it will be measured back to you,[42] since we are held to give an account for an entrusted talent.[43] One skilled in the law should, therefore, be cautious in counsel, faithful in advocacy, and just in judgment. But so that a richer supply of allegations and judg-

---

38. Cf. Psalm 58 (57):1(2).
39. John 7:24.
40. Wisdom of Solomon 1:1.
41. Matthew 16:27.
42. Cf. Matthew 7:2 and Mark 4:24.
43. Cf. Matthew 25:14ff.

ments is available, to the honor of God and the holy Roman Church, and for the utility of those studying, I Bernard, provost of Pavia, compiled *extravagantia* from the old and the new law under titles, imploring pardon from the reader for the imperfection of the work.

2. Preface to the *Summa decretalium* of Bernard of Pavia on the First Compilation, ante 1198. Ed. E. A. T. Laspeyres, *Bernardus Papiensis Faventini episcopi Summa decretalium* (Regensburg, 1860; rpt. Graz, 1956), 1–2.

The glory of a father is a wise son,[44] the glory of a master is the progress of a student, who ought not hide the lamp of teaching under a bushel,[45] ought not conceal the grain[46] of the word, ought not block up the fountain of knowledge but should channel it outside to others.[47] Impelled especially by this consideration, and with a view toward utility in the schools, I, Bernard, who as provost of Pavia compiled decretals and *extravagantia,* now, although unworthy, as bishop of Faenza undertake to produce, with Christ as guide, a little summary of the same small work, pardon having been asked for a poor job.

[Prooemium][48]

In the name of Christ. The book was titled *extravagantia;* for the most part [they are] decretals. In introducing it we should describe the subject matter, intention, utility, and order of proceeding. The subject matter is made up of decretals and certain useful provisions which Gratian left out—saving fruit new

44. Cf. Proverbs 15:20.
45. Matthew 5:15.
46. Cf. Proverbs 11:26.
47. Cf. Proverbs 5:16.
48. Laspeyres supplied this title between paragraphs, although noting that he did not find it in any manuscript.

and old for us[49]—in the corpus of canons, in the register of Gregory, and in Burchard. The intention is to collect the aforementioned into one volume, and according to their decisions to arrange them under appropriate titles. The utility is clear, because through knowledge of this work we will be more prepared for deliberating, citing texts, and judging. The order of proceeding is as follows. The work is divided into five books. The first of these treats ecclesiastical constitutions, ordinations and duties of clerics, and background material for judgments; the second treats judgments and the process of judgments; the third treats the life of clerics and their possessions, and the status of monks and their possessions; the fourth treats marriages; the fifth treats crimes and punishments.

3. Preface to the Collection of Decretals compiled by Rainier of Pomposa, c. 1201: dedicatory letter to the papal chaplain John. Ed. Etienne Baluze, *Epistolarum Innocentii III . . . libri*, 1 (Paris, 1682), 543 (rpt. in J.-P. Migne, *Patrologia Latina*, 216 [Paris, 1891], 1173–74).

Rainier, deacon and monk of Pomposa [wishes] attainment of the joy of eternal felicity, after the propitious successes of the present life, to the venerable man lord John, outstanding in knowledge and virtue of morals, by the grace of God priest and monk, reverent chaplain of the lord pope.

Some who come from diverse and even the farthest parts of the world to the apostolic see to hear the wisdom of the Solomon of our time,[50] and also many other virtuous and knowl-

49. Cf. Song of Songs 7:13.
50. For Innocent as Solomon, see anon., "Novus regnat Salomon in diebus malis: Une satire contre Innocent III," *Festschrift Bernhard Bischoff zu seinem 65. Geburtstag*, ed. Johanne Autenrieth and Franz Brunhölzl (Stuttgart, 1971), and for this passage p. 376.

edgeable men who at present dwell with us, desire to have his laws and judgments in writing. Along with you, by their own pleas they likewise urged me that, stealing a certain space of time from my other occupations, I should expend it in ordering and compiling them in one volume under specific titles. I obeyed those wishes devotedly and humbly, as I should, considering the subservience of my situation, and for the praise and glory of his name and for the benefit of readers, selecting from the first, second, and third years of his registers, I gathered in this work all the best things, with fullest authority as far as decretal and decrees are concerned. But I decided that some, because they contain[51] various legal issues, should be cut up, so that they could be distributed under the titles appropriate to them. Extracting from the judgments and certain of the letters only those sections which are pertinent for law, I properly arranged the aforementioned. And I sent the designated work first of all to you, because more than the others you insisted in a way that scarcely permitted me, although ill, to refuse, and you are joined to me by a bond of closer love. I put the titles of the same [work] in one list so that I have provided a kind of compendium for searching out each subject which it contains.[52]

4. Bull of promulgation by Pope Innocent III to the Decretals of the Lord Pope Innocent, or the Third Compilation, compiled by Peter of Benevento, 1209/1210. Ed. Aemilius Friedberg, *Quinque compilationes antiquae* (Leipzig, 1882; rpt. Graz, 1956), 105.

51. Migne 216.1173: *in se continens;* Baluze 543: *in se continent.* (See references above at head of translation.)

52. See the end of the preface to Dionysius Exiguus's first collection of councils (chap. 2). The edition of Rainier's collection prints immediately following the preface a list of forty titles, which will not be translated.

Innocent bishop, servant of the servants of God, to all the masters and scholars residing at Bologna, greetings and apostolic benediction.

By notification of the present letter let it be known that the decretal letters faithfully compiled by our beloved son Master Peter, subdeacon and notary, and collected under appropriate titles, are contained in our registers up to the twelfth year. We decided that as a precaution they ought to be sent to you under our seal, so that you can use the same without any scruple of doubt, when it is necessary, both in judgments and in the schools.

5. Bull of promulgation by Pope Honorius III to the Fifth Compilation, compiled by Tancred, May 2, 1226. Ed. Aemilius Friedberg, *Quinque compilationes antiquae* (Leipzig, 1882; rpt. Graz, 1956), 151.

Honorius bishop, servant of the servants of God, to [our] beloved son Master Tancred, archdeacon of Bologna, greetings and apostolic benediction.

New questions of emerging cases need to be resolved by new decisions, so that proper remedies having been chosen for individual illnesses, each person in a healthful manner is accorded his own rights.[53] Although through those [cases] which were decided in their own times procedure for future cases was carefully given by some of our predecessors, nevertheless because the profligate nature of things accompanying a great variety of legal problems daily produces new cases,[54] we arranged for cer-

---

53. See Justinian, *Institutes* 1.1.1 and 1.1.3–4, in *Institutiones,* ed. P. Krueger (Corpus Iuris Civilis 1; Berlin, 1928), 1. Honorius's text, and the *Institutes,* read *ius suum,* but the plural "rights" seems a better English translation.

54. See Justinian's Constitution *Cordi,* par. 4 on the promulgation of

tain decretal letters to be collected about these which, having arisen in our time, we settled through ourselves or our brothers, and we decided that they ought to be sent to you under our seal. Wherefore through apostolic script we command you, a careful man, that without any scruple of doubt you use these, having formally been published, and that you arrange for them to be received by others both in judgments and in the schools.

6. Bull of promulgation by Pope Gregory IX to the Compilation of Decretals of the Lord Pope Gregory IX, compiled by Raymond of Peñafort, O.P., September 5, 1234. Ed. Aemilius Friedberg, *Corpus Iuris Canonici,* 2 (Leipzig, 1881; rpt. Graz, 1959), 2–3.

Gregory bishop, servant of the servants of God, to his beloved sons, all the doctors and scholars residing at Bologna, greetings and apostolic benediction.

The peaceful king arranged with tender compassion for those subject to him to be virtuous, peaceful, and honorable. But unrestrained greed, profligate of its own substance, the rival of peace, the mother of lawsuits, the source of quarrels, daily generates so many new disputes that unless justice by its own virtue restrained its [greed's] efforts and unraveled its tangled questions, abuse by litigants would destroy the basis of the human covenant, and a writ of divorce having been issued, concord would be exiled beyond the boundaries of the world. Therefore written law is produced, so that harmful desire can be limited under a rule of law through which the human race is instructed that it should live honorably, should not injure another, and should accord to each person his own rights.[55] But various con-

---

the *Code,* found at the beginning of the *Code,* in *Codex Iustinianus,* ed. P. Krueger (Corpus Iuris Civilis 2; Berlin, 1914), 4.

55. See n. 53, above.

stitutions and decretal letters of our predecessors, dispersed in diverse volumes, have seemed to induce confusion, some because of excessive similarity, some because of contradiction, some even because of prolixity; others have been wandering around outside of the aforementioned volumes and as uncertain texts frequently tottered in judgments. [Thus] for the common utility and especially for those studying, we have taken care, superfluous things having been cut out, that these should be collected into one volume through our beloved son Brother Raymond, our chaplain and penitentiary, and we are adding our constitutions and decretal letters through which some matters are settled which in earlier ones were uncertain. Intending, therefore, that everyone use only this compilation in judgments and the schools, we firmly prohibit that anyone presume to make another without the express authority of the apostolic see.

7. Preface by Bartholomew of Brescia to his revision of the Ordinary Gloss to Gratian's *Decretum* by Johannes Teutonicus, dated soon after 1245.[56] Translated from *Decretum Gratiani . . . una cum glosis* (Venice, 1595), 1.

Since new remedies should be brought to bear for new cases which emerge, therefore I, Bartholomew of Brescia, trusting in the magnanimity of the Creator, decided that the apparatus to the decrees ought to be put in better form, not by removing anything, nor attributing to myself glosses which I did not compose, but only by supplying what is needed where correction seemed necessary, either due to the omission or shortening of decretals, or because of laws which newly appeared. Sometimes I also inserted solutions which were overlooked by Johannes. I did this for the honor of omnipotent God and the Roman Church, and for the common utility of all those studying in canon law.

56. For the date, see Kuttner, *Repertorium,* 103.

SELECT BIBLIOGRAPHY

The following works have been cited with an abbreviated form of
reference. Of necessity, works on the history of canon law in several
languages have been used, but an effort has been made to include
especially titles in English which provide further bibliography.

For the abbreviations JK, JE, and JL, see Jaffé, below.

Bellomo, Manlio. *The Common Legal Past of Europe, 1000–1800* (Studies
  in Medieval and Early Modern Canon Law 4; Washington, D.C,
  1995).
Berger, Adolf. *Encyclopedic Dictionary of Roman Law* (Transactions of the
  American Philosophical Society, New Series 43.2; Philadelphia, 1953).
Brasington, Bruce C. "Prologues to Canonical Collections as a Source
  for Jurisprudential Change to the Eve of the Investiture Contest,"
  Frühmittelalterliche Studien 28 (1994): 226–42.
Brundage, James A. *Medieval Canon Law* (London, 1995).
Chodorow, Stanley. "Law, Canon: After Gratian," *Dictionary of the
  Middle Ages,* 7 (New York, 1986), 413–17.
Duggan, Charles. *Twelfth-Century Decretal Collections and Their Impor-
  tance in English History* (University of London Historical Studies 12;
  London, 1963).
Fournier, Paul. *Mélanges de droit canonique,* ed. Theo Kölzer, 2 vols.
  (Aalen, 1983).
Fournier, Paul, and Gabriel LeBras. *Histoire des collections canoniques en
  Occident,* 2 vols. (Paris, 1931–32).
Fransen, Gérard. *Les Décrétales et les collections de décrétales* (Typologie des
  sources du Moyen Age occidental 2.A-III.1*; Turnhout, 1972).
García y García, Antonio. *Historia del derecho canonico 1: El Primer Milenio*
  (Salamanca, 1967).
Gaudemet, Jean. *Les Sources du droit de l'église en occident du IIe au VIIe
  siècle* (Paris, 1985).
Gouron, André. "Sur les sources civilistes et la datation des Sommes de

Rufin et d'Etienne de Tournai," *Bulletin of Medieval Canon Law* 16 (1986): 55-70.

Gratian, *Decretum Magistri Gratiani*, ed. Aemilius Friedberg, *Corpus Iuris Canonici* (Leipzig, 1879), vol. 1.

Jaffé, Philipp, and Wilhelm Wattenbach. *Regesta pontificum Romanorum ab condita ecclesia ad annum post Christum natum MCXCVIII*, 2d ed. (Leipzig, 1885-88). Papal letters generally will be cited according to this register; entries to the year 590 compiled by F. Kaltenbrunner (JK prefixes); to 882 by P. Ewald (JE prefixes); and to 1198 by S. Loewenfeld (JL prefixes).

Kalb, Herbert. *Studien zur Summa Stephans von Tournai* (Forschungen zur Rechts- und Kulturgeschichte 12; Innsbruck, 1983).

Kelly, J. N. D. *The Oxford Dictionary of the Popes* (Oxford, 1986).

Kuttner, Stephan. *Harmony from Dissonance: An Interpretation of Medieval Canon Law* (Wimmer Lecture 10; Latrobe, Pa., 1960) (rpt. in Kuttner, *The History of Ideas and Doctrines of Canon Law in the Middle Ages* [Variorum Reprint CS113; London, 1980]).

―――. *Repertorium der Kanonistik, 1140-1234. Prodromus corporis glossarum I* (Studi et testi 71; Vatican City, 1937, rpt. Rome, 1972).

Landau, Peter. "Kanonisches Recht und Römische Form," *Der Staat* 32 (1993): 553-68.

Mordek, Hubert. *Kirchenrecht und Reform im Frankreich* (Beiträge zur Geschichte und Quellenkunde des Mittelalters 1; Berlin, 1975).

Reynolds, Roger E. "Law, Canon: To Gratian," *Dictionary of the Middle Ages*, 7 (New York, 1986), 395-413.

Southern, R. W. *Scholastic Humanism and the Unification of Europe I: Foundations* (Oxford, 1995).

Stickler, Alfonsus M., S.D.B. *Historia iuris canonici Latini I: Historia fontium* (Rome, 1950).

Tierney, Brian. *Crisis of Church and State, 1050-1300* (Englewood Cliffs, 1964 [rpt. Medieval Academy Reprints for Teaching 21; Toronto, 1988]).

Van de Wiel, Constant. *History of Canon Law* (Louvain Theological & Pastoral Monographs 5; Louvain, 1991).

Van Hove, A. *Prolegomena*, 2d ed. (Commentarium Lovaniense 1.1; Malines, 1945).

Weigand, Rudolf "Frühe Kanonisten und ihre Karriere in der Kirche," *Zeitschrift der Savigny-Stiftung für Rechtsgeschichte*, Kanonistische Abteilung 76 (1990): 135-55.

INDEX

SCRIPTURAL REFERENCES

Acts 1:1	167	Ex 18:13-27	166
Acts 9:15	42	Ex 20:12	138
Acts 10:34	149	Ex 20:13-14	138
Acts 15:19-22	141	Ex 25:23ff	185
Acts 16:3	142	Ex 33:7ff	190
Acts 20:1ff	140, 209	Ez 13:19	134
		Ez 18:20	149
1 Cor 5:7	38	Ez 18:23	39
1 Cor 6:3	158	Ez 44:22	43
1 Cor 6:4	181, 195		
1 Cor 7:2	136	Gal 2:11ff	141
1 Cor 7:27	137	Gal 5:2	141
1 Cor 7:28	137	Gn 3:12	181, 195
1 Cor 9:15	187	Gn 4:17	182
1 Cor 9:20	142	Gn 10:8-9	182
1 Cor 14:38	121	Gn 11:1ff	182
1 Cor 15:31	140		
2 Cor 1:15ff	140, 209	Heb 6:16	139
2 Cor 1:17	141	Heb 7:19	192
2 Cor 1:23	141	Heb 13:4	136
2 Cor 11:10	140	Heb 13:9	119
2 Cor 11:29	41	Hos 4:6	121
Dt 6:5	138	Jb 28:1	119
Dt 15:12-17	183	Jer 1:10	155
Dt 19:15	181, 195	Jer 9:1	40
		Jn 7:24	230
Eph 4:5	37	Jn 14:2	186
Eph 5:27	41	Jn 21:17	122

239

1 Kgs 10:1ff	190	Prv 5:16	231
		Prv 11:26	231
Lk 6:39	119	Prv 15:20	231
Lk 9:62	136	Prv 22:28	94
Lk 10:4	140, 209	Ps 19(18):8	192
Lk 22:32	122	Ps 25(24):10	133, 167
Lk 22:35–36	140, 209	Ps 49(50):18	43
Lk 24: 13ff	77	Ps 58(57):1(2)	230
Lv 19:18	138	Ps 80(81):11(10)	77
Lv 20:7	41	Ps 101(100):1	133
Lv 21:13–14	43	Ps 110(109):4	139
		Ps 141(140):2	188
Mk 4:24	230	1 Pt 3:15	187
Mt 5:15	77, 231	2 Pt 2:22	39
Mt 5:17	41		
Mt 5:19	138	Rom 1:8	124
Mt 5:28	163	Rom 8:8–9	42
Mt 5:37	139	Rom 8:33	149
Mt 7:2	230	Rom 13:10	157
Mt 7:12	134	Rv 14:1–5	187
Mt 11:30	77		
Mt 13:52	77	Sg 7:13	232
Mt 15:14	103, 119		
Mt 16:18–19	155, 122	Ti 3:10	208, 138, 198
Mt 16:27	230	1 Tm 3:2	43
Mt 19:12	136	1 Tm 3:6	142
Mt 19:21	136, 207		
Mt 25:14ff	230	Wis 1:1	230
Nm 1:52	190		

PERSONS, COUNCILS, AND WRITTEN WORKS

Abbo of Fleury, abbot, 71–72, 97, 98n; *Apologeticus*, 98; Canons (*Canones*), 71–72, 75; preface text, 97f

Agatho, pope, 89

Agobard of Lyons, bishop, 62

Alcuin of York, 59, 81

Alexander I, pope, 127

Alexander III, pope, 176, 215, 216, 217

Alger of Liège, 105, 117–18, 165; Mercy and Justice (*De misericordia et iustitia*), 105, 117–18, 172; preface text, 165ff

Ambrose, 104, 128, 197

Anaclet I, pope, 84, 127

Anastasius, emperor, 24n

Anastasius I, pope, 23

Anastasius II, pope, 26

Anastasius "Bibliothecarius," 127, 127n, 147n

Ancyra, Council of (314), 25

Angilramnus, Chapters (*Capitula*), 64

Ansegisus of Fontanelle, abbot, 66

Anselm of Lucca, bishop, canonical collection of, 107

Anselm II of Milan, archbishop, 70, 94

Antioch, Council of (330 or 341), 25, 50

Apostolic Constitutions, 11

Arius, 55, 90, 183

Arles, Council of (314), 37n

Athanasius of Alexandria, bishop, 122, 154

Atto, cardinal, 105, 108–9, 118; Breviary of, 105, 108–9; preface text, 118ff

Augustine of Hippo, bishop, 64, 104, 128, 134, 138, 143, 144, 149, 167, 168, 197, 202; *Contra epistulam Parmeniani*, 144n; *De baptismo*, 53n; *De bono coniugali*, 149n; *Epistola 73*, 168n; *Epistola 139*, 145n; *Epistola 148*, 168n; *Epistola 185*, 139n, 143n; *In epistolam Iohannis*, 134n; Rule of, 162

Autgar of Mainz, archbishop, 79

Bartholomew of Brescia, 218, 228–29, 236; Revision of the Ordinary Gloss on Gratian's *Decretum*, 218, 228, 229; preface text, 236

Benedict of Aniane, 70, 71n

Benedict the Deacon, 64, 65, 66, 67, 68; False Capitularies, 64, 66–67, 92n; preface text, 78ff

Benedict of Nursia, 104, 127n; Rule of, 71

Bernard of Clairvaux, 214

Bernard of Compostella, Roman Collection (*Collectio Romana*), 217n, 222, 223

Bernard of Pavia, 214n, 217, 218–20, 221, 226, 228n; Breviary of *Extravagantia* or First Compilation, 218–19, 222, 229; preface text, 230f; *Summa decretalium* on the First Compilation, 217, 219–20, 229; preface text, 231f

Bernold of Constance, 115, 117

Boniface, pope, 26

Boniface, St., 66

Boniface VIII, *Liber Sextus*, 213n, 229

Boniface of Mainz, archbishop, 80–81, 91

Braga, First Council of (561), 30, 31

Braga, Second Council of (572), 30, 31, 54n

Brunicho of Worms, 99

Bulgarus, 177, 177n

Burchard of Worms, bishop, 64, 70, 71, 72–75, 99, 105, 107n, 115, 120, 121n, 171, 172, 220; *Decretum* of, 70, 72–75, 109, 151n, 174; preface text, 99ff

Caesarius of Arles, 134n

Canons of the Apostles, 11, 19, 25,

Canons of the Apostles (cont.)
25n, 26, 33, 33n, 47, 49, 50, 56,
84, 84n, 104, 131
Carloman, 81, 91
Cassiodorus, 23, 128
Celestine I, pope, 9, 10, 26, 50, 121,
126
Celestine III, pope, 220
Chalcedon, Council of (451), 7,
12, 23, 56, 125, 126, 196; canons
or decrees of, 25, 32, 48, 49, 50;
letter of Pope Leo to, 85–86
Charlemagne (Charles), emperor,
59, 60, 61, 62, 65, 66, 69, 78, 79,
81
Charles the Bald, emperor, 68, 152
Chrisogonus, pseudo pope, 132
Chrysostom, John, 151, 154
Cicero, 184
Clement I, pope, 84, 126, 127, 128
Clement III, pope, 218, 220
Clementine Decretals, 213n
Collectio Britannica, 113n
Collectio Dacheriana, 63
Collectio Dionysio-Hadriana, see
Hadrian I
Collectio Romana, see Bernard of
Compostella
Collectio vetus Gallica, 15
Collection of Châlons-sur-Marne,
First, 117
Collection of Châlons-sur-Marne,
Second, 116–17; preface text,
164ff
Collection Dedicated to Anselm
(*Collectio Anselmo dedicata*), 29,
70, 73n, 74; preface text, 94ff
Collection in Five Books, 107n
Collection in 74 Titles (*Diversorum
patrum sententie*), 107

Collection in Ten Parts, 116, 117,
165n; preface text, 158ff
Comp. I, *see* Bernard of Pavia,
Breviary of *Extravagantia*
Comp. II, *see* John of Wales,
Second Compilation
Comp. III, *see* Peter of Benevento,
Decretals of the Lord Pope
Innocent
Comp. IV, *see* Johannes Teutoni-
cus, Fourth Compilation
Comp. V, *see* Tancred, Fifth Com-
pilation
Concordance of Discordant
Canons (*Concordia discordan-
tium canonum*), *see* Gratian,
Decretum
Constans, emperor, 22
Constantine, emperor, 6, 55, 60,
89, 90, 131, 183, 196
Constantinople, First Council of
(381), 7, 22, 48, 55, 87, 90, 196
Constantinople, Fourth Council of
(869–70), 123
Constantinople, Second Council
of (553), 29n, 89
Constantius, emperor, 22, 37n
Corpus of Canon Law (*Corpus
iuris canonici*), 213, 213n, 229
Corpus of Civil Law (*Corpus iuris
civilis*), 213n
Cresconius, 21, 24, 27–29, 35, 50,
51n, 70, 95, 115, 122n; Concord
of Canons (*Concordia Canonum*),
13, 27–29, 61, 75, 179n; preface
text, 50ff
Cyprian, 123
Cyril of Alexandria, 29n, 147

Damasus I, pope, 20, 32, 35

Decree of Gelasius (*Decretum Gelasianum*), 25n, 33n
Decretals of Boniface VIII, *see* Boniface VIII, *Liber Sextus*
Decretals of Gregory IX, *see* Raymond of Peñafort
Deeds of Pope Innocent III (*Gesta Innocentii papae tercii*), 221
Desiderius of Monte Cassino, abbot (Pope Victor III), 110
Deusdedit, cardinal, 109-10, 111, 116, 122; Book of Canons (*Liber canonum*), 109-10; preface text, 122ff
Devotioni vestrae, see Innocent III
Didache (Teaching of the Twelve Apostles), 10
Didymus, 89
Diego Gelmírez of Santiago de Compostela, bishop, 110, 129
Dionysius the Areopagite, 120
Dionysius Exiguus, 14, 16, 19, 21, 23-27, 30, 32, 33, 50, 108n, 122n; translation of the Canons of the Apostles, 10-11; collections (*Collectio Dionysiana*), 24-27, 31, 56n, 84n, 213, 222, 233n; Cresconius's use of, 28; preface texts, 46ff
Dioscorus, 56, 90
Dunstan of Canterbury, archbishop, 71

Ebbo of Reims, archbishop, 63, 64, 76, 77, 99n
Ephesus, Council of (431), 7, 55, 90, 125, 196
Eugene III, pope, 214
Eusebius of Caesarea, bishop, 85
Eutyches, 56, 90

Evagrius, 89
Evaristus, pope, 84

Felix II, antipope, 122
Ferrandus of Carthage, deacon, 28, 29, 51, 95; Breviary of Canons (*Breviatio canonum*), 28
Five Old Compilations (*Quinque compilationes antiquae*), 216-18, 219, 229, 230. *See also individual compilations*

Gangra, Council of (343), 25, 50
Gelasius I, pope, 23, 24, 25n, 26, 50, 149, 152, 153
Gratian, 118, 170-73, 175, 180, 184n, 185, 189, 192f, 194, 198n, 199, 200f, 201, 202, 203, 207, 209ff, 214, 215, 217; *Decretum* (Concordance of Discordant Canons or *Concordia discordantium canonum*), 15, 21, 65n, 114, 163n, 164n, 170-73, 199n, 213n, 220; decretists' commentaries on, 174-80; and demarcation of "old law," 219; study of in Bologna, 225; and *Rex pacificus*, 227-28; Ordinary Gloss on, 228; Revision to the Ordinary Gloss on, 218, 228
Gregorian Decretals, *see* Raymond of Peñafort, Decretals of Gregory IX
Gregory, cardinal, 110-11, 129; *Polycarpus*, 110-11; preface text, 129ff
Gregory I ("the Great"), pope, 7, 63, 74, 126, 132, 146, 156; decrees, 84; homilies, 129; letters, 70;

Gregory I ("the Great") (cont.)
Pastoral Rule, 129; register, 126,
220; sayings, 104

Gregory VII, pope, 108, 109, 110,
111, 114, 115, 232

Gregory IX, pope, 213, 225, 226,
227, 229, 235; *Rex pacificus*, 213,
217, 218, 226, 227, 228; text, 235f;
see also Raymond of Peñafort,
Decretals of Gregory IX

Hadrian I, pope, 60, 126, 155; *Collectio Dionysio-Hadriana*, 60, 61,
63, 67

Halitgar of Cambrai, bishop, 62–
64, 67, 72, 73n, 76, 77, 99n, 105,
115; Penitential (*Penitentiale*),
62–64, 108n; preface text, 76ff

Hatto of Mainz, archbishop, 69,
92

Henry IV, emperor, 109

Henry V, emperor, 110

Himerius of Tarragona, bishop, 4,
9, 10, 20, 21, 35

Hispana Gallica Augustodunensis,
64, 67

Honorius III, pope, 217, 223n,
224, 225, 227, 229, 234; *Novae
causarum*, 224; text, 234f; *see also*
Tancred

Hormisdas, pope, 14, 26, 49, 149

Hosius of Córdoba, bishop, 22

Hugh Capet, 71, 97

Ibas of Edessa, 29n, 152

Innocent I, pope, 21, 26, 50, 87,
145, 151, 154, 202n

Innocent III, pope, 13, 14, 217, 221,
225, 227, 228, 232n; decretals of,

218, 220, 222, 224; registers of,
221, 222, 223; *Devotioni vestrae*,
223, 225; text 233f; *see also* Peter
of Benevento

Irish Collection of Canons (*Collectio canonum Hibernensis*), 13, 16,
19, 33–36, 61, 62, 67, 115; preface
text, 58

Isaac of Langres, bishop, 68;
Chapters (*Capitula*), 68, 69, 81n;
preface text, 91f

"Isidore the Merchant" (*Isidore
Mercator*), *see* Pseudo-Isidore

Isidore of Seville, bishop, 22, 32,
64–65, 168

Ivo of Chartres, bishop, 111–12,
117, 133, 159, 171, 172, 173; *Decretum*, 112, 113–14; *Panormia*,
113–14, 116; Prologue, 114–15,
116, 117, 159, 172, 174, 178, 179,
197n, 207n; Prologue text, 132ff

Jerome, 104, 119, 121, 127, 167, 197,
202

Johannes Faventinus, 218

Johannes Teutonicus, 224, 228,
229; Fourth Compilation, 224,
225n, 299; Ordinary Gloss on
Gratian's *Decretum*, 228

John II, pope, 27, 132n

John VIII, pope, 127, 152, 156n

John XXII, pope, 213n

John the Scot, 120

John of Thérouanne, bishop, 158

John of Wales, 224; Second Compilation, 224, 229

Julian, priest of S. Anastasia, 26, 48

Julius I, pope, 21, 87, 89, 120, 123,
151

Justinian, emperor, 14, 29n, 89,
180, 227; Code, 234–35n; Corpus of Civil Law (*Corpus iuris
civilis*), 213n; Digest, 181n; Institutes, 157n, 234n; *Novellae*,
202n

Lanfranc of Bec, 112, 172
Laodicea, Council of (between 343
and 380), 25, 50
Lapsacus, Synod of (304), 86
Lateran Council of 1179 (Third),
217
Lateran Council of 1215 (Fourth),
217, 224
Lawrence, antipope, 23
Leo I ("the Great"), pope, 9n, 21n,
25, 26, 50, 85, 86, 119, 121, 126,
142, 152, 153n
Leo IX, pope, 106
Liber extra, see Raymond of Peña-
fort, Decretals of Gregory IX
Liber Pontificalis, 132n, 150n
Liber Sextus, see Boniface VIII
Liberinus, bishop, 28, 50
Liberius, pope, 9, 21, 37
Lothar I, 79
Lothar II, 163
Louis II, 79, 119
Louis the Pious, emperor, 62, 63,
65, 78, 79

Macedonius, 55, 90
Macharius, bishop, 89
Marcian, emperor, 56, 90
Martin of Braga, archbishop,
18, 27, 30, 31, 36, 53, 54n, 68n;
Chapters (*Capitula*), 30, 31;
preface text, 53f

Mercurius (Pope John II), 132

Neo-Caesarea, Council of (between 314 and 319), 25, 50
Nestorius, 56, 64, 90, 146, 147
Nicaea, First Council of (325), 6,
7, 12, 25, 32, 44, 55, 56, 84, 88,
90, 122, 125, 183, 196; canons or
decrees, 4, 21, 37n, 48, 49, 50,
84, 87, 89, 131, 146, 153; "Old
Roman version" of, 21–22; *Prisca*
or "Italian version" of, 23, 25, cf.
47n
Nicaea, Second Council of (787),
126n
Nicholas I, pope, 119, 152, 155
Nitigisius of Lugo, archbishop, 30,
53
Novae causarum, see Honorius III

Origen, 89
Otbert of Liège, bishop, 117
Otgar of Mainz, archbishop, 66
Otto III, emperor, 73

Paschal II, pope, 110, 111
Paucapalea, 174–76, 178, 185, 212,
220; *Summa* on Gratian's *Decre-
tum*, 175–76, 195n; preface text,
180ff
Paul the Deacon, 59
Paulinus of Aquileia, bishop, 81
Penitential of Bede, 104
Penitential of Theodore, 104
Pepin, 79
Peter of Benevento, 222–23, 234;
Decretals of the Lord Pope
Innocent (*Decretales domini
Innocentii papae*) or Third Com-

Peter of Benevento (cont.)
pilation, 223, 224, 225, 226, 227,
229; text of bull of promulgation, 233f
Peter Lombard, 179; *Sentences*, 174,
178
Photius, 152, 154, 155, 156n
Pseudo-Isidore, 13, 21, 64–66, 70,
214; Pseudo-Isidorian decretals,
5, 13, 64–66, 68, 69, 73, 74, 106,
108, 109, 113, 122n, 127n; preface
text, 82ff

Rainier of Pomposa, 218, 221–22;
Collection of Decretals, 220n,
221–22; preface text, 232f
Rathbod of Trier, archbishop, 69,
93
Raymond of Peñafort, 216, 225–
26, 229, 230, 235; Decretals of
Gregory IX (*Liber extravagantium* or *Liber extra*), 62,
213, 216, 217, 218, 219, 225–27,
228, 229, 230; text of bull of
promulgation, 235f
Regino of Prüm, 69–70, 74n, 75,
92, 172; Two Books Concerning Synodal Investigations and
Ecclesiastical Instructions (*Libri
duo de synodalibus causis et disciplinis ecclesiasticis*), 69–70;
preface text, 92ff
Rex pacificus, see Gregory IX
Riculf of Mainz, archbishop, 79
Rimini, Council of (359), 37
Robert Capet, 71, 97
Rolandus, 174, 176, 177, 178, 179,
202; *Stroma* on the *Decretum* of
Gratian, 176; preface text, 185ff

Roman Penitental, 63, 103, 108,
108n, 120, 121n
Rufinus, 174, 176, 177, 178, 179,
202; *Summa* on Gratian's *Decretum*, 176; preface text, 189ff

Sardica, Council of (343/344), 21,
22, 26, 32, 48, 50, 123; canons or
decrees of, 23, 25, 26, 49
Siricius, pope, 4, 9, 10, 20, 21, 26,
35, 37n, 40n, 50
Spanish Collection (*Collectio Hispana*), 13, 21, 22, 30, 31–33, 61,
64, 65, 69, 73, 75, 83n, 84n, 87n,
90n, 108n, 183n, 213; preface
text, 55ff
Statuta ecclesiae antiqua, 19n
Stephen of Salona, bishop, 25, 46,
47
Stephen of Tournai, 177–78, 179,
187n, 214n; *Summa* on Gratian's
Decretum, 175, 177–78, 179, 181n;
preface text, 194ff
Summa "Antiquitate et Tempore"
on Gratian's *Decretum*, 29, 175;
preface text, 202ff
Summa "Parisiensis" on Gratian's
Decretum, 175, 178; preface text,
201f
Sylvester, pope, 84, 91, 131, 132, 183
Symmachus, pope, 23, 86

Tancred, 224, 229, 234; Fifth Compilation, 224–25, 226, 227, 229;
text of bull of promulgation,
234f
Theodore of Mopsuestia, 29n
Theodoret of Cyrrhus, 29n
Theodosius I, emperor, 14, 55, 56n,
90

Theodosius II, emperor, 56, 90
Theophilus of Alexandria, patri-
    arch, 88
Theutberga, 163
Toledo, Fifth Council of (636), 32
Toledo, First Council of (397–
    400), 31
Toledo, Fourth Council of (633),
    32
Toledo, Third Council of (589), 33
Tribur, Council of (895), 40n
Tripartite Collection (*Collectio
    Tripartita*), 112–13, 114; preface
    text, 131ff

Urban II, pope, 110, 111

Valentinian I, emperor, 86
Victor III, pope, 109, 110, 122
Vitricius of Rouen, bishop, 87

Walter of Thérouanne, arch-
    deacon, 158

Zachary, pope, 80, 81, 91
Zosimus, pope (417–18), 22, 26, 50,
    126